T0377402

The Obama Doctrine

President Obama's first term in office was subject to intense criticism; many felt not only that he had failed to live up to his leadership potential, but that he had actually continued the foreign policy framework of the George W. Bush era which he was supposed to have abandoned. This edited volume examines whether these issues of continuity have been as prevalent during the president's second term as his first.

Is Obama still acting within the foreign policy shadow of Bush, or has he been able to establish his own approach towards international affairs, distinct from his predecessor? Within this context, the volume also addresses the idea of legacy and whether Obama has succeeded in establishing his own distinct foreign policy doctrine. In addressing these questions, the chapters explore continuity and change from a range of perspectives in International Relations and Foreign Policy Analysis, which are broadly representative of a spectrum of theoretical positions.

With contributions from a range of US foreign policy experts, this book will be of great interest to students and scholars of US foreign policy, Foreign Policy Analysis and American politics.

Michelle Bentley is Senior Lecturer in International Relations at Royal Holloway, University of London, UK.

Jack Holland is Associate Professor in International Security at the University of Leeds, UK.

Routledge Studies in US Foreign Policy

Edited by Inderjeet Parmar
City University
and
John Dumbrell
University of Durham

This new series sets out to publish high quality works by leading and emerging scholars critically engaging with United States Foreign Policy. The series welcomes a variety of approaches to the subject and draws on scholarship from international relations, security studies, international political economy, foreign policy analysis and contemporary international history.

Subjects covered include the role of administrations and institutions, the media, think tanks, ideologues and intellectuals, elites, transnational corporations, public opinion, and pressure groups in shaping foreign policy, US relations with individual nations, with global regions and global institutions and America's evolving strategic and military policies.

The series aims to provide a range of books – from individual research monographs and edited collections to textbooks and supplemental reading for scholars, researchers, policy analysts, and students.

The Obama Doctrine

A legacy of continuity in
US foreign policy?

Edited by
Michelle Bentley
and Jack Holland

Routledge
Taylor & Francis Group

LONDON AND NEW YORK

First published 2017
by Routledge
2 Park Square, Milton Park, Abingdon, Oxon OX14 4RN

and by Routledge
711 Third Avenue, New York, NY 10017

Routledge is an imprint of the Taylor & Francis Group, an informa business

© 2017 selection and editorial matter, Michelle Bentley and Jack Holland; individual chapters, the contributors

The right of Michelle Bentley and Jack Holland to be identified as authors of the editorial matter, and of the individual authors as authors of their contributions, has been asserted by them in accordance with sections 77 and 78 of the Copyright, Designs and Patents Act 1988.

All rights reserved. No part of this book may be reprinted or reproduced or utilized in any form or by any electronic, mechanical, or other means, now known or hereafter invented, including photocopying and recording, or in any information storage or retrieval system, without permission in writing from the publishers.

Trademark notice: Product or corporate names may be trademarks or registered trademarks, and are used only for identification and explanation without intent to infringe.

British Library Cataloguing in Publication Data
A catalogue record for this book is available from the British Library

Library of Congress Cataloging in Publication Data
Names: Bentley, Michelle, editor. | Holland, Jack, 1947– editor.
Title: The Obama Doctrine : a legacy of continuity in US foreign policy? / edited by Michelle Bentley and Jack Holland.
Description: New York : Routledge, 2016. | Series: Routledge studies in US foreign policy | Includes bibliographical references and index.
Identifiers: LCCN 2016024036 | ISBN 9781138831223 (hardback) | ISBN 9781315731346 (ebook)
Subjects: LCSH: United States–Foreign relations–2009– | Obama, Barack–Influence. | War on Terrorism, 2001–2009–Influence.
Classification: LCC E907 .O2215 2016 | DDC 327.73009/05–dc23
LC record available at https://lccn.loc.gov/2016024036

ISBN: 978-1-138-83122-3 (hbk)
ISBN: 978-1-315-73134-6 (ebk)

Typeset in Times New Roman
by Wearset Ltd, Boldon, Tyne and Wear

Contents

Contributors

Michelle Bentley is Senior Lecturer in International Relations at Royal Holloway, University of London.

Nicolas Bouchet is TAPIR Research Fellow at the German Marshall Fund of the United States.

Maxine David is Lecturer at Leiden University.

Jason Douglas is a PhD Researcher at University College Cork.

Ben Fermor is a PhD Researcher at the University of Leeds.

Christopher Fuller is Lecturer in Modern History at the University of Southampton.

Andrew Futter is Senior Lecturer in International Politics at the University of Leicester.

Jack Holland is Associate Professor in International Security at the University of Leeds.

Richard Jackson is Deputy Director of the National Centre for Peace and Conflict Studies at the University of Otago.

Lee Jarvis is Reader in International Security at the University of East Anglia.

Nicholas Kitchen is Assistant Professorial Research Fellow in the United States Centre, London School of Economics.

Michael Lister is Reader in Politics at Oxford Brookes University.

Jonna Nyman is Teaching Fellow at the University of Leicester.

Adam Quinn is Senior Lecturer in International Politics at the University of Birmingham.

Ty Solomon is Lecturer in International Relations at the University of Glasgow.

Chin-Kuei Tsui is Postdoctoral Fellow at the Institute of Strategic and International Affairs, National Chung Cheng University.

Oliver Turner is Hallsworth Research Fellow at the University of Manchester.

Introduction

Jack Holland and Michelle Bentley

In 2009, President Barack Obama was inaugurated under the highest of expectations. Hailed as a dynamic and effective political operative who would reverse the controversial extremes that had characterised the George W. Bush era, Obama was held up as an 'antidote' to the War on Terror and the contentious foreign policy decisions associated with the 'Bush Doctrine'. Obama's first term, however, was subject to intense criticism; many felt not only that he had failed to live up to his leadership potential, but that he had actually continued – and in some cases intensified – the foreign policy framework he was supposed to have abandoned. Far from a 'change we can believe in', US foreign policy under Obama comprised a case of ingrained political continuity; the ideas of his predecessor were alive and well. Indeed, Obama's failure to bring about wholesale change at the White House was one of the reasons why his prospects for re-election in 2012 were initially considered so uncertain. Obama was re-elected, however; and this edited volume examines whether, with a solid re-election under his belt, these issues of continuity have been as prevalent during the president's second term. Has Obama continued to act in the foreign policy shadow of his predecessor, or has he been able to establish his own approach towards international affairs, distinct from the Bush Doctrine? Is there an Obama Doctrine? And what is its legacy?

This book builds on our previous edited volume – *Obama's Foreign Policy: Ending the War on Terror* – which focused on Obama's foreign policy changes and continuities during his first term. This book examines the entirety of Obama's time in office, including his second term, assessing the wider context and impact of his presidential legacy. Of course, a number of Obama's signature foreign policy achievements have been delivered late in his second term, including a nuclear deal with Iran (see Chapter 8), agreement on climate change in Paris (see Chapter 13), and the normalisation of US–Cuba relations (see Chapter 14). The book brings together a range of academic authors, each working in their area of expertise, in order to explore the most pressing issues Obama has faced in office and deploying a range of cutting-edge theoretical approaches in doing so. In the following chapters, Obama's personality and policy preferences are located in a variety of contexts in order to identify and examine his contestable development of a distinct Obama Doctrine. Topics include nuclear weapons, energy security and economics, alongside analyses of US relations with Iran, China and Russia. Drawing on frontier work in International Relations and Foreign Policy Analysis, theoretical approaches applied include: discussions of systemic constraint (relative American decline in the international system); economic and strategic realignment (a neo-classical realist analysis of shifting international and domestic imperatives); rhetorical coercion and entrapment (embedded narratives on terrorism and counter-terrorism); cultural constraints (understandings of terrorism in the media, popular culture and everyday life); emotion and affective investment (the emotional commitment to longstanding policies and ways of thinking); comparative analyses of change and continuity in specific policy areas (nuclear weapons, drones and energy security); and reflection on the drivers of change and 'use' of time as a discursive resource (by presidents and scholars).

This is an important task. Obama's legacy is fiercely contested. For those who would hold Obama's record up as evidence of presidential success, however, this legacy is derived largely derived from his multiple domestic victories: healthcare reform, economic recovery, and the creation of a more perfect union. Nonetheless, Obama's foreign policy has also been highly significant and, arguably, a necessary, if imperfectly realised, remedy for the excesses of the Bush Doctrine. Where the Bush Doctrine introduced pre-emptive military solutions to potential security threats before they were fully manifest, Obama has exercised caution and a preference for diplomatic solutions when possible. Where the Bush Doctrine hoped for allies but did not rely upon them, Obama has, at times, been noted as leading from behind and keen to see US allies do their part in burden sharing. Where Bush pursued a 'one percent doctrine' (preparing for low-probability, high-impact events) in the wake of 9/11, Obama has played a far longer game that embraces the complexity and uncertainty of the international system as inherent and unavoidable conditions of the modern world to be managed, not removed. And yet Obama leaves office having destabilised Libya through airstrikes and with American warplanes bombing Syria, with US boots on the ground. One of the most reluctantly interventionist US presidents in history leaves office with US forces fighting Islamic terrorists and extremists in the Middle East, including in the very country in which he lambasted his predecessor's war as 'dumb'. For a president guided by the informal slogan of 'don't do stupid shit', this is surprising. How has a president fixated on refocusing and then ending the War on Terror ended up in this position? What is the nature of Obama's complex foreign policy legacy? Is it a legacy of continuity in US foreign policy?

Of course, the issue guiding this book above all others concerns an effort to make sense of an 'Obama Doctrine'. Is there one? What is its nature? What characterises and defines it? Usually the term 'doctrine' is seen to encompass a set of beliefs or a stated principle, which might guide policy and teach others. The term appears in religious, legal, military and political guises. While all four realms have influenced the formation of an Obama Doctrine, it is the political or foreign policy doctrine that concerns us here. Broader than the specific notion of a military doctrine, this formation is concerned with Obama's overarching stated and implied approach to foreign policy. It is a guiding vision that structures and informs how foreign policy is conceptualised, articulated, prioritised, formulated and enacted. To illustrate, it is possible to identify the implementation of a specific military doctrine – shock and awe – during the presidency of George W. Bush. This specific military doctrine was designed to impact an enemy's physical and psychological resources, through rapid escalation and deployment: in short, the use and demonstration of overwhelming military superiority. It formed a relatively small component of a much broader approach to foreign policy, which has been characterised as comprising key policy preferences, such as pre-emption (the nullification of threats before they are fully manifest, which has at times been defined as *the* Bush Doctrine) within a post-9/11 context of lowered thresholds for the toleration of acceptable risk (sometimes called the 'one percent doctrine', in which highly unlikely but potentially consequential eventualities – such as terrorist attacks – are treated as certainties). More broadly still, the Bush administration has been understood by a range of analysts to possess overarching stated and implicit principles which guided their approach to foreign policy. These include muscular unilateralism, Wilsonianism with boots, Anything But Clinton, Just Say No, and a philosophy of neoconservatism, to name only a few. These terms attempt to label and summarise the 'Bush Doctrine' at the broadest level of an orientation towards foreign policy, itself composed of more specific military doctrine(s). It is in this broadest sense – at the level of a general, stated or implicit, foreign policy orientation – that we ask, 'What is the Obama Doctrine?'

To answer this question, the book is structured in four parts. In Part I, 'Power and tradition: situating Obama's foreign policy', the book locates Obama's foreign policy in a range of relevant contexts. In Chapter 1, Nicholas Kitchen considers Obama's position within US political, economic and military history. For Kitchen, the Obama administration has been mindful that the response to 9/11 and the strategic preoccupation with terrorism had thrown the US off course. It therefore sought to refocus US foreign policy around a more limited conception of the national interest rooted in a more realistic appraisal of the limits, not just of American power, but of state power itself. As a result, the Obama administration's approach to international security has been one of issue management as opposed to the problem-solving approach of the Bush and, to a lesser extent, Clinton administrations. In Chapter 2, Adam Quinn offers the related but divergent argument that economics has been at the heart of the development of an Obama Doctrine. He notes that the Obama presidency began with an economic crisis that sapped the resources of the state and created a political environment in which government spending was under pressure. Obama took over from a presidency that was notable both for expensive foreign interventions, vast expansion of the security budget, and a lax attitude to funding these commitments with revenue. Obama's legacy then is one of adjusting US foreign policy to meet fiscal restraints. In Chapter 3, Jack Holland situates Obama's foreign policy within a different context: that of traditions of American foreign policy. Holland argues that the Obama Doctrine 'has been Jeffersonian in formulation and prosecution', which has meant that it has often run up against 'the demands of world hegemony in the twenty-first century'. Fortunately, like Quinn and Kitchen, Holland notes that decline suits Obama's relative reluctance to go abroad in search of monsters to destroy. For these three authors, then, strategic reassessment, economic decline and the Jeffersonian tradition provide three potentially complementary drivers of a more cautious foreign policy approach.

Part II explores the legacy of the Bush Doctrine through Obama's linguistic and cultural inheritance. In Chapter 4, Michelle Bentley argues that Obama's presidency was initially constructed around the abandonment of the controversial phrase 'War on Terror', in an effort to break down the contentious linguistic constructions that had characterised the post-9/11 era. However, the language of war remained central to Obama's foreign policy discourse and has continued to characterise US foreign policy, albeit to a lesser extent. In Chapter 5, Richard Jackson and Chin-Kuei Tsui explore the origins, nature and evolution of this War on Terror discourse under Bush and Obama, noting the linguistic shifts of Obama's second term. They find that 'there is much greater continuity than change in US counterterrorism policy', with changes constituting minor adaptations at the periphery of the dominant paradigm, due to the unchanged structural conditions of the War on Terror, which trap Obama as the star of America's counter-terrorism *Groundhog Day*. In Chapter 6, Ben Fermor continues a constructivist focus on language and culture, also exploring the limited changes apparent in Obama's foreign policy discourse. He agrees with Jackson and Tsui that 'as Barack Obama took office in January 2009, his ability to shape American foreign policy was constrained by the discursive structures already in place' because the Bush Doctrine had helped to cement 'understandings of how America should conduct itself in a world inhabited by Osama bin Laden, al Qaida and "Islamic extremists"'. However, Fermor argues that Obama's legacy is one of increased multilateralism and 'intelligent interventionism', with a subtle shift in the core narratives of the War on Terror through a process of broadening and narrowing. Fermor shows how Bush's core identity markers – good Americans and evil terrorists – were reworked by Obama to fit into a colonial language of civilisation and barbarism. The result of this reworking, Fermor argues, has been the broadening definition of an American Self, which enables international collaboration, faced with a narrowed framing of a dehumanised Other, rendering the task of degrading and destroying America's enemies a political necessity. The productivity of discourse also features in Ty Solomon's chapter. In Chapter 7, Solomon explores the fact that Obama's administration is the first in nearly a decade to pursue official negotiations with Iran over its nuclear programme, despite the discursive difficulties of doing so. In contrast to most extant realist work, Solomon pursues an analysis of the confrontation as socially constructed and mutually constitutive of the US and Iran's international identities. Moreover, drawing on psychoanalytic theory, the chapter extends constructivist thinking about identities by incorporating the importance of affective dynamics in identity construction. Together, then, these chapters consider the role of language, culture, identity and emotion in Obama's formulation of a foreign policy doctrine, demonstrating a shared concern for the nature and limitations of the structural context and drivers of US policy.

The book's third part considers some of the most important and fundamental foreign policy challenges the Obama administration faced. In Chapter 8, Jason Douglas and Andrew Futter reflect on Obama's nuclear weapons legacy, noting that progress has been made on a number of issues, including the New START (nuclear arms reductions treaty), diversification in US deterrence capability, and agreement with Iran over its disputed nuclear programme. For Douglas and Futter, these achievements should be read as continuity with subtle change: evolution, not revolution. Yet Obama's greatest legacy may be as yet underappreciated: the re-emergence of nuclear disarmament as a genuine political goal and guiding principle for future administrations. In Chapter 9, Christopher Fuller addresses one of Obama's most notorious and divisive policy choices: the frequent and widespread use of unmanned aerial vehicles (drones, or remotely piloted air systems). The scale and extent of this programme are considerable as Obama has overseen the construction of arguably the most significant assassination programme in US history in terms of size, reach and use. Fuller explores the operation and justification of this key plank of Obama's foreign policy legacy and of an emerging Obama Doctrine. In Chapter 10, Nicolas Bouchet explores one of the foreign policy features most important to the Bush Doctrine: democracy promotion. Analysing the case study of Egypt, Bouchet argues that Obama's approach to democracy has blended a higher degree of realist pragmatism into liberal concerns than did his predecessor. In Chapter 11, Maxine David explores US–Russia relations throughout Obama's presidency. David paints a mixed but broadly pessimistic picture of US–Russia relations, contrasting early successes such as the New START and increasing cooperation in Afghanistan with later difficulties such as the Magnitsky Act, the Edward Snowden affair and, in particular, proxy conflict in Ukraine and Syria. In Chapter 12, Oliver Turner considers US foreign policy towards China. Despite being debated by politicians as a real or potential threat to US interests in both of Obama's presidential campaigns, US–China policies have remained relatively cautious and pragmatic. Turner argues that Obama has had to work hard to avoid alienating states which are no doubt nervous about China's rise, but which benefit greatly from it. In Chapter 13, Jonna Nyman analyses Obama's energy security legacy. Nyman argues that Obama was elected on a promise of renewed leadership on climate change that would strengthen American security. However, in office, Obama's energy security strategy 'not only continued but *expanded* exploration and exploitation of conventional and unconventional fossil fuels'. For these authors, then, Obama's legacy is of altered rhetoric, but little substantive impact.

The book's fourth and final part explores the Obama Doctrine's place in history. Chapter 14, by Lee Jarvis and Michael Lister, explores the nature of the Obama Doctrine and its discursive position as a historical legacy. First, Jarvis and Lister reflect on efforts to articulate Obama's foreign policy record from within his administration, exploring the construction of major successes and failures. Like the majority of contributors to this volume and commentaries on US foreign policy, they note that two principal features have defined the Obama Doctrine – incrementalism (in the pursuit of otherwise lofty goals) and retrenchment – as driven by economic woes and evidenced, for example, in leading from behind in Libya and apparent hesitancy in Syria. By way of explanation, they consider the possibilities of structurally driven continuity, cyclical variations between transformationalists and incrementalists, and the potential uniqueness of every presidential doctrine. Second, and in particular, Jarvis and Lister focus on efforts to situate the Obama administration's legacy historically. In his second term, what has been remarkable has been the return to the theme of change, constructed through appeals to particular (punctuated and disjunctive) conceptualisations of time. Obama has gone out of his way to suggest that his legacy will include the ending of the War on Terror and rectifying the failings of his predecessor, most obviously in Iraq but also in Afghanistan. As well as frequently referencing historical American failures and successes, Obama has also looked to the future to situate his legacy, promising a prosperous twenty-first century shaped by capable people, as was the twentieth. A combination 'of historical providence, national character and presidential determination is that which … explains Obama's certainties about the successful future awaiting the US'. On the latter, as Republicans and Democrats gear up their election campaigns, the stakes could not be higher and choices clearer. Obama's legacy is consequential but not irreversible.

Part I

Power and tradition

Situating Obama's foreign policy

1 Ending 'permanent war'

Security and economy under Obama

Nicholas Kitchen

In my contribution to *Obama's foreign policy: ending the War on Terror* (Kitchen 2013), I argued that the domestic war-weariness of the American public had enabled Obama to jettison the War on Terror as a strategic concept and to refocus on the structural realities of the global economy, most obviously with the rebalance to Asia. At the same time as concluding that in the Obama presidency we were witnessing a reorientation of the geographic focus of American foreign policy, I offered the tentative suggestion that we might also be at the beginning of a change in the nature of American primacy itself: from unipolar dominance to a form of divested hegemony, where allies and partners were increasingly called upon to contribute to the provision of global public goods. If pursued, this deeper strategic shift, I predicted, would be met with political and bureaucratic resistance within the United States, a resistance reinforced in public discourse by America's cultural reverence for its military institutions.

This chapter revisits this theme, at the end of Barack Obama's second term in office, and prompted by a remark in the president's 2014 State of the Union address. 'America', Obama said, 'must move off a permanent war footing.' This statement had clear implications for the conduct of the United States' campaign against violent extremism, completing the strategic refocusing and political rebranding of the Global War on Terror (GWoT). But Obama's rhetoric has deeper implications for the conduct of American foreign policy, since 'permanent war' has been the strategic norm for the United States for the past seventy years. Has Obama's time in office laid the groundwork for such a significant strategic shift in American foreign policy, or will the legacies of the Cold War and the War on Terror continue to loom large over US strategy?

Establishing permanent war: the United States after 1945

Permanent war is not a natural condition for the United States. Geographically secure since the European powers had been warned off the American hemisphere, the United States had neither the pressing need nor the political desire for sustaining significant federal military structures, and, of course, the Constitution permitted the federal government only limited war-making powers. Although the United States was the world's largest economy by the outbreak of the First World War, Woodrow Wilson's reticence to involve the country in Europe's cynical and self-interested power politics was supported by the majority of his compatriots. Of course, the United States had gone to war for reasons of power and interest in the past, and would do so again in 1917, but following the war, as on previous occasions, the military establishment required for the task was in large part dismantled. From having had over 4 million men under arms at the end of the war, the US demobilised 3.25 million within nine months, and by the end of 1919 the army had been reduced to around 250,000 enlisted men. Military spending returned to pre-war levels of around 1 per cent of GDP by 1923.

If the 1920s and 1930s would later become characterised as a period of isolationism in US foreign policy, the Japanese attack on the American navy at Pearl Harbor laid to rest the debate between neutrality and interventionism. The United States entered the war with far greater designs on the nature of postwar order than those that had accompanied the country's entry into the First World War. However, in completing the interwar period's unfinished transition from British to American hegemony, it was far from clear that this would mean permanently maintaining the kind of significant military establishment usually associated with hegemonic powers. Although the United States emerged from the Second World War with overwhelming preponderance – as Mikhail Gorbachev would later lament, 'the only big country that had waxed fabulously rich on the war' (Kimball 1992) – American planners had approached the end of the war with a vision of order-building that embedded its power in a system of multilateral institutions (Ikenberry 2001, pp. 163–214). Drawdown proceeded unfettered, with military spending dropping from a peak of $83 billion in 1945 to $9 billion in 1948, with active duty personnel falling from 12 million in 1945 to 1.4 million in 1950.

The speed and depth of the United States' postwar drawdown might be considered surprising, particularly since US strategists appear to have reached consensus that the power of the Soviet Union represented a compelling threat in the first months of 1946.[1] Yet drawdowns of this sort were the norm in the American experience (Boot 2012). War was very much a temporary condition, and wartime dispensations granted by legislators to the executive branch were treated as strictly limited exceptions. But by the time of the Korean War, after which active-duty service personnel fell by nearly one-third, much of this could be accounted for by Eisenhower's New Look strategy that prioritised nuclear forces, and overall defence spending was maintained.

What had happened was that *NSC 68*, 'the first comprehensive enunciation of American security policy' and a document that amounted 'to an American declaration of permanent Cold War', had begun to be implemented (US National Security Council 1950; Brands 1989). Defence spending had increased from just under 5 per cent of GDP in 1950 to double-digit levels during the war, and would average almost 9 per cent from the end of the war through to the end of the 1960s, a period in which the US economy grew by an average of 6.5 per cent a year. If *NSC 68*'s purpose had been, in Dean Acheson's phrasing, 'to so bludgeon the mass mind of "top government" that not only could the President make a decision but that the decision could be carried out' (Acheson 1969, p. 374), its success was evident in the debate around whether investment in defence capabilities should trump the requirement to balance the federal budget.

Yet the requirements of strategists could only be met if the political conditions would permit them. Containment was constructed as much as an expression of the universal nature of American values as the necessary requirements of the zero-sum logic of a security dilemma (Jervis 2001). The political conditions that enabled containment resulted from domestic coalition-forming that tacked together Dean Acheson's Europe-first internationalists with the Asia-first school of Robert Taft in order to sustain general support for American internationalism, particularly among Congressional opinion (Snyder 1991, pp. 255–304). Driven by the likes of John Foster Dulles and Dean Rusk, a global anti-communist consensus, rooted in strategic ideas such as the domino theory and monolithic communist expansionism, demonstrated how the 'cross-currents of uniqueness and universality' in American identity could be simultaneously integrated into grand strategy (Foley 2007, p. 435).

For over forty years containment would swing between activism and détente, a reflection of the balance of power and ideas between hawks and doves (Gaddis 2005). The experience of Vietnam raised doubts about American ideals on the one hand and American capabilities on the other, animating American politics from the presidential candidacy of George McGovern to the songwriting of Bob Dylan, and from the revisionist history of William Appleman Williams to Henry Kissinger's concerns about overextension that underpinned détente (Nelson 1995). In response to a perceived collective failure of nerve by the Nixon and Carter administrations, neoconservatives argued for a revival of moral purpose and the assertion of American material power (Halper and Clarke 2004, pp. 55–58). Such arguments were heated, and produced significant changes in strategy, but they were shifts of degree. Throughout the Cold War, the goal of containing the Soviet Union, and the need for the United States to maintain a state of perpetual readiness for war, remained constant. Containment became a basic assumption of American political life, a grand strategy that defined not just American internationalism but American culture. Anti-communism energised politics in the United States from unions to universities and from movies to churches. It infected American society and culture with pathologies of nationalism, intolerance and suspicion (Whitfield 1996).

The missing drawdown: failing to end the Cold War

The Cold War had expanded the American state, leaving a more powerful presidency, a more secretive government and less constraining Congress. Believing democratic decision-making to be an inherent weakness in such an ultra-securitised climate, policy-makers had adopted, and the public had largely accepted, unprecedented privations of traditional American liberties (Maynes 1990). The power of the military-industrial complex, the designation of enemy ideologies, the annexation of constitutional powers by the executive from Congress, the culture of classifying information, the secret institutions of the national security infrastructure: all had redefined the American people's relationship with their government to the detriment of their constitutional rights (Halperin and Woods 1990).

Some in the political commentariat saw the end of the Cold War as an opportunity for a peace dividend. In this reading, the Cold War was an anomaly, the bulk of a 'seventy year detour' from the main road of American diplomatic history (Moynihan 1990). The editor of *Foreign Affairs*, William Hyland, wrote that 'for the first time in half a century, the United States has the opportunity to reconstruct its foreign policy free of the constraints and pressures of the Cold War' (Hyland 1990). 'The peace dividend', wrote his counterpart at *Foreign Policy*, was 'not just about the money that will be freed up' but also about 'the categories of thought that will finally be opened up' (Maynes 1990).

This approach in many ways mirrored the views of the American public, a reality that was reflected on either side of party-political divide in the presidential primaries in 1991 and 1992. Democrat Paul Tsongas focused on the scale of the budget deficit necessitated by high military spending, arguing that 'if our security needs have lessened, our level of military spending should reflect that change' (Clymer 1991). For the Republicans, Pat Buchanan made a serious challenge for the sitting president's party nomination, a campaign that made possible Ross Perot's independent candidacy in the general election itself, in which the latter would define himself as an economic nationalist committed to balancing the federal budget.[2]

So as the Soviet Union fell, both Washington insiders and the country at large felt the need to debate the balance of American political life: the roles of the executive branch, the media and the military, the balance between government secrecy and freedom of information, and the need to restructure domestic liberties and industrial organisation as part of a clear transition from war to peace (Moynihan 1992; Pessen 1993). Yet there is little evidence that these kinds of questions were seriously addressed in government itself, or within the foreign policy bureaucracy that owed its twentieth-century growth to the grand strategy of anti-communist containment. Among the major foreign affairs think tanks, those outliers such as the CATO Institute and Heritage Foundation that did take retrenchment seriously, and academic voices such as Eric Nordlinger (Nordlinger 1991, 1995), were marginal to the debate, their advocacy of a drawdown dismissed by the new president's National Security Advisor in a major foreign policy speech, as 'the rhetoric of Neo-Know-Nothings' (Lake 1993). In the 1990s, American governing elites were concerned not with how to dismantle containment, but with how to replace it.

Defence spending did fall somewhat in the 1990s as certain Cold War commitments were scaled back, but levelled off by the middle of the decade and by the end of the Clinton presidency had begun to rise again. The Clinton administration's proffered grand strategy – democratic enlargement – essentially sought to globalise the Western order that had been built in opposition to the Soviet bloc, with the president likening the strategy to the domino theory in reverse: encouraging and supporting rather than preventing a succession of mutually reinforcing societal changes that were in the interests of the United States (Brinkley 1997). Whilst such a strategy was motivated by and reflected a set of liberal goals deeply influenced by ideas of democratic peace and globalisation, underpinning it was the simple, brute fact of American dominance.

What International Relations theorists began to describe as structural unipolarity was a curious condition, particularly as it appeared to be reinforced rather than eroded during the course of the 1990s (Layne 1993, 2006; Thompson 2006). But for those in the policy establishment here was confirmation that what they tended to refer to as primacy could be sustained (Wohlforth 1999). Perversely, a consequence of such dominance might be to reduce a state's sense of its own security – the extent of its perceived limits means that all sorts of disturbances can threaten it (Jervis 2006). Permanent war was therefore maintained in the 1990s not because the United States itself continued to be threatened by foreign enemies, but because American policymakers came to identify the unipolar structure of the system, and America's place in it, as the object of defence.

In practice, this resulted in a security discourse that was both expansive and vacillated with events: a nervous hyperactivity that reflected a definition of American interests that was global in scope and that therefore apparently regarded each and every occasion where America's interests were not met in full as representing a reduction of American power. Revisionist great powers, rogue states, failed states, proliferation of weapons of mass destruction, ethnic conflict, civil war, genocide and mass atrocities, violations of human rights, drugs, organised crime, resource conflicts, migration, pandemics, natural disasters: in American political discourse it seemed any number of issues could be securitised and advanced as threats to national security, requiring the United States to remain ever alert (Buzan 1998).

For some, this was perfectly reasonable: a safety-first approach to a dangerous world. As Robert Kagan put it, 'there is no certainty that we can correctly distinguish between high-stakes issues and small-stakes issues in time to sound the alarm' (Harries 2000, p. 28). For Colin Powell, Chairman of the Joint Chiefs of Staff, the level of uncertainty as to the threat you might face meant 'putting it in the mind of an opponent that there is no future in trying to challenge the armed forces of the United States' (House Armed Services Committee 1992). Indeed, maintaining forces into the post-Cold War world recognised that the main threat to the United States arose from its being perceived abroad as weak and irresolute (Gaffney Jr. 2000). Therefore, however challenged, the United States had to be able to respond emphatically. Powell again: 'I believe in the bully's way of going to war. I'm on a street corner, I got my gun, I got my blade, I'ma kick yo' ass' (Gates Jr. 1995).

In the face of this approach, conservatives and realists in this period complained of a 'frantic' search for new missions and visions for United States foreign policy, efforts that the CATO Institute concluded 'are so wide ranging as to constitute a campaign of threat procurement' (Carpenter 1992). Permanent war had created inertias and path-dependencies that had a deep influence on strategic debate. The very language of foreign policy debate was inherently internationalist (Clarke and Clad 1995, pp. 49–63), and the notion that United States might not be engaged in an enduring battle to sustain world order was not one that foreign policy professionals were minded to admit. Just as academic Sovietologists had not been able to conceive of the subject of their discipline ceasing to exist (Cox 2009), so America's foreign policy experts remained resolutely unable to detach themselves from notions of credibility and leadership, despite the radical structural shift in the United States' strategic environment (Steel 1995, pp. 113–114). The Cold War may have ended, but the United States proved unable to end the Cold War.

Purpose renewed: the Global War on Terror as grand strategy

The Global War on Terror was in many ways a strategic concept explicitly constructed to fill the vacuum that anti-communist containment had left during the 1990s. Indeed, such was the determination of former Cold Warriors within the Bush administration to solve the threat deficit problem of the prior decade that they sought explicitly to cast the War on Terror as a 'long war', a defining struggle that would act as a lode star for the conduct of US foreign policy: in short, a grand strategy for the United States.

Whilst the United States strategic environment hadn't changed, the events of 9/11 shifted society and policy-makers' perception of threat in a way that allowed the country and the foreign policy elite to coalesce around a defined purpose for American foreign policy (Holland 2009). Part of the explanation for the nature of the post-9/11 shift lies with the personnel in the administration's senior foreign policy team, a mix of neoconservative democratic globalists and assertive nationalists, a number of whom had been hawkish Cold Warriors in the Reagan era and who were intensely comfortable with the notion of permanent war. And for a period, as Americans rallied round the flag and domestic politics created incentives for threat inflation, the Bush administration's 'vulcans' seemed to have finally settled on a new guiding principle for America's military might (Mann 2004).

The result was that counterterrorism was expanded through the Iraq war to encompass an attempt to comprehensively reorder the Middle East. This new overarching imperative of US foreign policy was pursued with overwhelmingly military tools, unsurprisingly, given the extent to which the Cold War security architecture had been maintained. At the same time, those means were not immediately clearly suited to addressing non-state actors, hence the early identification of terrorists with their state allies. The overthrow of the latter would inaugurate a fundamental remaking of the Middle East, draining the swamp of motivation for a disaffected Muslim youth long denied the benefits of political and economic freedom by their post-colonial authoritarian rulers.

Perhaps the most significant consequence of the War on Terror was the geographic focus it placed on the Middle East, particularly as the invasion of Iraq shifted resources and attention away from Al Qaeda's Afghanistan base. But the War on Terror both re-established norms and processes of permanent war in American politics and society and inaugurated new ones. Congress's 2001 Authorization for the Use of Military Force granted the president authority to use all necessary and appropriate force against those whom he determined 'planned, authorized, committed or aided' the 9/11 attacks – providing the overarching authority for military campaigns against an almost unlimited range of individuals and groups. International affirmation was forthcoming, with the language of post-9/11 United Nations Security Council resolutions reinforcing the legal basis for American military action that could potentially be carried out in anticipation of terrorist attacks (Byers 2002). Alongside the obvious shifts in the rhetorical tone of foreign policy – Bush was unashamed to be a 'war president' – the bureaucratic restructuring of the American national security apparatus amounted to a comprehensive updating of architecture of permanent war for a new era. The administration created a new Department of Homeland Security, strengthened the money-laundering controls of the US Treasury, and reallocated responsibilities between the various domestic and foreign intelligence and security services whilst granting them new powers of surveillance and detention.

The Bush administration also threw money at the War on Terror. The Department of Homeland Security was budgeted $43 billion, almost as much as the State Department. The seventeen agencies of the 'intelligence community' came to command a collective budget in excess of $80 billion. And the 'regular' defence budget, which excludes the 'exceptional' costs of wars in Iraq and Afghanistan, doubled in a decade from $267 billion in 2000 to £533 billion in 2010. Andrew Bacevich's concern that such extensive growth of the national security state might put the United States on the 'path to permanent war' if anything underplayed its impact, since it built upon a Cold War architecture of permanent war that had never been dismantled (Bacevich 2010). Such concerns were even shared by Secretary of Defense Robert Gates, who warned that

> America's civilian institutions of diplomacy and development have been chronically undermanned and underfunded for far too long.... when it comes to America's engagement with the rest of the world, it is important that the military is – and is clearly seen to be – in a supporting role to civilian agencies.
>
> (Tyson 2008)

Gates may have been preparing to leave the Pentagon when he made that statement in July 2008, but by November he had agreed to stay on under the incoming Democratic president, whose campaign had been explicit in rejecting many of the Bush administration's counter-terrorism tactics, and tapped into the public's war-weariness seven years on from 9/11. Ultimately the Global War on Terror failed to sustain itself as grand strategy in the way its proponents had hoped. Such an outcome was perhaps unsurprising, requiring a feat of 'macro-securitisation' that was always likely to be a herculean task, given its reliance on terrorists' capacity to continue to carry out large-scale attacks, the willingness of allies to accept a war paradigm, and Al Qaeda and its ilk's inability to pose a genuine ideological alternative to liberal order (Buzan 2006). That said, the War on Terror was responsible for two of the United States' three longest wars in its history, and sustained significant increases in defence, homeland security and intelligence spending, all on top of a missing drawdown from the country's last major conflict. The American economy may have seemed able to sustain it, but the long-term trend in America's military commitments continued steadily upward.

Pushback: dumb wars and debt

Obama's election was made possible by the financial crisis of 2008, a crisis that made America's leaders appear feckless and the United States' political and economic model inoperative. The clarion call of Obama's campaign rested on the hope that change was possible. Yet Obama's proposals for change were clearer and better developed in the sphere of foreign policy than in economic affairs. Here, candidate Obama ran hard on his opposition to the discredited Iraq war, contrasting the dumb war in Iraq with the necessary war in Afghanistan, and more generally proposing to return American foreign policy to a more consensual, multilateral variant, less reliant on the tools of military force.

Once in office, the administration's first steps were largely symbolic, designed to 'signal to the world that he is the unBush' (Freedland 2009). In the first hundred days of détente, Guantanamo Bay, the symbol of American lawlessness in the War on Terror, would be closed and torture repudiated; troops would be withdrawn from Iraq; former pariahs including Venezuela, Cuba, Iran and Syria would be offered the chance to come in from the cold; moderate Muslim opinion would be cultivated and international institutions re-engaged (Kitchen 2011).

At the same time, Obama was far more cautious than his predecessor in articulating doctrine as such. Bumper stickers for Obama's approach to strategy have been left to anonymous officials who pronounce that the administration 'leads from behind' or believes the key task of foreign policy is 'don't do stupid shit'. When pushed, the president has been willing to offer a 'strong belief that we don't have military solutions to every problem' (Yglesias 2015). This has been evident in the administration's willingness to push diplomatic and multi-lateral approaches to problem solving – most obviously with Iran – and to tone down exceptionalist rhetoric, usually with a hedge to the universalisability of American values which emphasises that different cultures may apply liberal norms differently.

The administration's caution is bound up in a sense of the limits of what American power can achieve. Whilst unwilling to describe himself as a realist, Obama is on record as admiring how the arch-realist foreign policy team of the George H.W. Bush administration managed the dying breaths of the Soviet

Union between 1989 and 1991 (Brooks 2008). Such an approach indicates that Obama's administration conceives of the United States' role in the world in profoundly different terms to its post-Cold War predecessors, which were prone simply to assert the righteousness of the United States' claim to international leadership. Obama has certainly paid lip-service to American idealism, but the conduct of his diplomacy continues to suggest that disparate issues need not be conflated for the purposes of moral clarity (Cohen 2009).

Some argue that behind the more limited ambitions of the Obama administration lies the reality of more limited means (Quinn 2013). Such arguments point to the level of US indebtedness incurred from persistent deficits – particularly since the Bush administration chose to combine its War on Terror security largess with unprecedented tax cuts; sequestered military spending; and greater constraints on US unilateral action imposed by a less unipolar balance of power. And indeed, Obama himself has emphasised that his is 'a US leadership that recognizes our limits in terms of resources, capacity' (Zakaria 2012). However, the reality of such constraint is far from clear. Federal debt as a percentage of GDP has been falling since the beginning of 2014, and federal borrowing is cheaper than at any time in history. And whilst defence spending has fallen from its 2010 peak, it remains higher than at any point during the Cold War, and greater than the total of the next nine states combined (IISS 2015). Few would suggest that should Obama's successor wish to return the United States to a more activist military approach to foreign policy, they would not be able to do so. Even Obama himself makes the point about resources with the caveat that 'the United States continues to be the one indispensable nation in tackling major international problems' (Zakaria 2012).

It therefore may be more accurate to understand the administration's talk of limits as political shorthand for its more circumscribed approach to the use of military force that rests on an analysis of the basic operation of international relations: an analysis which differs markedly from that of its predecessor. If the Bush administration saw American unipolarity as an inherently permissive condition that meant the United States could use its military dominance to impose its will, a basic cost-benefit analysis of its attempts to do so in Iraq and Afghanistan demonstrates the manifest falsehood of that belief (Stiglitz and Bilmes 2008). In an international system where conventional interstate war has been rendered obsolete as rational policy (Mueller 1990; Tertrais 2012), conflict is instead characterised by transnational contestation by state and non-state actors, processes which serve to blur notions of both territorial integrity and sovereignty, as well as the distinctions between different types of actors. Whilst some have theorised this evolution of the security environment as occurring within the context of unipolarity's demise (Haass 2008), the United States' military position, defined in terms of the usual metrics, remains dominant. Rather than the balance of power being at issue, it is the general capacity of states to exert control over this more disorderly security environment that underpins the United States' strategic thinking in the aftermath of the Bush doctrine (see Rogers 2000).

Obama's approach to international security is therefore characterised by a general scepticism of what it is, in practice, that large-scale military actions can achieve. From the very beginning of the Obama administration, this approach was set out in terms of 'smart power', an approach to international leadership that stressed the needs of followers to translate elements of hard and soft power into legitimacy and authority (Nye 2008, 2011). Emphasising the 'softer' tools of diplomacy and statecraft do not imply rejecting the use of force: a point Obama made himself in his Nobel acceptance speech and which has been confirmed by his willingness to use special forces, air power and drones – with the latter use of hard power in particular precipitating significant costs in terms of soft power (Boyle 2013). Bearing in mind that such trade-offs between means and ends are the very stuff of strategy, it is possible to isolate a number of ways in which the administration would at least claim that its approach reflects those 'smart' principles.

First, the use of drone technology has enabled the administration to turn the United States' approach to counter-terrorism from one of problem-solving to one of issue management. Under Obama, unmanned aerial vehicles (UAVs) have been deployed against terrorist targets in Pakistan, Somalia, Yemen, Libya, Iraq and Syria. Whilst it is true that the drone campaign raises significant questions as to its moral and legal status, not to mention its wider effectiveness in reducing the terrorist threat to the United States (McCrisken 2011), it is also the case that it has allowed the administration to present itself as directly addressing the terrorist threat without having to resort to the types of large-scale boots on the ground undertakings that characterised the Bush administration. But although some regard the use of drone technology as a 'surrogate' (Krieg 2016), there can be no doubt that drones are perceived as the direct application of military force, both by the communities that have been regularly targeted by UAVs (Friedersdorf 2012) and by the operators themselves (Chatterjee 2015).

Second, and conditioned by the experience of the campaigns in Iraq and Afghanistan, is a profound scepticism about the ability of American military capabilities to solve political problems, particularly in the Middle East. Military power can be used for containment of situations (for example, the use of air-power to arrest the territorial expansion of ISIS) or for signalling and structuring purposes – as has been the case in the South China Sea. But the administration has consistently demurred when it has been suggested that American military force may be used to extract compliance from, or compel behaviour change in, either state or non-state actors.

Third, the administration has sought to focus more on deeper strategic issues in terms of system management than on tactical battles against asymmetric enemies. In this reading, the War on Terror has been a strategic 'detour', which blinded American policy-makers to the underlying reality of structural change in the international system that was dictating that Asia would be the key geopolitical arena of Obama's tenure and beyond (Lizza 2011). Behind this lies a return to Clinton-era ideas that geoeconomics rather than geopolitics is ultimately determining of (inter)national success, evidenced by the amounts of domestic political capital the administration has been prepared to spend to secure deals on the Trans-Pacific Partnership (TPP) and the Transatlantic Trade and Investment Partnership (TTIP).

Fourth, and a corollary from these latter two points, has been the administration's confidence in the capacity of economic tools to deliver political outcomes. Sanctions regimes, of course, are slow, gradual tools, and require political commitment to sustain, though American diplomats regularly point out in private that military routes have yielded a similar experience in the recent past. Certainly most experts agree that the multilateral sanctions imposed on Iran from 2010 contributed significantly to the increasing Iranian flexibility on its nuclear programme that led to the Joint Comprehensive Plan of Action agreed in Vienna in July 2015 and adopted in October (Katzman 2014). The sanctions imposed on Russia in the wake of its annexation of Crimea and actions in Eastern Ukraine will be still harder to sustain to effectiveness, but there can be little doubt that they have added significant costs to Russia's endeavour, contributing to an annualised decline in Russian growth of 4 per cent, and massive capital flight.

These trends – the shift from problem-solving to issue management; scepticism about the utility of force as an instrument of compellence; a focus on deeper structural issues in the global economy; and confidence in economic tools of statecraft – suggest that the Obama administration's sense of the limits of power should be understood not in terms of American capabilities, but in terms of the kind of outcomes it is practically possible for any state's individual capabilities, directly applied, to deliver in international politics. Madeleine Albright notoriously questioned what the point of American military forces was if they weren't to actually be put to use, but the Bush administration's misplaced confidence in war as a tool of strategy drove home the reality that military tools can only achieve so much. The Obama administration has taken that message very much to heart.

Critics have argued that, taken together, this represents a curtailing of commitments and shifting of burdens that amount to a dangerous grand strategy of retrenchment, particularly in the Middle East (Drezner 2011; Gerges 2012). Realist advocates of retrenchment have been at pains to point out that the administration's policies fall far short of such a disengagement (Posen 2014; Walt 2014), and it is perhaps more appropriate to see the US shifting – progressively, as not all of the change has occurred under the Obama administration – from a relatively short-lived bout of unilateral world-making back to a more traditional internationalism. Under Obama that internationalism has been increasingly characterised by a strategy of divested hegemony in which the United States eschews direct American action in favour of engaging and facilitating allies and proxies. In the Asia-Pacific, that has involved encouraging its traditional partners – particularly Japan – to make more of a contribution to their own security, with the United States offering symbolic shows of strength in the South China Sea and renewed commitment to regional trade and governance structures in return.

In the Middle East, the original geography of the War on Terror that Obama had sought to reroute the United States away from was renewed post-Arab

Spring in a new and shifting map of the region. In Egypt, Hosni Mubarak, a former bastion of (relative) stability and a reliable security partner, was jettisoned (see Chapter 10), a process made possible by the depth of American patronage within the Egyptian military. As the region has descended into wide-spread instability and conflict, the Obama administration has increasingly applied American capabilities indirectly with the goal of shaping the evolution of conflicts, in contrast to the approach of the early years of the War on Terror, where the explicit and direct involvement of US forces was tasked with attaining particular outcomes.

This more indirect application of American power has two distinctive features. First is the divesting of hegemonic responsibilities to regional allies. This was evident as early as 2011, when Saudi Arabia and the Gulf Cooperation Council (GCC) were tasked with propping up the ruling monarchy in Bahrain, the home of the US 5th Fleet. Later, in the Libya intervention, where an anonymous US official characterised the administration's approach as 'leading from behind' (Lizza 2011), the United States acted in support of France and the UK in a NATO context, although the nominal 'leaders' were reliant on US support for basic operational tasks such as air-to-air refuelling (Barry 2011). Since 2015, Saudi Arabia has led a coalition of nine Arab states seeking to influence the outcome of the Yemeni civil war, a campaign for which the US provides intelligence and logistical support, as well as supplying the necessary munitions.

Second, the administration has also preferred to engage proxy forces on the ground, limiting the direct US ground force presence to covert and special forces. In Libya and Syria, rebel forces have been supported by Gulf states with American approval, at the same time as the US has engaged in directly training and equipping Syrian forces in Turkey and Qatar, and providing the Kurdish *peshmerga* with advanced weaponry. The administration has even employed Iranian forces as the necessary ground complement to US air strikes against ISIS in Iraq (Krieg 2016, p. 106).

By divesting its hegemony in this way, the United States has sought to reduce its exposure to crises, and in particular to blowback consequences from the actions that are necessary for the management of peace and security. Free-riding by allies and others on the hegemonic public goods of the global commons was not an issue for the United States in the Cold War and post-Cold War period, since the blowback consequences of American actions to sustain a benign security environment were minor. That is no longer the case. The spread of insecurity across borders and the disintegration of the division between state and non-state actors has led American strategists to seek to inure the United States to an environment in which resistance to hegemonic control is pervasive and violent. Neither the American public nor US policy-makers continue to value the privileges of unilateralism in the ways they once did.

Yet even as it attempts to divest itself of particular strategic assets and responsibilities and to supplant its exposure onto others, the United States has also sought to retain the option on ownership, and to direct the goals and conduct of operations carried out by others. With Western allies in NATO this has to a large extent worked, particularly as the administration's focus on Asia creates pathologies in European capitals.[3] With others, such as Qatar and Saudi Arabia, the United States has had to stomach a culture of operations that, for example, is far less sensitive to Western notions of collateral damage. And support for non-state proxies, of course, has a long history of rebounding on great powers.

Conclusion

The Obama administration's relative reticence when it comes to the direct application of American military force may have avoided getting the United States into any more 'dumb wars' – so far. Obama has extracted the United States from the wars he inherited, although the ongoing conflict with ISIS in Iraq and Syria may be seen as a continuation of the events set in train by the US invasion in 2003. But the shutting down of the Bush administration's wars cannot be seen as taking the United States off the path of permanent war, since America's strategic overloading on the tools of war has its roots not in the War on Terror, but in the failure to draw down after the Cold War.

Indeed, it may be best to understand Obama's call for the United States to move off a permanent war footing less as a call to close down the national pathology of the War on Terror, than as a warning: the Obama withdrawals don't mean that future American leaders couldn't take the United States into more ill-judged military adventures; and the US's over-reliance on the military instrument is something the country as a whole needs to address. In this sense it echoes another president with whom history may most closely compare Obama: Dwight Eisenhower, and the counsel in his farewell address to guard against unwarranted influence by the military-industrial complex, not that this administration has been any more reticent than its predecessors to sell American arms around the world (Gould *et al.* 2015; and see also Chapter 3 below). The deeply embedded political and bureaucratic culture of enormous defence budgets, and a wider militarism in American society, surely militate against a return to the kind of civil–military relations that characterised the United States before NSC-68. But if the key lesson of the Bush administration for US foreign policy was that unipolarity does not mean omnipotence, the Obama administration's legacy in defence may be that having capabilities does not entail using them.

Notes

1 The key elements in the Western strategic assessment of the Soviet Union took shape in the space of seventeen days in February and March 1946. The discovery of Soviet spies in the Manhattan Project was swiftly followed by George Kennan's Long Telegram, which was the first systematic intelligence appraisal of the USSR's attitudes and intentions. Less than two weeks later, Churchill, with the tacit approval of Truman, set out with typically vivid imagery the communist challenge to liberal civilisation.
2 It is easy to forget that Perot was the early front-runner, achieving as high as 39 per cent in the polls in June 1992, with 49 per cent believing he could win the election when he dropped out of the race in July (Eldersveld and Walton 2000).

3 The US Ambassador to NATO and the Supreme Allied Commander Europe, somewhat
   unsurprisingly, described the Libya campaign as a 'model intervention' (Daalder and
   Stavridis 2012).

References

Acheson, D., 1969. *Present at the creation: my years in the State Department*, New York:
   Norton.
Bacevich, A.J., 2010. *Washington rules: America's path to permanent war* 1st edn, New
   York: Metropolitan Books.
Barry, B., 2011. Libya's Lessons. *Survival*, 53(5), pp. 5–14.
Boot, M., 2012. Overspending the Peace Dividend. *Los Angeles Times*. Available at:
   http://articles.latimes.com/2012/jan/08/opinion/la-oe-boot-defense-20120108.
Boyle, M.J., 2013. The Costs and Consequences of Drone Warfare. *International Affairs*,
   89(1), pp. 1–29.
Brands, H.W., 1989. The Age of Vulnerability: Eisenhower and the National Insecurity
   State. *The American Historical Review*, 94(4), pp. 963–989. Available at: www.jstor.
   org/stable/1906591.
Brinkley, D., 1997. Democratic Enlargement: The Clinton Doctrine. *Foreign Policy*, 106,
   pp. 110–127.
Brooks, D., 2008. Obama Admires Bush. *New York Times*, 16 May.
Buzan, B., 2006. Will the 'Global War on Terrorism' Be the New Cold War? *International Affairs*, 82(6), pp. 1101–1118. Available at: www.jstor.org/stable/4122087.
Buzan, B., de Wilde, J. and Waever, O. 1998. *Security : a new framework for analysis*,
   Boulder, CO: Lynne Rienner.
Byers, M., 2002. Terrorism, the Use of Force and International Law after 11 September.
   International Relations, 16(2), pp. 155–170. Available at: http://ire.sagepub.com/
   content/16/2/155.abstract.
Carpenter, T.G., 1992. *A search for enemies: America's alliances after the cold war*,
   Washington, DC: Cato Institute.
Chatterjee, P., 2015. A Chilling New Post-traumatic Stress Disorder: Why Drone Pilots Are
   Quitting in Record Numbers. *salon.com*. Available at: www.salon.com/2015/03/06/a_
   chilling_new_post_traumatic_stress_disorder_why_drone_pilots_are_quitting_in_
   record_numbers_partner/.
Clarke, J. and Clad, J., 1995. *After the crusade: American foreign policy for the post-superpower age*, Lanham, MD: Madison Books.
Clymer, A., 1991. Bush's Arms Plan; New Weapons Cuts May Prompt More Than Bush
   Wants. *New York Times*, 30 September.
Cohen, R., 2009. Moralism on the Shelf. *Washington Post*, 10 March.
Cox, M., 2009. Why Did We Get the End of the Cold War Wrong? *British Journal of
   Politics & International Relations*, 11(2), pp. 161–176. Available at: http://dx.doi.
   org/10.1111/j.1467–856X.2008.00358.x.
Daalder, I.H. and Stavridis, J.G., 2012. NATO's Victory in Libya. *Foreign Affairs*, 91(2),
   pp. 2–7.
Drezner, D.W., 2011. Does Obama Have a Grand Strategy: Why We Need Doctrines in
   Uncertain Times. *Foreign Affairs*, 90(4), pp. 57–68.
Eldersveld, S.J. and Walton, H., 2000. *Political parties in American society*, Boston:
   Bedford/St Martin's. Available at: www.loc.gov/catdir/bios/hol057/99064268.html.

Foley, M., 2007. *American credo: the place of ideas in US politics*, Oxford: Oxford University Press. Available at: www.oxfordscholarship.com/oso/public/content/political-science/9780199232673/toc.html.

Freedland, J., 2009. After a Flurry of Early Activity, the Obama Doctrine is Taking Shape. *Guardian*. Available at: www.guardian.co.uk/commentisfree/2009/mar/11/barack-obama-doctrine-us-foreign-policy.

Friedersdorf, C., 2012. 'Every Person Is Afraid of the Drones': The Strikes' Effect on Life in Pakistan. *The Atlantic*.

Gaddis, J.L., 2005. *Strategies of containment: a critical appraisal of American national security policy during the Cold War*, New York: Oxford University Press. Available at: www.loc.gov/catdir/enhancements/fy0640/2004065459-d.html.

Gaffney Jr., F.J., 2000. American Power – For What? A Symposium. *Commentary*, 109(1), pp. 21–47.

Gates Jr., H.L., 1995. Powell and the Black Elite. *New Yorker*, 73, 25 September.

Gerges, F.A., 2012. *Obama and the Middle East: the end of America's moment?*, Basingstoke: Macmillan.

Gould, J., Judson, J. and Mehta, A., 2015. Pentagon Agency Handled Record Foreign Arms Sales in 2015. *Defense News*, 18 October.

Haass, R.N., 2008. The Age of Nonpolarity. *Foreign Affairs*, 87(3), pp. 44–56. Available at: http://search.ebscohost.com/login.aspx?direct=true&db=bth&AN=31700689&site=ehost-live.

Halper, S. and Clarke, J., 2004. *America alone: the neo-conservatives and the global order*, Cambridge: Cambridge University Press.

Halperin, M.H. and Woods, J.M., 1990. Ending the Cold War at Home. *Foreign Policy*, 81, pp. 128–143. Available at: www.jstor.org/stable/1148812.

Harries, O., 2000. American Power – For What? A Symposium. *Commentary*, 109(1), pp. 21–47.

Holland, J., 2009. From September 11th, 2001 to 9–11: From Void to Crisis. *International Political Sociology*, 3(3), pp. 275–292. Available at: http://dx.doi.org/10.1111/j.1749-5687.2009.00076.x.

House Armed Services Committee, 1992. Hearing of the House Armed Services Committee, 6 February.

Hyland, W.G., 1990. America's New Course. *Foreign Affairs*, 69(2), pp. 1–12. Available at: www.jstor.org/stable/20044300.

IISS, 2015. *The military balance 2015*, Abingdon: Routledge.

Ikenberry, G.J., 2001. *After victory: institutions, strategic restraint, and the rebuilding of order after major wars*, Princeton, NJ: Princeton University Press.

Jervis, R., 2001. Was the Cold War a Security Dilemma? *Journal of Cold War Studies*, 3(1), pp. 36–60.

Jervis, R., 2006. The Remaking of a Unipolar World. *The Washington Quarterly*, 29(3), pp. 7–19.

Katzman, K., 2014. *Achievements of and outlook for sanctions on Iran*, Washington DC: US Congressional Research Service.

Kimball, W.F., 1992. U.S. Economic Strategy in World War II: Wartime Goals, Peacetime Plans. In W. F. Kimball, ed. *America unbound: World War II and the making of a superpower*. New York: St. Martin's Press, pp. 139–157.

Kitchen, N., 2011. The Obama Doctrine – Detente or Decline? *European Political Science*, 10(1), pp. 27–35. Available at: http://dx.doi.org/10.1057/eps.2010.71.

Kitchen, N., 2013. Structural Shifts and Strategic Change: From the War on Terror to the Pivot to Asia. In M. Bentley and J. Holland, eds. *Obama's foreign policy: ending the War on Terror*. London and New York: Routledge, pp. 61–75.

Krieg, A., 2016. Externalizing the Burden of War: The Obama Doctrine and US Foreign Policy in the Middle East. *International Affairs*, 92(1), pp. 97–113.

Lake, A., 1993. From Containment to Enlargement. *US Department of State Dispatch*, 4(2), pp. 658–664.

Layne, C., 1993. The Unipolar Illusion: Why New Great Powers Will Rise. *International Security*, 17(4), pp. 5–51.

Layne, C., 2006. The Unipolar Illusion Revisited: The Coming of the United States' Unipolar Moment. *International Security*, 31(2), pp. 7–41.

Lizza, R., 2011. The Consequentialist: How the Arab Spring Remade Obama's Foreign Policy. *The New Yorker*, 2 May.

McCrisken, T., 2011. Ten Years on: Obama's War on Terrorism in Rhetoric and Practice. *International Affairs*, 87(4), pp. 781–801. Available at: http://dx.doi.org/10.1111/j.1468–2346.2011.01004.x.

Mann, J., 2004. *Rise of the Vulcans: the history of Bush's war cabinet*, New York and London: Viking.

Maynes, C.W., 1990. America without the Cold War. *Foreign Policy*, 78, pp. 3–25. Available at: www.jstor.org/stable/1148626.

Moynihan, D.P., 1990. The Peace Dividend. *New York Review of Books*, 37(11).

Moynihan, D.P., 1992. End the 'Torment of Secrecy'. *The National Interest*, 27, pp. 18–21.

Mueller, J., 1990. The Obsolescence of Major War. *Security Dialogue*, 21(3), pp. 321–328.

Nelson, K.L., 1995. *The making of détente: Soviet–American relations in the shadow of Vietnam*, Baltimore, MD: Johns Hopkins University Press.

Nordlinger, E.A., 1991. America's Strategic Immunity: The Basis of a National Security Strategy. In R. Jervis and S. Bialer, eds. *Soviet–American relations after the cold war*. Durham, NC: Duke University Press, pp. 239–261.

Nordlinger, E.A., 1995. *Isolationism reconfigured: American foreign policy for a new century*, Princeton, NJ, and Chichester: Princeton University Press.

Nye, J.S., 2008. *The powers to lead*, Oxford: Oxford University Press.

Nye, J.S., 2011. *The future of power* 1st edn, New York: PublicAffairs.

Pessen, E., 1993. *Losing our souls: the American experience in the cold war*, Chicago: I.R. Dee.

Posen, B.R., 2014. *Restraint: a new foundation for US grand strategy*, Ithaca, NY: Cornell University Press.

Quinn, A., 2013. US Decline and Systemic Constraint. In M. Bentley and J. Holland, eds. *Obama's foreign policy: ending the war on terror*. London and New York: Routledge, pp. 45–60.

Rogers, P., 2000. *Losing control: global security in the twenty-first century*, London: Pluto.

Snyder, J.L., 1991. *Myths of empire: domestic politics and international ambition*, Ithaca, NY: Cornell University Press.

Steel, R., 1995. *Temptations of a superpower*, Cambridge, MA: Harvard University Press.

Stiglitz, J.E. and Bilmes, L.J., 2008. *The three trillion dollar war: the true cost of the Iraq conflict*, New York: W.W. Norton.

Tertrais, B., 2012. The Demise of Ares: The End of War as We Know It? *The Washington Quarterly*, 35(3), pp. 7–22.

Thompson, W.R., 2006. Systemic Leadership, Evolutionary Processes, and International Relations Theory: The Unipolarity Question. *International Studies Review*, 8, pp. 1–22.

Tyson, A.S., 2008. Gates Warns of Militarized Policy. *Washington Post*, 16 July.

US National Security Council, 1950. *NSC 68: United States objectives and programs for national security*, Washington DC.

Walt, S.M., 2014. Do No (More) Harm. *Foreign Policy*, 7 August.

Whitfield, S.J., 1996. *The culture of the Cold War*, Baltimore, MD: Johns Hopkins University Press. Available at: www.loc.gov/catdir/bios/jhu051/95023468.html.

Wohlforth, W.C., 1999. The Stability of a Unipolar World. *International Security*, 24(1), pp. 5–41.

Yglesias, M., 2015. The Obama Undoctrine. *Vox*. Available at: www.vox.com/2015/2/9/8001459/obama-undoctrine.

Zakaria, F., 2012. Inside Obama's World: The President talks to TIME About the Changing Nature of American Power. *Time*, 19 January.

2 Restraint and constraint

A cautious president in a time of limits

Adam Quinn

Presidents make their own policy but not in circumstances of their own choosing, and so it has been for Barack Obama. He came to office in 2009, succeeding a president, George W. Bush, whose administration displayed great confidence in the scale and utility of American military power and worried little about resource constraints. President Obama's administration has served as a counterpoint in both regards. Indeed, its tenure could justly be read as a reaction against what went before. The United States remains by far the most powerful single state in the international system, and its role as founder and leader of the liberal order brings with it certain expectations of engagement and activism. Obama could not escape those if he tried, and in some regards he has been quite happy to fulfil the demands of casting. But in seeking to do so he has been, when compared with his predecessor, both more pessimistic about what the application of military force can achieve and more restrained in his actions and diplomatic posture. These are, one would suppose, not unrelated facts.

In my contribution (Quinn 2013) to a previous volume by the same editors as this book, which discussed President Obama's first term, I made two main points. The first was that even primarily structural theories of International Relations allow scope for agency when it comes to the behaviour of states. Kenneth Waltz's neorealism (Waltz 2010), the best known and most purely structural, does not propose that all states can be relied upon to behave in a set way. It simply posits that over the long term states on aggregate are socialised towards behaving in a conservative, *realpolitik*-oriented manner by the combined effect of an anarchic environment and their overriding drive for self-preservation. Combine this understanding with knowing the distribution of international power at a given time, and you have a useful but not infallible basis for expectations regarding particular instances of national behaviour. My second proposition was that the Obama administration had an inclination towards restraint that dovetailed well with the period in which it was called upon to govern, i.e. one of relative decline in America's power advantage over other states.

In such a period, I suggested, the United States would increasingly be required to make choices harder than had been forced upon it for some time regarding allocation of funds for the demands of national security. No longer would American leaders have the luxury of assuming the nation could afford to be incontinent in its prioritisation and promiscuous in its interventions without serious risk of exhausting its resources. The track record of administration policy has continued to grow in the years since that chapter appeared; at the time of writing the end of Obama's time in office draws near. As is so often the case with presidencies, events have resisted policymakers' efforts to neatly apply their preferred hierarchy of priorities. Nevertheless, in the face of challenges, the administration has continued to display the same quality of circumspect restraint noted above, and apparent intuitive comfort with the need to plan for a world in which American power is less pre-eminent than in the recent past. This being the case, it would be fair to conclude that the analysis provided last time remains robust.

Rather than litigate the same points again here, this chapter will consider the points made in that previous contribution to be stipulated, and this new instalment will seek to do three things: first, briefly to note any major changes in trends affecting the United States' relative international position; second, now that we have almost the complete track record of this administration in office as a basis for judgement, to survey the extent to which there has been continuity in security policy between Bush and Obama, to the surprise and disappointment of some. Third and finally, it will argue that the key difference between the administrations was reluctance to begin major new overseas operations, and that this was motivated by concerns over both efficacy and cost.

The power position of the United States

The George W. Bush administration, especially after September 2001, was notable for the ambition of its grand strategy and for holding office during a period of high confidence regarding the scale and utility of the United States' international power. In this sense its choices and national circumstances appear mutually reinforcing in retrospect.

The signature strategic document of the administration's tenure was the 2002 National Security Strategy (NSC; White House 2002). This set it as the objective of the United States to prevent the rise of any new concentration of power capable of rivalling America, characterised the world order as one of harmonious concert between all major powers in the context of US primacy, and laid the ground for what would soon become publicly known as the doctrine of 'pre-emption' regarding use of force against hostile states or other actors. This escalation in the scope and explicitness of US hegemonic ambition was underlined in a series of public presidential pronouncements, including speeches before Congress (Bush 2002a) and at West Point (Bush 2002b) in which Bush developed the same themes as well as naming the 'Axis of Evil' as the primary focus of American attention. The most expansive – some would say strident – articulation of the administration's desire to exercise power for transformative purposes internationally came in Bush's second inaugural address (2005), in which he set 'ending tyranny in our world' as the ultimate end of American strategy.

This was not only manifested in the realm of ideas. The administration launched two major ground wars, first in Afghanistan and then in Iraq, which would vary in size over time but which at their peaks involved 100,000 and 166,000 troops respectively (*New York Times* 2011). These overseas operations were sizeable in their ambitions – to create functioning systems of representative, accountable and pro-American government that could be sustained after a US departure – and equally sizeable in cost. In addition to these commitments, the administration was confrontational in its relations with Iran, sufficiently so to lead many analysts to consider a further war there a non-trivial possibility (Knowlton 2007). During the course of this period, US defence spending increased by hundreds of billions per year (Korb *et al.* 2011), to a level $100 billion higher than average yearly spending during the Cold War, while the administration remained resolutely and deliberately unconcerned about identifying current income to pay for its overseas operations. On fiscal matters it applied a philosophy articulated, hyperbolically, by one very senior figure as 'deficits don't matter' (Garofalo 2008).

The Bush administration was not an outlier in its confidence regarding US power. Rather, it was leaning into the zeitgeist. The early years of the twenty-first century saw a wave of bold claims regarding the nature, extent and likely longevity of American world domination. Indeed, for a time the concept of 'American empire' became accepted currency within mainstream discourse on both left and right (Bacevich 2002; Cox 2004, 2005; Ferguson 2004; Mann 2003). Certainly debate was engaged frequently over the desirability of American pre-eminence and the capacity of the US to pursue imperial projects with ultimate constancy and efficacy. And there were those such as Joseph Nye (2002) who, while proposing the importance of 'soft power', argued that paradoxically the United States might have increasing difficulty translating its advantage in relative capabilities into desired outcomes, even as those capabilities loomed larger than ever. Still, the supposition of American dominance on an imperial scale was a commonplace of the intellectual and political milieu in the midst of which the Bush administration charted the course outlined above.

By the inauguration of Barack Obama in January 2009, this high-water mark for American power and confidence already seemed some way in the past. One reason was the very visible failure of American actions in Iraq and Afghanistan to produce the outcomes sought. After thousands of US casualties, tens of thousands of civilian deaths, and the expenditure of trillions of dollars (Crawford 2014), neither country was peaceful, stable or politically unified. As a result, the transformative global ambitions of the Bush administration's early and middle years – for a world peace built on a global wave of liberalism and democracy – had come to seem at best like overreaching, at worst fantastical, and certainly not achievable within the foreseeable future. The Iraq intervention might have succeeded in destabilising existing patterns of state order in the Middle East, but it certainly had not triggered the hoped-for cascade of liberalisation and democratisation. If anything, it appeared to have unleashed uncontrollable and dangerous new forces running contrary to US hopes, while in the process giving the

United States ownership of two expensive and failing expeditionary wars. The shortcomings of American military capabilities when applied in pursuit of transformative political goals were therefore in plain view before the end of Bush's term of office.

The second component in signalling a reconsideration of America's power position was the financial crisis of that same year, the near collapse of the economy after the bankruptcy of Lehman Brothers, and the subsequent Great Recession. The combined effect of these events was to significantly shrink US GDP, reduce government revenue, radically increase the national debt and deficit, and undermine confidence in the fibre of the US economy. This in turn set the stage for rancorous political argument within the US during the Obama presidency about levels of government spending and debt, with immense pressure placed on the president by Republicans in Congress to agree to substantial spending cuts (MacAskill 2011). Whether spending reductions were truly an imperative of the federal government's stretched fiscal position or merely the outgrowth of a surge in anti-government ideology is a matter of continuing debate. Nevertheless, the result was ultimately that the defence budget became one part of a wider political argument regarding spending restraint, leading to the imposition of meaningful cuts from 2013 onward (Cordesman 2015).

These were immediate, crisis-driven downturns in US economic growth and government capacity in the short term. But they served to compound anxiety over the effects of longer-term global trends: the movement of the world economy's 'centre of gravity' eastward (Quah 2011), China's rapid economic growth over several decades bringing it to the brink of being the world's largest economy, and the prospect of rising powers such as China investing their increased economic resources in enhancing their military capabilities. Domestically, meanwhile, there had long been concern in the United States about whether longstanding commitments to medical care and social security for an ageing population could be met from government revenues without significant tax rises. Such a crunch of spending priorities would make maintaining, let alone increasing, the budget for overseas national security projects a political challenge, given the categories of spending that would need to see cuts to make this possible.

Over the course of the final years of the Obama administration, these trends have slowed somewhat in ways advantageous to the United States, though without – for the time being at least – halting. Growth in China sputtered without stalling in 2015, with apprehension growing regarding the prospect of a full-blown future crisis with roots in its inflated stock market or opaque banking system. In the United States, meanwhile, annual growth rates recovered to passable levels, better than those most other developed Western economies are managing. Nevertheless, for the time being the rebalancing of the global economy towards Asia continues. Meanwhile in the United States a fiscally conservative Congress with power over appropriations ensures that tight restrictions on spending will remain in place in the absence of a major and unanticipated electoral realignment or an intruding external security crisis. For a variety of reasons, intellectual and political, it remains controversial to characterise the United States as being in the process of relative decline as an international power (Quinn 2011). But if we take that charged word out of the equation, there is widespread agreement that what is unfolding is a long-term narrowing of the GDP gap between the United States and certain rising powers, and that considerations of resource and priority will be more keenly felt by the United States now and in the future than they were during the first decade of this century.

Constraint and continuity: the persistence of the counterterror framework

President Obama was elected in large part on the back of a sustained and effective critique of Bush-era foreign and security policy. Obama had opposed the war in Iraq – albeit from outside the constraints of elected office at the national level – before it started (NPR 2009), and continued to do so through to 2008. He condemned the use of 'enhanced interrogation techniques', i.e. torture, by the US government (Mikkelsen 2008). He criticised the apparently open-ended nature of the 'War on Terror' as a legal and ideological framework, on the grounds that it conferred broad and 'unchecked' authority on the presidency in the use of force and gathering of intelligence so long as there was an asserted connection between the targets and the threat of terrorism, expansively defined (Obama 2007). And he chided the administration for having depleted the stock of international goodwill towards the United States through its penchant for confrontation and unilateralism (Pew Research Center 2008).

In government, Obama has in some instances pursued meaningful change. Interrogation practices were reformed to exclude methods such as waterboarding. Immediately upon assuming office he directed the CIA to close secret prisons and ordered the closure of the detention facility at Guantanamo Bay (Warrick and DeYoung 2009). He reduced and ultimately liquidated the American military presence on the ground in Iraq (Baker 2009). He visited Cairo to make a speech calling for better relations between the US and the Muslim world based on a new commitment to mutual respect (Obama 2009a). He signalled his desire to open dialogue with the government of Iran with a view to resolving peacefully the standoff over its pursuit of nuclear technology (BBC News 2009). He rejected the 'Global War on Terror' as a guiding framework for policy, and in 2013 made an extended speech arguing that presidential pursuit of counter-terrorism policy should operate within a framework more bounded and less open-ended than the Authorization for Use of Military Force (AUMF) put in place during the fearful and febrile political context of September 2001 (Obama 2013).

Notwithstanding these important points, President Obama ultimately did embrace continuity in security policy to a greater extent than many won over by Candidate Obama's critiques had hoped (McCrisken 2011, 2013). Enabled by technology, he greatly scaled up the United States' use of armed unmanned aerial vehicles (drones) to kill targets in territories where the US was not officially at war, including Pakistan and Yemen (*The Intercept* 2015). Though perhaps reined in from their scale and profile during the Bush administration, the practices of 'rendition' and extrajudicial detention of individuals suspected of terrorist activity, broadly defined, have continued to take place under the Obama administration (ProPublica 2012). Beset by practical and political barriers, Obama had not as of late 2015 either closed Guantanamo Bay or repealed or replaced the AUMF. As his administration drew down the US presence in Iraq, he in fact increased the US presence in Afghanistan during his first term (Litpak and Koran 2015). By the end of his second term he had decided, reversing his previous plan, that a residual US troop presence in Afghanistan would continue indefinitely (Rosenberg and Shear 2015). Meanwhile US air power was being used once again in Iraq, as well as in Syria, in response to the Islamic State threat that rose up there in the aftermath of American withdrawal (DoD 2015). It had previously been deployed in Libya in 2011, where it was indispensable – along with special forces – in bringing about the fall of the Gaddafi regime to its domestic enemies (Barry 2011). Furthermore, as the revelations of Edward Snowden in 2013 made clear, the Obama administration put in place a surveillance apparatus at home and abroad of shocking scope, relying on extremely expansive legal readings of the executive's authority as the basis for doing so (*Guardian* 2015).

To some extent this disconnect between pre-inauguration hope and later action reflects the fact that some projected onto Obama a breadth of liberal or even pacifist principle that simply was not justified by any statements made by the candidate himself (McCrisken 2011, 2013). Obama always believed military force could be necessary and justified under the right circumstances, a point he made prior to his election and underlined in the acceptance speech he delivered after the peculiar decision to award him the Nobel Peace Prize only months into his first term (Obama 2009b). He may have been opposed to wars he considered 'dumb' in conception or execution, but not to all war. Likewise, he was committed from the outset to continuing to use the institutions of the security state to pursue tough measures against terrorist and extremist groups and individuals. Critical though he was of some of the specifics of how Bush had characterised and pursued his 'war' on terror, Obama only ever promised a more effective counterterrorist campaign, not a radical deconstruction of the enterprise of counterterrorism itself, discursive or practical (Obama 2007).

This does not account entirely for the degree of continuity, however. It also seems to be the case that upon assuming office Obama became persuaded of the reality and seriousness of the threat posed by terrorism and extremism, and thus became a supporter of policies he might have opposed while campaigning as an opposition candidate. Indeed, the escalation of government policy in some areas, such as surveillance and targeted killing by drone, was linked to his desire to turn the page on other approaches, such as major ground operations. One could read this either as the co-optation of the new president by the national security establishment into which he was inducted upon arriving in office, or as the success of experts with inside knowledge in convincing the new commander in chief of the necessity and legitimacy of some of their ongoing programmes.

Either way, it would be reasonable to characterise this outcome as a type of structural influence on the course of policy, moderating the impulses towards change of a new chief executive. One can see evidence of this willing acceptance of significant elements of the national security establishment's worldview in at least one extended interview on the subject in the latter part of his presidency (*Vox* 2015).

We might also add the domestic ideological and political climate as a factor affecting the president's course on certain issues. His inability to follow through on closing the facility at Guantanamo Bay stemmed in large part from Congressional resistance. His decision to increase troop numbers in Afghanistan was heavily influenced by a campaign of pressure orchestrated by key actors in the military (Woodward 2010). We cannot be certain of Obama's reasons for being willing to embrace the legitimacy and methods of the counterterrorist apparatus. Aside – presumably – from genuine conviction as to its effectiveness, he may have been influenced by a calculation that in the prevailing domestic political context there were only very low political risks associated with persevering with a 'tough' approach, and higher costs associated with the arguments that would follow a notable winding down of the security apparatus (Roth 2015).

When it comes to the question of how his second term compared with his first, we might plausibly say that at the outset of his first term President Obama was engaged in a struggle to reconcile his prior critiques of President Bush's 'War on Terror' approach with the pressures towards continuity that come with office. Although he did make some consequential changes – as far as we know no one has been waterboarded by a US government employee since January 2009, and American troop presence in both Iraq and Afghanistan has been drastically reduced – when it comes to the counterterror framework as a whole, on balance the gravitational pull of continuity has proved stronger than the drive to change. Obama has articulated the desire for a more constrained and transparent executive branch when it comes to the waging of the campaign against terrorism, but has been unable to give this solid institutional or legal form beyond the administration's own assurances that within the vast sphere of presidential discretion it will be sober and scrupulous in its decisions regarding the use of force and the application of surveillance. Meanwhile an apparatus for the identification, targeting and killing of perceived threats has grown up that tacitly accepts the premise that the campaign against terrorism is something akin to war, even while seeking to be more restrained than Bush in the scope of the objectives pursued and more surgical in the tools employed. In the absence of external scrutiny or binding legal constraints, any changes in this area are contingent for their sustainability on the decisions of subsequent presidents and the political climate of the time. Obama's second term ultimately confirmed him as a president who accommodated and operated within the parameters of preference of the national security establishment more than he sought to bend it to any agenda which that establishment's liberal critics might have hoped to see implemented.

A tilt towards restraint: 'don't do stupid stuff' or expensive stuff

An important reason for the expansion of those aspects of security policy to which the Obama administration has committed on a large scale, such as drone strikes and surveillance, is that they appear cost effective when compared with the major ground operations in Iraq and Afghanistan. None of the principal decision-makers in the Bush administration predicted that those ground operations would last as long or cost as much as they did. But even were we to suppose they might have had an inkling that the missions would prove more expensive than the initially avowed plan indicated, the Bush presidency's freedom of action was greatly enhanced by the US government's perceived enjoyment of significant slack in terms of both the total national resources available and the level of deficit spending available without Congressional obstruction. During the Obama presidency, this was no longer the case.

In the aftermath of the bailout of the banking system following the financial crisis, the cost of stimulus spending approved in 2008 and 2009, and the shrinkage of government revenue caused by the recession, the centre ground of American politics from 2010 onwards regarded the federal government as being extended to its fiscal limits. In view of the Iraq experience, President Obama was already sceptical about the efficacy of major ground operations as a means of achieving sustainable political results, even more so once cost-benefit analysis was taken into account. But even if he had not been so disappointed by outcomes obtained, the sheer cost of such operations would have ruled them out of serious consideration – bar the intrusion of an unambiguous security emergency – given the fiscal climate in which Obama was required to govern. Though Republicans in Congress were more favourably disposed towards authorisation requests for defence spending than domestic entitlement spending, much of the debate over budgets in this period took the form of arguments about the headline level of spending for the total budget. (For a flavour of the period see Kane *et al.* 2011). In the absence of willingness on the president's part to trade domestic spending priorities for overseas military ones, nothing comparable to Bush-era war spending could have been seriously considered by Obama without a major external event disrupting the terms of the political argument over the budget.

As a consequence of the budgetary argument as it actually did unfold, the later years of the Obama administration witnessed meaningful real-terms cuts in defence spending for the first time in a generation (Walker 2014). It should be noted as a caveat that these cuts fell on a budget that had swollen significantly during the Bush years, affected by the scale on which war was waged during that period. Nevertheless, the cuts imposed were sufficient to lead those holding a brief for the Department of Defense to warn of significant implications for capabilities. It is also worth noting that below the headline spending figure, the defence budget has been put under stress by rising costs in areas that do not contribute directly to any margin of military superiority over rival states, e.g. healthcare, which consumed nearly 10 per cent of the budget in 2013. This trend led

Secretary of Defense Robert Gates to complain that 'health-care costs are eating the Defense Department alive' (Kokulis 2013; Pincus 2012). In recent years the Republican-controlled Congress has sought to boost the defence budget, but in 2015 the president blocked its efforts, accurately perceiving them as a means to loosen the strictures imposed on defence by earlier agreements, a Republican priority, while side-stepping the need for agreement on domestic spending. Until either a comprehensive agreement can be reached between the parties on spending, or Republicans can fully capture both executive and legislature, potentially opening the door to a new budgetary settlement favourable to defence at the expense of domestic programmes (Davis 2015).

We should see Obama's response to national security in this context, particularly in reference to cases where he displayed reluctance to initiate new overseas military interventions, even while subject to political pressure to do so. This has been a major feature of his presidency, and is likely to be remembered as one of its signature qualities. As noted above, he came to office powered in no small part by publicly articulated scepticism regarding the wisdom of the American presence in Iraq, and pursued a determined course of drawing down troops there. He approved significant troop increases in Afghanistan, but this decision was heavily influenced by pressure from key military figures, and was tied to a timetable for subsequent drawdown that signalled future disengagement so strongly that many worried that it undercut the strategic value of the initial deployment (Obama 2011b). Libya in 2011 presented a case that might by historical standards have been thought tailor-made for US intervention: a serious rebellion against an erratic dictator with a long history of anti-Americanism (albeit moderated in later years), combined with high probability of mass executions of rebel forces in the absence of outside intervention, and strong likelihood that US intervention would be decisive in determining the outcome of the conflict. Nevertheless, even with all these factors in place, the United States was slow to act, lagging behind the interventionist posture adopted by the UK and France, and ultimately did so only when it became apparent that no other actor could play the necessary role and that total defeat for its favoured local forces would result from inaction. In the speech explaining his decision to commit US airpower, Obama went out of his way to underline the reluctance with which he had approved military action, and the intervention was explicitly limited to the objectives of saving the rebels and facilitating their toppling of Gaddafi, ruling out the commitment of resources analogous to the Afghan effort to support any new order in Libya (Obama 2011b). This was the policy episode that gave rise to the infelicitous characterisation of the US approach by someone inside the administration itself as 'leading from behind', and while the words were poorly chosen the impression they conveyed was not inaccurate (Lizza 2011).

Subsequent events have only further confirmed the administration's minimalism in cases where military intervention was a plausible policy option. We should exercise some care in identifying cases that supposedly demonstrate a level of American restraint peculiar to Obama. In the case of Russia's annexation of Crimea, for example, and its use of 'hybrid' warfare to destabilise eastern

Ukraine, given the geographical and logistical constraints no remotely viable military response existed for consideration by US policymakers, and therefore it is highly unlikely that an administration of any stripe would have considered escalating the military dimension of the situation. In this regard, the Bush administration's relative passivity in the face of the Russian incursion into Georgia in 2008, in spite of strong administration sympathy for the Saakashvili government, is instructive. But in other cases, most especially in Syria, the United States clearly could have acted, considered acting, was pressed by some to act, but ultimately decided to act only to the minimum extent necessary.

When first confronted with the choice of whether or not to intervene in the Syrian civil war, the Obama administration decided against any meaningful intervention, motivated by what this chapter has characterised as its twin guiding principles: scepticism that American military deployment could deliver superior and sustainable political outcomes on behalf of US interests, and fear of being drawn into an extended entangling engagement at greater cost than could be justified by attainable gains. In both regards administration posture reflected the legacy of Iraq. Subsequently, US involvement was once again seriously considered when it appeared Bashar al-Assad's government had used chemical weapons against its domestic enemies. Meanwhile, the extent of other foreign powers' involvement, including Russia, Iran and the latter's Lebanese proxies, made it seem to some that the United States was paying a price for its reserve, reducing its capacity to shape the ultimate outcome relative to those states which bought a stake through military support. The rise of the Islamic State as a fighting and quasi-governmental force in both Syria and Iraq was decisive in shoving the administration towards greater activism, going beyond its (failing) efforts to train favoured local actors towards direct use of American force and – small but real – US presence on the ground, including deployment of special forces (Baker *et al.* 2015). Still, at each stage it is striking that this administration has opted to minimise the US footprint, limiting its escalations to the smallest scale compatible with what it perceived to be necessary and with the imperative to be seen to act. In this aversion to major overseas action, and the reasons for it – concerns over efficacy and cost that explicitly derive from the Bush administration's experience in Iraq (Obama 2016) – we find the key shift in security policy under the Obama administration.

We might note that this does not imply that the Obama administration had any principled aversion to the cultivation of military power or the maintenance of America's extensive overseas security architecture. In east Asia, for example, the administration embraced the importance of a US presence as a force for stability, and made plans for further investment in long-term capability (Ratnam and Brannen 2015). The important point is that it saw this in the context of a need to prioritise: investment in America's ability to provide for future stability in the Asian theatre would be furthered by avoiding draining embroilment in Middle Eastern wars of a type essentially peripheral to the global balance of power.

Conclusion

At the risk of signalling a banal truth, all administrations represent a combination of continuity and change. No one gets to begin the world again. Nor does anyone get to retread old steps exactly; the path they are required to walk can never precisely replicate that of the past. In view of these foundational truths, we can say that President Obama's policies fell into a familiar schema of categories. He continued some things from Bush-era security policy because he came to believe them necessary. In this category we might place targeted killing and surveillance. He also continued others, at least for a time, that he might have preferred to change; such are the constraints of office in a system where the branches of government divide powers and the executive branch is large and diverse in its interests. In this category we might place detention at Guantanamo Bay, and perhaps the commitment of troops to Afghanistan. He changed course on some issues where he both had strong and clear views and was able to command that they be implemented as policy. Here we might file his prohibition on waterboarding and other forms of torture. He also strongly favoured the removal of US troops from Iraq and saw that objective through in the face of resistance (though we should note that this was already agreed, on paper at least, by the Bush administration in 2008).

In the final category, the greatest shift between the Bush and Obama eras represented a coming together of both presidential preferences and national circumstances in complementary mutual reinforcement. President Obama governed in the shadow of the legacy of Bush's Iraq decisions, and did so during a time of increasingly sharply felt fiscal constraints. That is to say, the largest part of his foreign policy inheritance was a war that appeared to have achieved little of lasting benefit to the US national interest while incurring vast financial cost (to say nothing of the cost in human life, American and Iraqi). And he came into this inheritance at a time when the husbanding of resources was a high priority. From this starting point, his pessimistic views about what it was possible to achieve politically through the use of US military force, combined with the pessimistic views of the US government as a whole regarding what the country could afford in the way of new overseas adventures, put something close to a veto on the launch of major new ground operations during the Obama presidency. This was a period in which the United States felt more constrained than it had for at least two decades by resource considerations, and its leaders had been made conscious of the questionable track record of efficacy of its military power as an applied tool for achieving transformational political ends. It was also a period in which it had leadership disposed to show more restraint, being possessed of a more circumspect awareness of its own limitations than some. In this regard, presidential disposition was a good complement to national circumstances during these years. Whether this will continue to be the case under President Obama's successor is uncertain, as is so much in international politics – who could have foreseen all the events of the Bush presidency from the vantage point of 2000? But the question of whether the United States can achieve a strategy that adequately matches its leaders' ambitions to its national resources will assuredly be of great consequence, not only for America itself but for the world that its behaviour so disproportionately affects.

References

Bacevich, A. (2002) *American Empire: The Realities & Consequences of US Diplomacy*, Cambridge, MA: Harvard University Press.

Baker, P. (2009) 'With Pledges to Troops and Iraqis, Obama Details Pullout', *New York Times*, 27 February, www.nytimes.com/2009/02/28/washington/28troops.html.

Baker, P., Cooper, H. and Sanger, D. (2015) 'Obama Sends Special Operations Forces to Help Fight ISIS in Syria', *New York Times*, 30 October, www.nytimes.com/2015/10/31/world/obama-will-send-forces-to-syria-to-help-fight-the-islamic-state.html.

Barry, J. (2011) 'America's Secret Libya War', 8 August, *Daily Beast*, www.thedaily-beast.com/articles/2011/08/30/america-s-secret-libya-war-u-s-spent-1-billion-on-covert-ops-helping-nato.html.

BBC News, (2009) 'Obama Reaches out to Muslim World', 27 January, http://news.bbc.co.uk/1/hi/world/middle_east/7852650.stm.

Bush, G.W. (2002a) State of the Union Address, 29 January, http://georgewbush-whitehouse.archives.gov/news/releases/2002/01/20020129-11.html.

Bush, G.W. (2002b) Graduation Speech at West Point, 1 June, http://georgewbush-whitehouse.archives.gov/news/releases/2002/06/20020601-3.html.

Bush, G.W. (2005) Second Inaugural Address, 20 January, http://georgewbush-whitehouse.archives.gov/news/releases/2005/01/20050120-1.html.

Cordesman, A. (2015) 'Tracking the Defense Budget: US Defense Budget Cuts, Sequestration, the FY2014 Budget, and the FY2014–FY2022 Forecast', *Center for Strategic and International Studies*, 16 July.

Cox, M. (2004) 'Empire, Imperialism and the Bush Doctrine', *Review of International Studies*, 30:4, pp. 585–608.

Cox, M. (2005) 'Empire by Denial: The Strange Case of the United States', *International Affairs*, Jan 2005, 81:1, pp. 15–30.

Crawford, N.C. (2014) 'U.S. Costs of Wars Through 2014: $4.4 Trillion and Counting', Watson Institute, 25 June, http://watson.brown.edu/costsofwar/files/cow/imce/figures/2014/Costs%20of%20War%20Summary%20Crawford%20June%202014.pdf.

Davis, J.H. (2015) 'In Wielding Rarely Used Veto, President Obama Puts Budget Heat on Republicans', *New York Times*, 22 October, www.nytimes.com/2015/10/23/us/politics/obama-vetoes-defense-bill-deepening-budget-fight-with-gop.html.

Department of Defence (DoD) (2015) 'Operation Inherent Resolve', October, www.defense.gov/News/Special-Reports/0814_Inherent-Resolve.

Ferguson, N. (2004) *Colossus: The Rise and Fall of the American Empire*, London: Allen Lane.

Garofalo, P. (2008) 'Six Years After Cheney Said "Deficits Don't Matter", the National Debt Hits a 50-Year High', *ThinkProgress*, 2 October, http://thinkprogress.org/economy/2008/10/02/172396/cheney-deficit-debt/.

Guardian (2015) 'The NSA Files', www.theguardian.com/us-news/the-nsa-files.

The Intercept (2015) 'The Drone Papers', https://theintercept.com/drone-papers/.

Kane, P., Montgomery, L. and Branigin, W. (2011) 'Obama–Boehner Talks Collapse; Each Side Blames the Other', *Washington Post*, 22 July, www.washingtonpost.com/business/economy/senate-rejects-conservative-budget-proposal-as-obama-boehner-reach-for-grand-bargain/2011/07/22/gIQAzskYTI_story.html.

Knowlton, B. (2007) 'Nuclear-armed Iran Risks "World War III," Bush Says', *New York Times*, 17 October, www.nytimes.com/2007/10/17/world/americas/17iht-prexy.4.793 2027.html.

Kokulis, J.L. (2013) 'Preserving the Military Health Care Benefit: Needed Steps for Reform', American Enterprise Institute, 17 October, www.aei.org/publication/ preserving-the-military-health-care-benefit-needed-steps-for-reform/.

Korb, L.J., Conley, L. and Rothman, A. (2011) 'A Historical Perspective on Defense Budgets', Center for American Progress, 6 July, www.americanprogress.org/issues/ budget/news/2011/07/06/10041/a-historical-perspective-on-defense-budgets/.

Lieberthal, K. (2011). 'The American Pivot to Asia', *Foreign Policy*, 21 December, www.foreignpolicy.com/articles/2011/12/21/the_american_pivot_to_asia?wp_login_ redirect=0.

Litpak, K. and Koran, L. (2015) 'Obama Makes Final Push to Close Guantanamo', *CNN*, http://edition.cnn.com/2015/10/23/politics/guantanamo-bay-prison-closure-obama/.

Lizza, R. (2011) 'The Consequentialist', *New Yorker*, 2 May.

MacAskill, E. (2011) 'Barack Obama Announces $1.1tn Spending Cuts', *Guardian*, 14 February, www.theguardian.com/world/2011/feb/14/barack-obama-spending-cuts.

McCrisken, T. (2011) 'Ten Years on: Obama's War on Terrorism in Rhetoric and Practice', *International Affairs*, July, 87:4, pp. 781–801.

McCrisken, T. (2013) 'Obama's War on Terrorism in Rhetoric and Practice' in M. Bentley and J. Holland (eds), *Obama's Foreign Policy: Ending the War on Terror*, Abingdon and New York: Routledge, pp. 17–44.

Mann, M. (2003) *Incoherent Empire*, London: Verso.

Mikkelsen, R. (2008) 'Ex-generals to Urge Obama Action on Torture Issue', Reuters, 3 December, www.reuters.com/article/2008/12/03/us-usa-obama-torture-idUSTRE4B18 UY20081203.

National Public Radio (NPR) (2009) 'Transcript: Obama's Speech Against the Iraq War', 20 January, www.npr.org/templates/story/story.php?storyId=99591469.

New York Times (2011) 'American Forces in Afghanistan and Iraq', 22 June, www. nytimes.com/interactive/2011/06/22/world/asia/american-forces-in-afghanistan-and-iraq.html?_r=0.

Nye, J.S. (2002) *The Paradox of American Power: Why the World's Only Superpower Can't Go it Alone*, New York: Oxford University Press.

Obama, B. (2007) Speech at Woodrow Wilson Center, Council on Foreign Relations, 1 August, www.cfr.org/elections/obamas-speech-woodrow-wilson-center/p13974.

Obama, B. (2009a) Remarks by the President at Cairo University, White House, 4 June, www.whitehouse.gov/the-press-office/remarks-president-cairo-university-6–04–09.

Obama, B. (2009b) Nobel Lecture, 10 December, www.nobelprize.org/nobel_prizes/ peace/laureates/2009/obama-lecture_en.html.

Obama, B. (2011a) Remarks by the President in Address to the Nation on Libya, 28 March, www.whitehouse.gov/the-press-office/2011/03/28/remarks-president-address-nation-libya.

Obama, B. (2011b) Remarks by the President on the Way Forward in Afghanistan, 22 June, www.whitehouse.gov/the-press-office/2011/06/22/remarks-president-way-forward-afghanistan.

Obama, B. (2013) Remarks by the President at the National Defense University, White House, 23 May, www.whitehouse.gov/the-press-office/2013/05/23/remarks-president-national-defense-university.

Obama, B. (2016) Transcript: President Obama's Address to the Nation on the San Bernardino Terror Attack and the War on ISIS, *CNN*, 7 December, http://edition.cnn.com/2015/12/06/politics/transcript-obama-san-bernardino-isis-address/.

Pew Research Center (2008) 'Global Public Opinion in the Bush Years (2001–2008)', 18 December, www.pewglobal.org/2008/12/18/global-public-opinion-in-the-bush-years-2001–2008/.

Pincus, W. (2012) 'CBO says Military Health-care Costs Could Soar', *Washington Post*, 16 July, www.washingtonpost.com/world/national-security/cbo-says-military-health-care-costs-could-soar/2012/07/16/gJQAFLVQpW_story.html.

ProPublica (2012) 'The Best Reporting on Detention and Rendition Under Obama', 13 July, www.propublica.org/article/the-best-reporting-on-detention-and-rendition-under-obama.

Quah, D. (2011)'The Global Economy's Shifting Centre of Gravity', *Global Policy*, 2:1, http://onlinelibrary.wiley.com/doi/10.1111/j.1758–5899.2010.00066.x/pdf.

Quinn, A. (2011) 'The Art of Declining Politely: Obama's Prudent Presidency and the Waning of American Power', *International Affairs*, 87:4, pp. 803–824.

Quinn, A. (2013) 'US Decline and Systemic Constraint', in Michelle Bentley and Jack Holland (eds), *Obama's Foreign Policy: Ending the War on Terror*, Abingdon and New York: Routledge, pp. 45–60.

Ratnam, G. and Brannen, K. (2015) 'Against Other Threats, Obama's Security Budget Sticks to Asia-Pacific Pivot', *Foreign Policy*, 2 February, http://foreignpolicy.com/2015/02/02/793982budget-asia-pacific-syria-iraq-russia-ukraine/.

Rosenberg, M. and Shear, M. (2015) 'In Reversal, Obama Says U.S. Soldiers Will Stay in Afghanistan to 2017', *New York Times*, 15 October, www.nytimes.com/2015/10/16/world/asia/obama-troop-withdrawal-afghanistan.html.

Roth, K. (2015) 'Obama & Counterterror: The Ignored Record', *New York Review of Books*, February, www.nybooks.com/articles/2015/02/05/obama-counterterror-ignored-record/.

Vox (2015) 'Obama: the *Vox* Conversation, Part 2: Foreign Policy', www.vox.com/a/barack-obama-interview-vox-conversation/obama-foreign-policy-transcript.

Walker, D. (2014) 'Trends in U.S. Military Spending', Council on Foreign Relations, 15 July, www.cfr.org/defense-budget/trends-us-military-spending/p28855.

Waltz, K.N. (2010, originally 1979) *Theory of International Politics*, Long Grove, IL: Waveland Press.

Warrick, J. and DeYoung, K. (2009) 'Obama Reverses Bush Policies on Detention and Interrogation', *Washington Post*, 23 January, www.washingtonpost.com/wp-dyn/content/article/2009/01/22/AR2009012201527.html.

White House (2002) 'The National Security Strategy of the United States of America', September, http://georgewbush-whitehouse.archives.gov/nsc/nss/2002/.

Woodward, B. (2010) *Obama's Wars*, New York: Simon and Schuster

3   Obama as modern Jeffersonian

Jack Holland

Since 1993 the United States has been led by presidents representative of all four of Walter Russell Mead's (and David Hackett Fischer's) foreign policy traditions. First, Bill Clinton's foreign policy exhibited a Hamiltonian–Wilsonian tension, as he attempted to deliver the intoxicating vision of an expanded zone of peace and prosperity, through the promotion of democracy and laissez-faire capitalism. Second, George W. Bush's election flung the United States back onto a relatively isolationist footing, as the president embodied and performed a Jacksonian stance, sensitive to the dangers and sceptical of the entanglements that lurked beyond the water's edge. This, of course, was rapidly modified after 9/11, but American foreign policy remained more overtly Jacksonian in nature than is usually credited in a literature fixated on images of a 'neocon' presidency: a foreign policy of Wilsonianism with boots. Third, Obama's foreign policy has been Jeffersonian in formulation and prosecution. The only footnote to add is that such a stance is, arguably, fundamentally irreconcilable with the demands of world hegemony in the twenty-first century. Obama has recognised this and governed as a 'modern Jeffersonian': an internationalist, wary of the domestic implications of internationalism. This approach has enabled him to enjoy about as much foreign policy success as is possible for a Jeffersonian president of the world's only superpower in a hyper-globalised world.

American foreign policy traditions from Bush Senior to Bush Junior

Conceptualising US foreign policy

This chapter mobilises a theoretical framework developed by two principal authors. Walter Russell Mead's ambitious book, *Special Providence* (2002), builds on David Hackett Fischer's seminal tome, *Albion's Seed* (1989). Fischer (1989) outlines four folkways in the United States that were transported to the North American continent in the language, culture and beliefs of four distinct groups who made their way to the United States in a series of large-scale population movements from Great Britain and Northern Ireland. The first accounts for the exodus of English Puritans from East Anglia to Massachusetts between 1629 and 1641. The second maps the movement of 'distressed Cavaliers and indentured servants' from southern England to Virginia from 1642 to 1675. The third traces migrants from the north Midlands to Delaware between 1675 and 1725. And the fourth notes the flight of the Scots-Irish from the Borderlands of Britain and Ulster, in a series of migration waves, from 1717 to 1775. These groups dispersed across distinct but overlapping territories in the United States, during a period in which the nation, its politics and customs were in formation. Although their numbers are significant they are dwarfed by the impact of these groups on the character and composition of the fledgling nation. As they evolved and took root in the United States, across a variety of measures – including language, dress, habit and belief – these four groups came to dominate American cultural and political life, suppressing minority alternatives.

Mead (1989) extends Fischer's (1989) dense historical unpacking of these complex and interwoven cultural predispositions to consider the impact these migrant groups had on the development of American foreign policy. Respectively, Mead (2002) has labelled these groups and their ideas after four great figures in American political history who best encapsulate their central tenets: Wilsonian, Jeffersonian, Hamiltonian and Jacksonian. Although imperfect, this labelling serves as a useful heuristic and shortcut to understanding their key policy preferences and likely interactions. Together, they offer a nuanced, socially rooted and culturally sensitive alternative to the traditional analytical language of International Relations and US foreign policy.

The best known of the four schools, Wilsonian foreign policy emphasises the spread of human rights through democracy promotion. Although agreeing on the ends of American foreign policy, the school splits on the preferential means by which to achieve them. So-called 'Soft Wilsonians' tend to privilege the role of international organisations such as the United Nations, valuing the efficacy and legitimacy of coalition action and good international citizenship. Their closely related but politically distant counterparts, 'Hard Wilsonians', are quicker to dismiss the limitations that accompany such institutions, and are more willing to use force – unilaterally, if necessary – in order to achieve the optimal foreign policy outcome of a democratised state. Far from being purely altruistic, Wilsonians contend that it is only necessary to consider Germany and Japan to recognise the national interest-premised benefits of a policy of democracy promotion. Crucially, the route to success looks overly optimistic for many Wilsonians, who focus on the heartfelt assumption that inside every enemy there is an American waiting to get out.

Jeffersonians, on the other hand, see themselves as the intellectual defenders of the common man. They revere the constitution and the division of powers that, if carefully and actively preserved, will ensure that the New World never falls prey to the tyrannies of the Old. Like the Wilsonians, Jeffersonians value human rights. In contrast to the Wilsonians, however, Jeffersonians focus first and foremost on the rights and liberties of American citizens. The reasons for this are simple: Jeffersonians do not share Wilsonian optimism regarding foreign adventurism. Foreign policy, for them, is the careful calculation and management of costs and risks, striving to prevent the overreach of the state and – above all else – the tyranny of an imperial presidency, emboldened through quests for geopolitical gain in the name of Empire. In this sense, the Jeffersonians and Wilsonians occupy a single axis, but sit at opposite ends of the spectrum. Both value democracy and human rights above all else, but Jeffersonians worry that their preservation at home requires an acknowledgement of the vulnerability of the United States. This fragility is threatened – potentially fatally – by overly assertive foreign policy. Since the ultimate Jeffersonian task is to continue to proactively build a more perfect union at home, it is better not to go abroad in search of monsters to destroy.[1]

Hamiltonians are America's capitalists. While they acknowledge the importance of human rights for all citizens, at home and abroad, they start with a focus on the material wealth of the American nation. This wealth is maximised by free trade, which will also bring the happy concomitant benefit of the greater protection of human rights abroad. For Hamiltonians, global flows of money, goods and people are what tie states together, prevent wars and ensure that the Unites States continues to sit atop a neoliberal world order. Of course, if needed, Hamiltonians will act hypocritically, assertively kicking open doors for trade around the world by arguing for low import taxes while hiking tariffs at home in order to protect fledgling or weakened American industries. It is not that Hamiltonians are uninterested in democracy and human rights, just that they privilege liberal capitalism as the most important and fundamental component of American security and wellbeing. They are internationalist, certainly, and focus foremost on pursuing the national interest, conceived as broadly synonymous with economic policy.

Last and least understood, Jacksonians harbour a clear, consistent and acute philosophy, which underpins the development of a sharply bifurcated foreign policy, based on military populism. At the end of the day, all that matters for Jacksonian America is the continued physical survival and wellbeing of the United States and its people. The fate of the rest of the world is only relevant if it impacts America. This binary underpinning generates a distinctive foreign policy approach, characterised on the one hand by indifference (easily confused with tolerance) and, on the other hand, by assertive unilateral displays of military force. A tendency to 'underplay' foreign policy when events only indirectly impact the US stands in stark contrast to gross overreaction when America's physical security is threatened. In this infrequent situation – such as Pearl Harbor, or 9/11 – Total War is a legitimate option for a policy response. America's armed forces should be fully equipped to deliver victory at all costs. As Jacksonians consider America's enemies to be beyond the protection of the law by virtue of having broken it, they have little time for international legalities or institutions. Once figuratively outlawed, the human rights of non-Americans are inconsequential at best and inexistent at worst; they may be punished or killed in the name of re-establishing America's physical security.

The 1990s and early 2000s

The 1990s were a remarkable decade for American foreign policy. Bush Senior's foreign policy is frequently underestimated in academic and popular literature, despite significant successes such as: helping to steer the US and the world through the end of the Cold War and into a new world order, where the certainties and rules of bipolarity no longer held true; helping to broker agreement on the reunification of Germany; helping to avoid significant entanglement in the cause of East European uprisings; and successfully preserving the norm of non-intervention and the ban on chemical weapons usage in Kuwait and Iraq, without creating a security vacuum at the heart of the region. And yet Bill Clinton successfully framed these multiple, challenging achievements as preoccupation: a failure, by a wonk-ish and distracted global diplomat, to acknowledge the domestic realities faced by struggling Americans. Bill Clinton was and remains a formidable politician.

In contrast to the pragmatism and realpolitik of George H. W. Bush and National Security Advisor Brent Scowcroft, Bill Clinton came to power on the back of one straightforward and resonant line more than any other: 'it's the economy, stupid'. Everything else played second fiddle. Through the promotion of free trade and emphasis on the benefits of globalisation, Bill Clinton embodied a Hamiltonian president. In order to situate this preference within a broader grand strategy, he spoke of engagement (broadly, diplomacy committed to internationalism) and enlargement. While the former was relatively empty in meaning (and benign), the latter encompassed two – potentially contradictory – foreign policy traditions. Clinton's policy of enlargement aimed to increase the size and scope of the zone of market democracies. Within this vision, capitalism and democracy were envisaged to go hand in hand; free markets, democracy and human rights were seen as intimately interwoven. Inevitably, this vision hit key sticking points, most notably in dealings with China. Clinton's (secondary) calls for a Wilsonian promotion of human rights led to an ill-advised Executive Order tying future Chinese trade conditions ('Most Favored Nation' status) to demonstrable progress in the realm of human rights. When this progress failed to materialise, Clinton's Hamiltonian preferences were made abundantly clear as, rather than risk damaging trade relations, human rights concerns were relegated. For Clinton, Wilsonian policy was to be pursued and welcomed, but only when and where it complemented the Hamiltonian underpinnings – the economic imperatives – of America's foreign policy.

Clinton's intoxicating foreign policy vision of peace and wealth, achieved through an internationalist US foreign policy, was brought to an abrupt end with the election of George W. Bush. America's forty-third president was elected, in part, due to the framing of Clinton's humanitarian misadventures as squandering America's great resources and unnecessarily risking the lives of US troops for reasons only tangentially related to the US national interest. Bush assured the American people that limited interventions for altruistic purposes would not feature in his foreign policy; never again would US troops be sent to fight with one hand tied behind their backs. When engaged for the right reasons, US troops would have only one mission: to win. Bush's presidency therefore began with a series of attempts to roll back the agreements and internationalism of the Clinton years, as he sought to retrench the US and reduce overseas entanglements. Bush campaigned and then governed for eight months as a Jacksonian president.

Of course, 9/11 would alter America's footing from relative reluctance to engage the world beyond its borders to proactive and increasingly pre-emptive foreign policy. The limits of tolerable risk were lowered as a Jacksonian president assessed all necessary means to eviscerate the newly apparent threat to the American nation (Daalder and Lindsay 2003; Holland 2009, 2013b). Congress shared such considerations, with near-unanimous support for the Authorization for the Use of Military Force, permitting the president to do whatever might be necessary in the logic of the response. Five weeks later, the United States intervened in Afghanistan, a state accused of harbouring those guilty of perpetrating the events of 11 September 2001. This was the first of two '9/11 wars' (Burke 2011) that Obama would inherit. While he supported the first, the second – begun eighteen months later in Iraq – he infamously termed 'a dumb war'. This war brought together a dangerous coalition of foreign policy traditions. Jacksonian vengeance fused seamlessly with the zeal of Hard Wilsonian policy, as Bush's foreign policy morphed from the isolationist preferences of his habitual Jacksonian leanings into an increasingly interventionist approach, influenced by a narrowed neoconservative philosophy and belief in the possibility of democratisation through the use of force. With no link established between Saddam Hussein and 9/11, despite the rhetorical justification for the conflict, Obama would come to power opposed to one enduring military intervention in Iraq and seeking to refocus another in Afghanistan. He would seek to improve, and then end, both.

Obama as modern Jeffersonian

'Jeffersonian foreign policy is no bed of roses' (Mead 2010). Fearing and actively avoiding the consequences of military conflict can readily lead to accusations of wimpishness, not least in the context of a highly charged and partisan domestic political landscape. Yet accusations of timidity on the part of Obama are misleading and have frequently been (justifiably) deflected for three reasons. First, Obama achieved that which Bush had failed: he got Osama bin Laden, whose extrajudicial assassination was both the remit of Jeffersonian cost-benefit calculation and the ultimate tonic for vengeful Jacksonian America (Jarvis and Holland 2014). This single incident helped to silence and appease some of Obama's most vitriolic opponents. Second, Obama is not a president solely motivated by the avoidance of armed conflict. Rather, he is a president who will commit American forces to action, in a manner carefully arrived at, when he considers the cause to be just and practical. In this, he is no different from other presidents before him. It is simply that his cost-benefit calculations err on the side of caution, not least compared with his immediate predecessor's preferred war-fighting style. Third, Obama has been an internationalist president. Far from focusing exclusively on the creation of a more perfect union at home, Obama has seen himself as a uniquely positioned global statesman, leading the world's only superpower, in a dangerous and increasingly interconnected world.

Two features of Obama's foreign policy follow from these arguments and are vital to conceptualising the Obama Doctrine. The first is an appreciation of the duration of change and global context; the necessity of pursuing a modest pace of change in a world where freedoms are relatively recent, hard won and increasingly demanded. The Wilsonian tide of history does not run smoothly or without interruption – one need only consider the rise of Islamic State to realise that – but the ebb and flow of world events have drifted steadily in the direction of universal human rights, democratic freedoms and market capitalism. Obama is certainly no King Cnut. He has not resisted this historical impulse, demanding the tide turn back. Rather he has sought to ride the wave of history, without ever getting out too far ahead of it. Recognition of the dangers and limitations of forcing more rapid positive historical developments – abroad, if not at home[2] – has been at the heart of Obama's approach to the presidency. He has achieved significant foreign policy successes because of a necessary willingness to recognise the frustratingly slow pace of international change; this willingness accompanies a strongly held conviction that more rapid transitions (delivered through unilateral action) would require an utterly undesirable situation: an imperial presidency. Obama therefore recognises that the United States does indeed play a unique role in this ever-changing world: a position that elevates America above other states, as freedom's guarantor and protector. Neither he, nor any other president, could ignore issues beyond the water's edge. His options do not extend to whether to engage or not, but rather how best to perform America's unique role in the historical arc of freedom's evolution (Bouchet 2013; Dunn 2005). This approach has borne fruit, with a number of Obama's major achievements coming late in his second term: for example, a deal with Iran on nuclear weapons; multilateral agreement in Paris on climate change; and the normalisation of relations with Cuba. All of these came about following lengthy diplomatic efforts; Obama has played the long game well.

Second, performing this role has required Obama to decide how best to occupy America's unique global position: how best to be exceptional? Obama, like all American presidents, has been required to strike a balance between competing impulses which attempt to influence the means of US internationalism. 'The seemingly paradoxical idea of a state being exceptional by virtue of uniquely being built on universal principles' lies at the heart of this tension (Bouchet 2013: 37; see also McCrisken 2003). American exceptionalism – the notion that America is unique and superior – is a key and widely understood feature of American foreign policy. Despite ill-advised musings on the limits of uniqueness,[3] Obama has publicly and repeatedly reiterated a shared understanding and appreciation of American exceptionalism. Again, in this, he is like all American presidents. The decision Obama has had to make is on how best to act and here he, like those before him, has attempted to strike a balance between exemplarist and vindicationist strands of American exceptionalism (Brands 1998).

Both vindicationists and exemplarists share an appreciation of America's exceptionalism and role to play in changing the world for the better – for both altruistic and self-interested reasons. They differ, however, on the best means for doing so. 'Recalling Thomas Jefferson, in his Cairo speech to Muslims world-wide, Obama quoted the founding father: "I hope that our wisdom will grow with our power, and teach us that the less we use our power the greater it will be"' (Obama 2009, also cited in Marsden 2011). Like Jefferson, Obama most naturally occupies an exemplarist position, whenever circumstances permit. The shining light of America's example – a beacon of freedom visible to the rest of the world – is the optimal means by which to encourage democratic transition. Obama is certainly politically opposed to the Hard Wilsonian, vindicationist leanings of his predecessor, who was more inclined to use American military superiority to force change on others. However, like all of Obama's foreign policy, this is a careful balancing act; a shade of grey, rather than black and white; context- and fact-dependent, rather than ideologically wedded to one extreme position. Just as Jefferson did, Obama will pursue policies about which he harbours significant fears, if and when he calculates that they are in America's best interests. This is because, as many observers have noted, Obama is a 'results-driven pragmatist ... attuned to complexity and nuance' (Milne 2012). He is the fox following on from his predecessor hedgehog.

The central argument this chapter makes is that Obama is a modern Jeffersonian: an internationalist president, by necessity, acting with notable caution, in a world where the United States stands as the defender and promoter of electoral and economic freedoms. He is a Jeffersonian by background, inclination and belief. He is a modern Jeffersonian by virtue of the pressures exerted on him: from America's hegemonic position; from an American national identity, premised on exceptionalism; from a Democratic Party, more internationalist and Wilsonian than he; and from a polarised domestic political landscape, where inaction is framed as dithering or timidity. Obama's challenge – and considerable success – has been in reconciling these contradictory demands, whilst staying true to his Jeffersonian convictions.

Bush's wars: Iraq and Afghanistan

Obama's immediate inheritance from his predecessor of two large, regional conflicts, amidst the context of a global War on Terrorism, have dominated his foreign policy, framing and constraining his options. On Iraq, Obama's message was clear and concise: this was a dumb war, which the United States should not have begun, and from which the United States should extricate itself. On Afghanistan, however, Obama has always been far more committed to the cause and therefore prepared to use American military force (McCrisken 2011). As Aaronson (2013), like McCrisken (2011, 2013), notes, on the campaign trail in 2007 Obama was explicit that 'we will wage the war that has to be won ... getting out of Iraq and on to the right battlefield in Afghanistan and Pakistan' (Obama 2007); in this, Obama demonstrated a steadfast commitment (e.g. Holland 2013c).

When it comes to waging war in Afghanistan, Obama has never been a pure, old-fashioned Jeffersonian in the mould of his eighteenth- and nineteenth-century counterparts. Rather, he has always acknowledged America's unique internationalist imperatives and global role. Even when inheriting Bush's wars, he was at pains to state, on the campaign trail, that ending those conflicts was a long-term goal. To start with, and particularly in Afghanistan, fighting smarter to deliver on the requirements of national security was always his focus. Afghanistan was always a war Obama believed in fighting. His approach was that of a modern Jeffersonian in three principal respects. First, Obama sought to reconceptualise the geography and geopolitics of the conflict, in order to fight the war in a manner he considered to offer greater likelihood of ultimate success. Obama reshaped the geopolitics of the Afghanistan conflict, reconceptualising the war around the AfPak label, to include Pakistani territory – 'in particular the Northwest Frontier Province and Baluchistan, incorporating Tribal and Pashtun regions along the Afghan border' (Holland 2013c: 12). Unlike Bush's war, Obama's prosecution of it neither counted nor relied upon Pakistani assistance: it doubted it (Holland 2013c).

Second, despite clear disdain for the decision to invade Iraq in 2003, Obama was prepared to learn lessons from the conflict. In Afghanistan, Obama was prepared to replicate the strategy of a troop surge, previously used in Iraq. Obama contemplated and deliberated this strategy for ninety days, following a request from military leaders. If the deliberation and compromise on troop numbers (Stanley McChrystal got 10,000 fewer American troops than requested) were Jeffersonian in nature, the ultimate decision to deploy 30,000 additional US troops is indicative that Obama is a modern Jeffersonian, prepared to commit sizeable forces to conflicts perceived to be in the national interest and following careful consideration, even when his natural inclination is to avoid putting Americans in harm's way. In this instance, Obama calculated that the possibility of stabilisation and security through a sufficient troop-to-territory ratio outweighed a personal desire to avoid putting Americans in harm's way.

Third, Obama officially ended combat operations in Afghanistan in 2014, with the handover of security responsibility from the US and NATO's International Security Assistance Force (ISAF) to Afghanistan. The nature of the withdrawal, as well as its very fact, is further evidence of Obama's successful creation of a form of Jeffersonian foreign policy, fit for the United States in the twenty-first century. Ten thousand troops will remain in Afghanistan until at least the end of 2015. They are tasked with the limited and mobile counter-terrorism efforts that Obama, had he been in power in 2001, would have prosecuted from the outset. Finally, in 2015, he had the kind of conflict he was advocating on the campaign trail eight years earlier: 'I will not hesitate to use military force to take out terrorists ... I will ensure that our military becomes more stealthy, agile, and lethal in its ability to capture or kill terrorists' (Obama 2007). But, as a modern Jeffersonian, he would avoid full-scale, boots-on-the-ground wars in countries that are very difficult to pacify and reform.

Obama's wars: Libya, Syria and beyond

There is one war that is truly Obama's, and that is Libya. This is ironic, since the conflict was 'initiated and legitimised, not by the United States but, principally, France and, to a lesser extent, Britain' (Holland 2013c). This, however, is highly representative of Obama's reluctance to engage in military conflict, getting out ahead of the Wilsonian waves of history. The war's successful prosecution was nonetheless wholly reliant on US participation and leadership, even if Obama's pre-ferred (unofficial) position was to 'lead from behind'. Here, again, we see that Obama embodies the presidency of a modern Jeffersonian. Addressing the nation and justifying military intervention in the first conflict of his own choosing, Obama clearly and succinctly articulated a modern Jeffersonian rationale for war, espousing caution and reluctance, but, ultimately the (global and national) obligation to act:

> For generations, the United States of America has played a unique role as an anchor of global security and as an advocate for human freedom. Mindful of the risks and costs of military action, we are naturally reluctant to use force to solve the world's many challenges. But when our interests and values are at stake, we have a responsibility to act To brush aside America's responsibility as a leader and more profoundly our responsibilities to our fellow human beings under such circumstances would have been a betrayal of who we are. Some nations may be able to turn a blind eye to atrocities in other countries. The United States of America is different. And as President, I refused to wait for the images of slaughter and mass graves before taking action.
>
> (Obama 2011; see also Aaronson 2013 for further analysis)

Libya was a war of choice, pursued primarily for altruistic motivations (even though appeals to national interest were made for instrumental reasons (see Holland and Aaronson 2014)). It was fought through overwhelming air power supporting indigenous forces on the ground. A modern Jeffersonian determined to preserve American lives, Obama repeatedly stressed that there was no possib-ility of US ground forces becoming involved. Haunted by Bush's mistakes in Iraq, he also explicitly ruled out US-sponsored regime change, which was declared to be outside the mission's direct objectives.

> If we tried to overthrow Gaddafi by force, our coalition would splinter. We would likely have to put U.S. troops on the ground to accomplish that mission, or risk killing many civilians from the air. The dangers faced by our men and women in uniform would be far greater. So would the costs and our share of the responsibility for what comes next.
>
> To be blunt, we went down that road in Iraq.
>
> (Obama 2011)

'In Libya, Obama's desire to fight the good fight, and to fight it right, came together' (Holland 2014). Libya was a model intervention for a modern Jeffersonian seeking to pay a limited cost and bear a limited burden (Quinn 2011: 819). 'It minimised the costs and risks to American life, by concentrating efforts on the lofty heights of exceptionalist rhetoric and American airpower. It was the ideal type intervention of a slowly solidifying Obama Doctrine' (Holland 2013c). Libya was an ideal type modern Jeffersonian conflict – one pursued reluctantly because America could not avoid involvement. The pressures to intervene came only partly from Obama; more significantly they resulted from America's exceptional identity, public and international outrage, and partisan domestic pressures. The conflict was fought in a modern Jeffersonian style, utilising all available technological sophistication, coupled with elegant and lofty rhetoric, in order to minimise the costs and risks to the United States.

The second conflict that is Obama's own, but not yet fully owned by Obama, is the crisis in Syria. If 'Obama's first term was marked by a satisfactory intervention in Libya', then his second term has followed with 'mounting frustration over Syria' (Aaronson 2013). In Syria, the Wilsonian optimism of the Arab uprisings has met the teleological reversals of international terrorism's most despised creation to date. However, before we get to this point, it is important to note that the conflict in Syria is not a single war. Rather, it has evolved through three phases, each frustrating in different ways. It is: civil war and humanitarian disaster; a conflict threatening to spill over into further and unabashed chemical weapons usage, undermining global norms and international treaties inhibiting such usage; and the latest battleground of the global war on terror, fought as counter-insurgency.

In its first guise, the Syrian Civil War began in spring 2011, within the context of the regional Arab uprisings. Following protests and government retaliation, the situation rapidly escalated to armed conflict. Rebel groups fighting Bashar al-Assad's government forces include(d) the Free Syrian Army. At this stage, calls for and pressures to intervene centred on humanitarian concerns, due to the rising death toll and number of displaced persons. In its second guise, following Assad's use of chemical weapons in 2012, the US and UK called, initially, for intervention. Obama's 'red line' on chemical weapons use was arguably a case of rhetorical self-entrapment, as the administration was coerced by its own bold statements to support an interventionist line out of step with Obama's usual reluctance to seek military solutions to global crises. A route out of this 'intervention trap' was presented by a combination of the political posturing of Ed Miliband's Labour Party in the UK, Secretary of State John Kerry's hypothesising, and Russian Foreign Minister Sergei Lavrov's rapid strategic diplomatic manoeuvring. And when this unlikely escape route presented itself, Obama rapidly opted to take it. In its third guise, the rise of Islamic State in 2014 has been a game-changer, shifting the Syrian conflict from the context of the Arab uprisings to the context of the enduring war against terrorism. As Islamic State seized towns and territory in Iraq, Obama opted to act. Intervention has, once again, taken the form of targeted airstrikes, with America's president reluctant to commit troops on the ground, despite appeals from coalition states. In Syria, Obama's dilemma has become how best to resist calls to ramp up the military campaign from those who claim an air campaign has limited ability to solve the crisis decisively. The president is gambling that internal pressures will cause Islamic State to collapse. Given the rapid evolution of the Syria conflict through its three phases, perhaps it is reasonable to expect further (currently unforeseen) developments. But, at present, an uneasy and deadly stalemate has been reached, as Obama, more than many others, is prepared to recognise the need for a cautious approach which acknowledges the long duration necessary for positive change.

Finally, beyond Libya and Syria, America, under Obama, remains in conflict with states it is not at war with (e.g. in the Horn of Africa and elsewhere in the Middle East, see Ryan 2011). Obama's proclivity to maximise the use of technology in order to minimise the risks to American life has also been consistently evident in his choice to fight from the air and, in particular, to use remotely piloted aircraft systems (UAVs/drones). As Aslam (2013) points out, Obama's use of drones builds on Bush's second term policy, rather than constituting a total step-change in US foreign policy. Bush had ramped up the use of drones between 2005 and 2008, as the technology developed. What differs from his predecessor, however, is the frequency with which Obama has deployed drone strikes, in Yemen, Libya, Pakistan, and Somalia in particular. As Fuller notes in chapter 9 below, Obama will leave office having overseen the construction of the largest, most efficient and most deployed assassination programme the United States has ever seen. Obama is clearly not a 'squeamish' president; he has personally presided over kill lists, making tough calls on when to prioritise increased national security over civilian casualties. Remotely piloted air systems give Obama ability to continue the War on Terror in countries the US is not at war with (e.g. Yemen, see Ryan 2011), in a manner that largely eliminates the risks of combat for American troops. This is an ability that, as a modern Jeffersonian, he has seized and maximised.

Conclusion

Tony Smith argues that, after 2000, the US entertained a 'progressive imperialist' form of democracy promotion. In contrast and opposition to this position, Obama's 2010 National Security Strategy insisted, 'America will not impose any system of government on another country'. The corollary, 'but our long-term security and prosperity depends on our steady support for universal values' (NSS 2010, see also Bouchet 2013), reflects a number of the key themes of Obama's modern Jeffersonian foreign policy. Regime change, imperial foreign policy, and gung-ho interventionism are consigned to the past in Obama's foreign policy; they are mistakes that he has attempted to remedy. Military intervention, for Obama, is rarely the answer to international questions and crises. Yet history, and America's exceptional role in its unfolding, demand that the US takes action. In these situations, circumstances must be carefully and patiently analysed, with a strategy reached that prioritises American life. When no good options present themselves, it is usually better to wait for the circumstances to change than search for new and bolder courses of action.

Obama's caution is now infamous. As Quinn argues in Chapter 2 above, while there have been important continuities in policy between Obama and his predecessor, not least in some of the principles of executive discretion it has brought to bear in counterterrorism, a key element of his policy has been its reluctance to enter into new entanglements which might bear significant cost.

Kitchen in Chapter 1 above also accurately situates this caution and 'issue management' in direct contradistinction to his predecessor. He argues that the Obama administration's approach to international security has been one of issue management as opposed to the problem solving approach of the Bush, and to a lesser extent Clinton administrations. Where Obama has engaged America's armed forces, he has done so with significant reluctance. In Syria, intervention was rendered necessary because of: the security vacuum inherited in Iraq; the evolution of the conflict to become recontextualised within discourses of chemical weapons norms and then the War on Terror; and domestic and partisan calls for action which draw on embedded notions of American exceptionalism. In Libya, intervention was rendered necessary because of: international pressure from allies; America's identity as freedom's protector; the impossibility of effective action without the US; domestic calls and pressure from public opinion and partisan voices to take action against a widely known and disliked tyrant in order to prevent a potential massacre; and Obama's own belief that this was a distinct possibility.

Obama's presidency

> confirms that, for all the difficulties and contradictions it produces, US presidents persistently fall back on democracy as a theme and goal of their foreign policy.... Had he wanted to, Obama would have had a hard time breaking away from this bipartisan tradition, just as Bush did after criticizing Bill Clinton for his democracy promotion.
>
> (Bouchet 2013: 31–32)

Here we see, again, that questions of structure and agency are central to making sense of US foreign policy. As a strategic agent, Obama is a Jeffersonian. As a strategic agent located in a strategically selective context, he is a modern Jeffersonian (see Hay 2002). He has adapted and updated a Jeffersonian foreign policy in the only way that is possible in the context of leading a sole, exceptional, superpower in a globalised world. This is his legacy. The Obama Doctrine is modern Jeffersonian: the least dangerous foreign policy currently possible for the greatest superpower the world has ever known.

Notes

1 In contrast to other schools which understand that America once had a revolution, both Wilsonians and Jeffersonians believe that America is and remains a revolutionary country (Mead 2002: 178).

2 Here, in this divergence, we see the quintessential Jeffersonian contrast between the revolutionary zeal of domestic policy, relative to the gradual and creeping change

apparent in foreign policy. Passing the Affordable Care Act; ending Don't Ask, Don't Tell; and facilitating gay marriage, all constitute radical change for American society and serve the purpose of creating a more perfect union at home.

3   'In April 2009, when asked whether he subscribed to the notion of American exceptionalism, the new President replied: I believe in American exceptionalism, just as I suspect that the Brits believe in British exceptionalism and the Greeks believe in Greek exceptionalism.' The critics who pilloried him for this apparently un-American thought chose to ignore the fact that he continued his answer by speaking of America's 'continued extraordinary role in leading the world towards peace and prosperity' (Bouchet 2013: 38).

References

Aaronson, M. (2013) 'Interventionism in US Foreign Policy', in Bentley, M. and Holland, J., eds. *Obama's Foreign Policy: Ending the War on Terror* (Abingdon: Routledge).

Aslam, W. (2013) 'Drones and the Issue of Continuity in America's Pakistan Policy under Obama', in Bentley, M. and Holland, J., eds. *Obama's Foreign Policy: Ending the War on Terror* (Abingdon: Routledge).

Bouchet, N. (2013) 'The Democracy Tradition in US Foreign Policy and the Obama Presidency', *International Affairs*, 89(1), 31–51.

Brands, G. (1998) *What America Owes the World: The Struggle for the Soul of Foreign Policy* (New York: Cambridge University Press).

Burke, J. (2011) *The 9/11 Wars* (London: Allen Lane).

Daalder, I. and Lindsay, G. (2003) *America Unbound: The Bush Revolution in Foreign Policy* (Chichester: Wiley and Sons).

Dunn, D. (2005) 'Isolationism Revisited: Seven Persistent Myths in the Contemporary American Foreign Policy Debate', *Review of International Studies*, 31(2), 237–261.

Fischer, D. (1989) *Albion's Seed: Four British Folkways in America* (Oxford: Oxford University Press).

Hay, C. (2002) *Political Analysis: A Critical Introduction* (London: Palgrave).

Holland, J. (2009) 'From September 11th 2001 to 9/11: From Void to Crisis', *International Political Sociology*, 3(3), 275–292.

Holland, J. (2013a) 'Foreign Policy and Political Possibility', *European Journal of International Relations*, 19(1), 48–67.

Holland, J. (2013b) *Selling the War on Terror: Foreign Policy Discourses after 9/11* (Abingdon: Routledge).

Holland, J. (2013c) 'Why is Change so Hard?', in Bentley, M. and Holland, J., eds. *Obama's Foreign Policy: Ending the War on Terror* (Abingdon: Routledge).

Holland, J. and Aaronson, M. (2014) 'Dominance through Coercion: Rhetorical Balancing and the Tactics of Justification in Afghanistan and Libya', *Intervention and State Building*, 8(1), 1–20.

Jarvis, L. and Holland, J. (2014) '"We [For]Got Him": Remembering and Forgetting in the Narration of bin Laden's Death', *Millennium – Journal of International Studies*, 42, 425–447.

McCrisken, T. (2003) *American Exceptionalism and the Legacy of Vietnam*, London: Palgrave.

McCrisken, T. (2011) 'Ten Years On: Obama's War on Terrorism in Rhetoric and Practice', *International Affairs* 88(5), 993–1007.

McCrisken, T. (2013) 'Obama's War on Terrorism in Rhetoric and Practice', in Bentley, M. and Holland, J., eds. *Obama's Foreign Policy: Ending the War on Terror* (Abingdon: Routledge).

Marsden, L. (2011) 'Religion, Identity and American Power in the Age of Obama', *International Politics*, 48, 326–343.

Mead, W. (2002) *Special Providence: American Foreign Policy and How It Changed the World* (New York: Knopf).

Mead, W.R. (2010) 'The Carter Syndrome', *Foreign Policy*, 4 January.

Milne, D. (2012) 'Pragmatism or What? The Future of US Foreign Policy', *International Affairs*, 88(5), 935–951.

NSS (2010) National Security Strategy of the United States of America, httn://osce.usmission.gov/national security strategy 2010.html.

Obama, B. (2007) Speech at the Woodrow Wilson Centre, 1 August, Washington DC, www.cfr.org/elections/obamas-speech-woodrow-wilsoncenter/p13974.

Obama, B. (2009) 'A New Beginning', 4 June, Cairo University, Cairo.

Obama, B. (2011) Remarks by the President on Libya, 23 February, National Defense University, Washington DC.

Quinn, A. (2011) 'The Art of Declining Politely: Obama's Prudent Presidency and the Waning of American Power', *International Affairs*, 87(4), 803–824.

Quinn, A. (2013) 'Us Decline and Systemic Constraint', in Bentley, M. and Holland, J., eds. *Obama's Foreign Policy: Ending the War on Terror* (Abingdon: Routledge).

Ryan, M. (2011) 'War in Countries We Are Not at War With: The War on Terror on the Periphery from Bush to Obama', *International Politics*, 48(2/3), 364–389.

Smith, T. (2013) 'Democracy promotion from Wilson to Obama', in Cox, M., Lynch, T.I. and Bouchet, N., eds. *US Foreign Policy and Democracy Promotion: From Theodore Roosevelt to Barack Obama* (London: Routledge).

Part II

The language and culture of the war on terror

4 Ending the unendable

The rhetorical legacy of the war on terror

Michelle Bentley

Barack Obama's presidency was initially constructed around the abandonment of the controversial phrase 'war on terror', specifically where this signalled a public rejection of the George W. Bush administration's presentation of foreign policy as an act of war. In removing the phrase from political discourse, Obama sought to break down the contentious linguistic constructions that had characterised the post-9/11 era, and replace these with a more pragmatic and considered rhetorical approach. Obama was marking a clear line between his time in the White House and the extremes of US foreign policy that had preceded him, and that so many Americans had voted against in the 2008 election. Bush's antagonistic 'war' was over. It had ended.

Except that it hadn't. Obama consistently failed to realise this conceptual rebuff during his first term in office (Bentley 2013). While the exact phrase 'war on terror' was largely dispensed with, Obama continued to depict foreign policy as this specific form of conflict, thereby effectively imitating the rhetorical framework of the past. Given the political weight, dominance and pervasiveness of the 'war on terror' narrative, this is hardly surprising. The sheer strength of this was, and still is, incredible (Jackson 2005). Even its own architects failed to reverse it *c.*2005, when Bush attempted to reframe the narrative as the less offensive Global Struggle Against Violent Extremism (GSAVE) (Lynch 2010). Like some kind of Frankenstein's monster, the 'war on terror' had become so embedded within political dialogue that not even its originators could restrain it. Why then would Obama have been capable of doing so? Moreover, this was a time of significant policy continuity, with Obama facing the leftovers of Bush's highly military doctrine, notably the conflicts in Iraq and Afghanistan. The persistence of key issues – not least where these lay at the very heart of the 'war' itself – created bureaucratic and rhetorical commitments that could not easily be transcended. Within this context, it was difficult to shift away from the language that had framed these situations; and indeed, had framed them very successfully. Consequently, the 'war' was still very much alive, specifically where it continued to influence the development and implementation of US foreign policy aims. It was beyond Obama's capacity to discard such an intrinsic aspect of US politics. Simply put, the new president could not end what he could not control.

Yet with two major election successes under his belt and considerable distance established between him and the Bush era, could Obama now manage to undo this restrictive condition? In response, this chapter examines whether this situation continued into Obama's second term, or whether – following his re-election – the president managed to fracture the dynamics of continuity and reframe policy within an alternate context. Not least where it has been argued that the nature of the 'war on terror' is unwinnable – that where this effectively comprises a 'war' against an emotion or tactic, ending that conflict is complex, if not impossible – how has this played into Obama's efforts to disrupt that narrative since 2012? Has he succeeded in dismantling this rhetoric, or is the 'war on terror' so pervasive that it has continued to shape foreign policy even now? It concludes that Obama's success in waging control over US foreign policy rhetoric, although substantially more extensive than that seen in his first term, has remained limited. As circumstances have changed and new conflicts have emerged that have not been grounded in the 'war on terror' (most notably where these relate to the Arab Spring), so Obama has been able to capitalise on this in order to create new detachment from the controversial concept of 'war', especially as an act and/or vision of foreign policy. Yet the narrative trap remains. When addressing issues still relevant to the 'war on terror', and particularly the events of 9/11, Obama has continued to fall back on the same rhetoric as his predecessor, even to the extent that this has involved describing foreign policy as 'war'. Obama has moved on, but this narrative still haunts him.

The impossible victory

Rejecting the 'war on terror' was always going to be problematic in that the 'war' itself could not be won. While the inability to achieve a victory may sound like an ideal reason to abandon a particular strategy, this was a situation in which the 'war' was so vague as a form of conflict, and so ingrained within political thinking, that winning could be its only conclusion. The 'war' could not simply be halted. Logically that would comprise a defeat on the part of the US, and specifically a defeat by the terrorists. If the US did not win, then surely it must have lost. At the very least it would be deemed an ostensibly cowardly move to walk away from the 'battle'. However contentious the 'war on terror' is/was recognised to be, it still created certain expectations concerning what success would comprise, specifically where a refusal to engage with it could be taken as a sign of weakness and of having been vanquished in some respect. And yet there was no way either to win a victory, which would technically have provided an opportunity to get away from the 'war': i.e. if it had been won, it no longer existed. The 'war on terror' has long been criticised for being so ambiguous and poorly defined as to prove effectively unwinnable. Even Bush himself acknowledged this. In one of the more damning comments of the 2004 presidential election campaign, Bush admitted on national television that the 'war on terror' might never be won because of the unconventional nature of the threat (Borger 2004). In an interview with NBC, the president said: 'I don't think you can win it. But I think you can create conditions so that the – those who use terror as a tool are less acceptable in parts of the world.' It speaks volumes that even Bush recognised that US foreign policy had been structured in a way that could not be finished (however many 'Mission Accomplished' banners you put up).

There are three core aspects to this unwinnability. First, this was not technically or conventionally a war and, therefore, could not be won as a war. Popescu says this cannot really 'be conceptualized as a true *war* in th[e] instrumental (or strategic) understanding of the term' (2009: 102). This has been portrayed negatively as a situation in which the labelling of post-9/11 US foreign policy as 'war' resulted in, or at least facilitated, the promotion of actual physical conflict, especially in relation to Iraq (Stevenson 2013: 47). Employing the language and expectations of war vastly exaggerated the extent of US foreign policy to reflect this disproportionate rhetoric (Howard 2002: 9). The very language of war would shape the future scope and content of US foreign policy, and – more than this – would provide the basis of its justification, however questionable this was as a form of policy validation. Indeed, analysts have been keen to reject the idea that this was simply a rhetorical device designed to frame post-9/11 policy, maintaining that it was an ideational structure with the capacity to change the course of foreign policy (Roberts 2005: 114; Ralph 2006: 117; Mustapha 2011: 487). 'War' implies a very exact form of conflict, not least in the sense that those in charge are largely permitted to take extreme measures in order to secure a victory; everything and anything must be done to ensure that an enemy is conquered. It was within this context that calling US foreign policy a 'war' effectively gave Bush the green light to carry out programmes of invasion and intimidation that would otherwise have proved prohibitively contentious. This was a case not merely of framing, but of the actual construction and implementation of policy. As Gilles Andreani (2004: 31) argues, while the 'war on terror' had a clear metaphorical quality, '[T]he use of the word "war" has gone far beyond metaphor to acquire a strategic reality.' Within this context it is difficult to ascertain what a victory might comprise, given that this strategy of US foreign policy did not look like, or function as, a conventional war. If this is not a typical war then it could not have a typical victory – or indeed any kind of victory, necessarily.

Second, the nature of the enemy in respect to the 'war on terror' made it impossible to ascertain any criteria by which success could be measured. What target Bush had in mind is still unclear. Who or what was he fighting? The concept of 'terror' as an enemy is flawed, and analysis – both at the practitioner and the academic levels – has repeatedly highlighted that this cannot comprise a legitimate enemy. Specifically, terror is an emotion and/or a tactic – neither of which makes for a clear adversary (Perry 2005: 44). This is especially relevant in that a fight against such a vague enemy cannot be won. What could possibly qualify as having defeated terror (Gray and Wilson 2006: 25; Youngs and Widdows 2009: 3; Gills 2009: 158)? Eliminating all terrorism (assuming of course you have a clear definition of what a terrorist/terrorism is – itself a difficult issue to resolve (Hodgson and Tadros 2013))? Likewise, was this a situation in which victory required the emotional overcoming of terror itself, in the sense that people could go about their 'everyday' life without being scared of the terrorist threat? There was no clarification. Furthermore, this vagueness only encouraged the construction of the 'war on terror' as a 'floating signifier' that was applied to any threat the Bush administration wished to include (Zalman and Clarke 2009: 101). This can be seen in Bush's declared 'axis of evil' whereby rogue states, as well as terrorists, were now brought into this complex mix. Anything and everything could be 'terror' if Bush desired it to be.

Admittedly, Obama did try and clarify the exact nature of the enemy on taking office in 2008; explicitly, he sought to reframe this as a 'war' against al Qaeda, i.e. a clearly identified enemy. Yet this had significantly limited results and merely perpetuated the difficult notion of foreign policy as 'war' (Bentley 2013). Specifically, his definition was not accompanied by a shift away from targeting 'armies and paramilitaries, not terrorists' nor (despite the reference to al Qaeda) did it clearly promote a strategy for 'repressing, apprehending, killing, or bringing to justice those who struck the United States by devastating the World Trade Center and a wing of the Pentagon' (Foxell 2004: 488). This highlights the difficulty in attacking 'terror' by trying to attack an enemy, not least where core problems underpinning terrorism are disregarded, a factor that is argued to prolong the terrorist threat. As the Head of Israel's General Security Service (Shabak), Ami Ayalon, said, 'those who want victory' over terror without addressing underlying grievances 'want an unending war' (in Chomsky 2003: 118). Yet Foxell's analysis also highlights the very problematic nature of identifying enemies within the framework of terror, and how the concept of terror has moved the focus of US foreign policy away from the very people it was supposed to enact revenge on. Similar efforts also failed when former Secretary of Defense, Donald Rumsfeld attempted to place some kind of measurement on the 'war on terror': 'He concluded that success depended on whether the number of terrorists we were killing or deterring was greater than the number the enemy was recruiting' (Nye 2008: 1). As well as strongly suggesting that America had already lost, this represents another unsuccessful attempt to place some kind of tangible metric on the concept of terror. It certainly does not express a point at which the 'war' could be seen to be won in that it is dependent on an on-going analysis within what is implied to be an open-ended conflict. There was no way of qualifying the idea of terror as an enemy, even when policymakers attempted to narrow this down within the framework of the existing strategy. And without a clear enemy, there was no way to establish a win. As Nye continues: 'Small wonder, then, that as he was fired, even Rumsfeld finally expressed discontent with the term "war on terrorism".'

Third, an end to the 'war on terror' has also proved elusive thanks to the continuity surrounding the concept. The sheer dominance and success of this narrative should not be underestimated (Jackson 2005). Whatever controversy and scepticism it is viewed with now, and while the narrative is certainly not as extensive as in the concept's heyday immediately post-9/11, this does not undermine or devalue the incredible narrative strength inherent in the 'war on terror'. Jackson (2005) and Hodges (2011: 5) both refer to this narrative as a 'regime of truth': a strong and pervasive construction of understanding that shaped and defined thinking about security at both the political and the public levels. Specifically, what the regime established in the wake of 9/11 was more than a 'passing phase' in terms of foreign policy construction; it was intrinsic to US, and now even international, politics (Jackson 2005: 3). Furthermore, it also became institutionalised and normalised within American government and security departments such as Department for Homeland Security, the PATRIOT Act and security doctrine more widely (Jackson 2011: 394). And to the extent that so many of the events which had underpinned the narrative in the first place, and were defined by it – e.g. Iraq, Afghanistan – were still major aspects of foreign policy, so their rhetorical construction within the terms of the 'war on terror' would also persist. Consequently, the idea that anybody – Obama or otherwise – could reverse this rhetorical construct was optimistic at best. In effect, Obama was now trapped within the narrative and the expectations of the 'war on terror' that had been set down by his predecessor. In the absence of a clear win, this level of continuity effectively kept the 'war' going. It was not something that could be relied on to simply fade away, even with Bush now out of office. Consequently, in combination with the above factors, there was no clear or obvious way of bringing an end to the narrative and/or the 'war' itself. Within this context, and not least since Obama's abandonment of the concept had already failed during his first term, was this something the second term president could escape from? Could Obama find a way to end the unendable?

A change we can (finally) believe in?

The answer is: partially. While the 'war on terror' narrative has certainly retained its rhetorical strength, certain factors sustaining it no longer apply. Specifically, Obama is now dealing with a range of threats that do not hold any major historical association with the 'war on terror', such as Libya and Syria. This has created a limited opportunity to re-exert a sense of rhetorical control over the construction of US foreign policy, specifically, an opportunity to discuss and respond to these new situations through Obama's own personal brand of foreign policy ideology. While analysts have been reluctant to identify a specific 'Obama Doctrine', certain trends can be highlighted – particularly Obama's aversion to largely unilateral expressions of military might. Especially in his second term, Obama repeatedly espoused the idea that US foreign policy could no longer be based on armed intervention:

> As Commander in Chief, I have used force when needed to protect the American people, and I will never hesitate to do so as long as I hold this office. But I will not send our troops into harm's way unless it is truly necessary, nor will I allow our sons and daughters to be mired in open-ended

conflicts. We must fight the battles that need to be fought, not those that terrorists prefer from us: large-scale deployments that drain our strength and
may ultimately feed extremism.

(Obama 2014a)

This has played directly into the language of 'war', where this is the exact conflict he rejects – albeit where this relates to conventional war as opposed to the
'war on terror'. Obama (2013a) has repeatedly called for a shift away from the
'perpetual war mindset', which has supposedly dominated US thinking on
policy. While he has been keen for this not to be taken as putting American
safety at risk, it has been about demonstrating that 'our security cannot depend
on our outstanding military alone' (Obama 2014a). This has also been recognised as a fundamentally multilateral strategy:

But this is not America's fight alone. I won't commit our troops to fighting
another ground war in Iraq or in Syria. It's more effective to use our capabilities to help partners on the ground secure their own countries' futures.

(Obama 2014b)

This approach has been widely evident in Obama's relatively hands-off strategy on
Libya – where it consisted of a NATO mission led primarily by the UK and France
– and his refusal to intervene in Syria, even despite the use of chemical weapons by
dictator Bashar al-Assad. Yet this is not simply a difference in strategic method,
but also the construction of foreign policy discourse. It is notable that these emergent situations are not constructed within the rhetorical framework of the 'war on
terror'. Indeed, the extent of this can be appreciated when considering the involvement of Islamic State (IS) in Syria. Despite clear involvement by terrorists, this has
not been constructed as a situation in which the US should intervene:

Now, it will take time to eradicate a cancer like ISIL. And any time we take
military action, there are risks involved, especially to the service men and
women who carry out these missions. But I want the American people to
understand how this effort will be different from the wars in Iraq and
Afghanistan. It will not involve American combat troops fighting on foreign
soil. This counterterrorism campaign will be waged through a steady, relentless effort to take out ISIL wherever they exist, using our air power and our
support for partners' forces on the ground.

(Obama 2014c)

To meet a threat like this, we have to be smart. We have to use our power
wisely. And we have to avoid the mistakes of the past. American military
power is unmatched, but this can't be America's fight alone. And the best way
to defeat a group like ISIL isn't by sending a large number of American combat
forces to wage a ground war in the heart of the Middle East. That wouldn't
serve our interests. In fact, it would only risk fueling extremism even more.

(Obama 2014d)

While the actions of IS could be associated with the type of violence which inspired the 'war on terror', and which that strategy was supposed to prevent, Obama could still avert the old language of counter-terrorism to put forward a new rhetorical basis that favoured his so-called pragmatism. Particularly since Syria had not been part of the 'war on terror', Obama had something of a clean sheet in respect to its construction, although terrorism had become an intrinsic aspect of the crisis in that country. This crisis was not bound to an existing linguistic structure in the way that Iraq and Afghanistan had been. As such, there was an element of distance between the two, one in which a separation could be made between the controversial rhetoric of the past.

Moreover, whereas previous research has linked Obama's use of the 'war on terror' narrative to his need to retain a strong position of leadership in the post-9/11 era – where Bush set a standard of the strong war president, Obama required that same hardline language in order to present himself similarly as an effective leader (Bentley 2013) – in Syria certain rhetorical needs connected to enforced continuity no longer applied. That is, the strength of the 'war on terror' had previously compelled Obama to adhere to the concept in order to secure the impression of his presidency as strong. Despite the now clear opposition to the 'war on terror', anything less than a similarly hardline approach would be perceived as weakness, and even as 'letting the terrorists win'. Consequently, Obama was put in a position where continuing to adopt the narrative of the 'war on terror' was his best means of promoting presidential strength. Yet now, in his second term, Obama was in a fundamentally different place. By moving away from the wars in Iraq and Afghanistan towards new situations – situations in which he was specifically attempting to promote a non-interventionist stance – this narrative was no longer necessary. Importantly, this is not to suggest that continuity no longer existed, but Obama's greater freedom to create distance from the foreign policy issues of the past brought new opportunities for discursive construction. Obama did not want to be a war president any more. He wanted the exact opposite. And he found himself in a new conceptual environment in which this stance was at least permissible and in which he actively did not want to intervene militarily. Unlike the need to continue the conflicts in Iraq and Afghanistan – which had required further military action and, therefore, the supporting rhetoric of the 'war on terror' – Obama's interest now lay specifically in not being a war president. Hence, the constraints of the 'war on terror' became loosened. Additionally, in this new situation Obama has done much to reclaim the word 'war'. The vast majority of times when Obama has used this word since his re-election has been in reference to the physical act of war, as opposed to a foreign policy mission. He talks about the Iraq and Afghanistan interventions as wars, but only in the conventional sense: he does not include them under the 'war on terror' conceptual banner (e.g. Obama 2013b, 2014e). War has been restored to its original meaning.

Critically, however, this is not to suggest that Obama's new stance has not attracted criticism. Jonathan Stevenson (2014: 121) describes it thus: 'The United States' present Syria policy is perhaps the most vivid, and discomforting example of the Obama administration's realism.' The refusal to take action on Syria is a major point of contention within the US government, and Obama's refusal to intervene has frequently been regarded as cowardice and/or weakness. In this sense then, Obama is still not free of the expectations of the 'war on terror', where this exacerbated an American exceptionalist view of the role the US plays in the world, i.e. as guardian. Thus, Obama's attempt to implement a rhetorical shift has had far from complete success. In a rhetorical environment characterised by the 'war on terror', Obama's anti-war approach has not always been popular, even amongst those who would not consider themselves hawks. Consequently, Obama's new rhetoric was not universally acknowledged or accepted by his wider political and public audiences – specifically not to the extent that the 'war on terror' continues. It certainly was not sufficient to overcome the wider issues relating to the inability to reverse this narrative, which in effect amount to ending the 'war'. Obama's new discourse failed to tackle any of these, particularly the idea that he did not present his alternative narrative in a way that could be seen as a victory. Obama merely changed the terms of debate – of the three factors involved in the inability to end the war highlighted above, he only addressed the third and final one (the issue of continuity). Yet he needed to have dealt with all three in order to fully introduce a new form of rhetoric. By not doing so, his rhetoric remained bogged down in the expectations associated with the 'war'. He may not have viewed himself as the war president, and as such this may have reduced the value that the 'war on terror' narrative held for him. Yet that assumed everyone else was also ready to move on. But until Obama gave them a victory, there was no end to move on from.

Bush's legacy

This relative 'failure' of Obama's discourse is not the only issue in respect to continuity. At one level, this concerns the sheer extent to which the language of the 'war on terror' has become ingrained within political discourse. This includes the incorporation of the phrase at the legislative and funding levels:

> In accordance with section 5 of the Consolidated and Further Continuing Appropriations Act, 2013, I hereby designate for Overseas Contingency Operations/*Global War on Terrorism* all funding (including the rescission of funds) so designated by the Congress in the Act pursuant to section 251(b)(2)(A) of the Balanced Budget and Emergency Deficit Control Act of 1985, as amended, as outlined in the enclosed list of accounts.
>
> (Obama 2013c; emphasis added)

Furthermore, Obama allowed others to use the phrase, not just in administrative language, but as part of political dialogue. By permitting this phrase to be employed, Obama did nothing to challenge its persistence. What was the point of his own personal refusal to use it if everyone else could? Admittedly, Obama began to contest its use on occasion. For example, in one incident where he was asked a question in relation to the 'war', he replied by referring to it as the '*so-called* war on terror' (Obama 2013d; emphasis added). Yet it is clear that continuity still existed in that it remained part of everyday language, something that constrained the president. Indeed, he referred to both the attacks at the Boston Marathon and the assault on UK soldier Lee Rigby as 'acts of terror' (Obama 2013e, 2013f). This mirrors the rhetoric of the war narrative. Rhetoric about terrorism not connected to new situations (i.e. Syria) often returned to the ideals of the 'war on terror'.

The clearest example of this trend relates to Obama's framing of 9/11. Specifically, Obama has found it impossible to talk about this event without using the classic language of the 'war on terror'. Most significantly, this is a rhetoric that explicitly employs the concept of foreign policy as a 'war'. While Obama has committed himself to rejecting this premise, again he has not done so in either his first or his second term. He still uses the word 'war' to construct US foreign policy. This is not the physical act of war, but war as a US mission:

> And then, on September 11, 2001, we were shaken out of complacency. Thousands were taken from us, as clouds of fire and metal and ash descended upon a sun-filled morning. This was a different kind of war. No armies came to our shores, and our military was not the principal target. Instead, a group of terrorists came to kill as many civilians as they could. And so our Nation went to war.
>
> (Obama 2013g)

> Ever since that awful September morning when our nation was attacked, when thousands of innocent Americans were killed, we've been at war against Al Qaida.
>
> (Obama 2013h)

> The United States did not seek this fight. We went into Afghanistan out of necessity, after our Nation was attacked by Al Qaida on September 11, 2001. We went to war against Al Qaida and its extremist allies.
>
> (Obama 2014f)

Obama (2014g) also explicitly refers to the '9/11 generation' as being the soldiers involved in battle: 'By the end of this year, our war in Afghanistan will be over, and we'll welcome home this generation – the 9/11 generation – that has proven itself to be one of America's greatest.' And even where Obama does not employ the concept of 'war', he still refers to it as a fight against the terrorists (Obama 2013i); this remains a 'fight against terrorism in a way that respects our values and our ideals' (Obama 2013j). While 'fight' is clearly a very different concept to 'war', it is not employed in a conceptual vacuum. The understanding of the word 'war' that was introduced by the Bush administration has not disappeared, even with the election of a new president. In this context, therefore, 'fight' carries with it the expectations of a much greater conflict. An audience cannot help but make that connection, not least under conditions of such extreme rhetorical continuity. Again, this represents Obama's inability to overcome the previous narrative. Any attempt to redefine the debate simply fell back into the existing rhetorical framework.

This rhetoric is not limited to the concept of 'war', however. Indeed, Obama picks up on a number of linguistic devices that underpinned Bush's construction of the 'war on terror' narrative. Most explicitly, in discussing 9/11, he draws on the concept of innocence, which Jackson (2005) has identified as a key tenet of the 'war on terror' discourse. For example, in an emotion-laden speech that draws not only on the concept of innocence, but also echoes the exceptionalist discourse that was also employed by Bush, Obama says:

> No matter how many years pass, we will never forget the innocent souls stolen on that dark day: parents, children, siblings, and spouses of every race and creed.... But the stories of all those lost and the beauty of their lives shine on in those they left behind. The sacrifice of so many has forever shaped our Nation, and we have emerged a stronger, more resilient America. We stand tall and unafraid, because no act of terror can match the character of our Union or change who we are.
>
> (Obama 2014h)

In this way, Obama was still trapped – at least when engaging with 9/11 and other central aspects of the 'war on terror'. The events of 9/11 are still so emotive and politically relevant that they cannot be reframed in terms of discursive presentation. Critically, it is not just that 9/11 is still constructed in the same highly emotive terms as were used immediately after the attacks. That is, it is not simply that this event is deemed such a horrific chapter in US history that only the most poignant language may be employed to express it (if any language can truly express the horror that happened on that day). It is also that discussion of 9/11 cannot escape the wider foreign policy framework in which it was originally constructed. This is still a declaration of 'war'; the US went to 'war' in revenge. The 'war on terror' is so extensive that it defines everything that it has touched. Indeed, trying to frame it in any other way would risk appearing to deny the intensity of what occurred. While Obama may not agree with the disproportionate language that has developed around 9/11, he would risk appearing unfeeling, weak even, if he chose to present it in other terms – specifically more moderate terms. In the memory of 9/11 at least, the war will never be over.

Conclusion

Obama is like the younger sibling of an exceptional child. No matter what he achieved in his two-term presidency, it will always be in the shadow of his predecessor. The expectations placed on him would be defined by what had gone before. This is especially true of the 'war on terror' narrative, not just in terms of rhetorical continuity, but also in respect of the standards of strong presidential behaviour that it set. It was something that even Bush could not walk away from. In this context, it is difficult to see how Obama could have simply turned off this persistent narrative. His clear commitment to abandoning the language of the 'war on terror' was always overly optimistic. The most successful and strong narrative in foreign policy discourse could never have been completely abandoned, at least not immediately, particularly since continuity was entrenched by the fact that there has been no end to the conflict to provide a point to move on from. The construction of the 'war on terror' narrative is self-sustaining. Failure to identify a point at which the 'war' could be won has perpetuated the very narrative itself. Obama became trapped in a construct he could not possibly escape from fully.

Yet his second term has offered some new opportunities – not to end the war, but to deliberately avoid using the narrative for situations not previously included in the 'war on terror', such as aspects of the Arab Spring, notably Libya and Syria where intervention has been a major issue (either because it took place or because it did not). Obama's intention to construct a less aggressive foreign policy in respect of these conflict scenarios effectively created a conceptual space in which to create distance from the controversial rhetoric of 'war'. The extent to which Obama capitalised on this, however, is partial. His approach still conflicted with the pre-existing narrative of the 'war on terror', to the point at which his rhetoric was largely unable to overcome this. In a battle of the narratives, Obama's discourse was poorly received, at least in comparison to the runaway success enjoyed by the 'war on terror'. Moreover, his rhetorical control has been limited to a handful of foreign policy situations. While Obama may have been able to exert a modicum of control over the discursive presentation of these, his control only applies to what has occurred after Bush's time in office. The events that were initially constructed as part of the 'war' – particularly 9/11 – are still very much understood within their original context. Obama has never been able to get past this. And given the strength of the narrative, it remains to be seen whether his successor will be able to. The further we get from the war, the more it may – if not end – fade. But with 9/11 still fresh in the memory of the American public and the political system, the 'war on terror' narrative is unlikely to disappear completely anytime soon. While the next president will have the same freedoms as Obama did in respect of emerging incidents, and may be able to capitalise on them to a greater extent, he or she will also be bound by the 'war on terror' narrative. A new presidency was not enough to end the 'war' last time. And there is nothing to suggest that it will do so on 20 January 2017 either.

References

Andreani, G. (2004) 'The "War on Terror": Good Cause, Wrong Concept', *Survival* 46(4): 31–50.

Bentley, M. (2013) 'Continuity We Can Believe In: Escaping the War on Terror', in M. Bentley and J. Holland (eds) *Obama's Foreign Policy: Ending the War on Terror*, London: Routledge.

Borger, J. (2004) 'President Admits War on Terror Cannot be Won', *Guardian* 31 August. Available: www.theguardian.com/world/2004/aug/31/uselections2004.september111.

Chomsky, N. (2003) 'Wars of Terror', *New Political Science* 25(1): 113–27.

Foxell, J. (2004) 'What Went Wrong in the U.S. "War on Terror"?', *American Foreign Policy Interests* 26(6): 485–500.

Gills, B.K. (2009) 'The End of the War on Terror', *Globalizations* 6(1): 157–62.

Gray, J. and Wilson, M. (2006) 'Understanding the "War on Terrorism": Responses to 11 September 2001', *Journal of Peace Research* 43(1): 23–36.

Hodges, A. (2011) *The 'War on Terror' Narrative: Discourse and Intertextuality in the Construction and Contestation of Sociopolitical Reality*, Oxford: Oxford University Press.

Hodgson, J. and Tadros, V. (2013) 'The Impossibility of Defining Terrorism', *New Criminal Law Review* 16(3): 494–526.

Howard, M. (2002) 'What's in a Name? How to Fight Terrorism', *Foreign Affairs* 81(1): 8–13.

Jackson, R. (2005) *Writing the War on Terrorism: Language, Politics and Counter-Terrorism*. Manchester: Manchester University Press.

Jackson, R. (2011) 'Culture, Identity and Hegemony: Continuity and (the Lack of) Change in US Counterterrorism Policy from Bush to Obama', *International Politics* 48(2/3): 390–411.

Lynch, M. (2010) *Rhetoric and Reality: Countering Terrorism in the Age of Obama*, Washington DC: Center for a New American Security.

Mustapha, J. (2011) 'Threat Construction in the Bush Administration's Post-9/11 Foreign Policy: (Critical) Security Implications for Southeast Asia', *The Pacific Review* 24(4): 487–504.

Nye, J. (2008) 'Smart Power and the "War on Terror"', *Asia-Pacific Review* 15(1): 1–8.

Obama, B. (2013a) 'Remarks on Health Insurance Reform and an Exchange with Reporters in San Jose, California'. Available: www.gpo.gov/fdsys/pkg/DCPD-201300397/pdf/DCPD-201300397.pdf.

Obama, B. (2013b) 'Remarks at the Brandenburg Gate in Berlin, Germany'. Available: www.gpo.gov/fdsys/pkg/DCPD-201300439/pdf/DCPD-201300439.pdf.

Obama, B. (2013c) 'Letter to Congressional Leaders Regarding the Designation of Funds for Global Counterterrorism and Overseas Contingency Operations'. Available: www.gpo.gov/fdsys/pkg/DCPD-201300190/pdf/DCPD-201300190.pdf.

Obama, B. (2013d) 'Remarks at a Young African Leaders Initiative Town Hall Meeting and a Question-and-Answer Session in Johannesburg, South Africa'. Available: www.gpo.gov/fdsys/pkg/DCPD-201300477/pdf/DCPD-201300477.pdf.

Obama, B. (2013e) 'Remarks on the Terrorist Attack in Boston, Massachusetts'. Available: www.gpo.gov/fdsys/pkg/DCPD-201300246/pdf/DCPD-201300246.pdf.

Obama, B. (2013f) 'Statement on the Attack on a British Servicemember in London, England'. Available: www.gpo.gov/fdsys/pkg/DCPD-201300359/pdf/DCPD-201300359.pdf.

Obama, B. (2013g) 'Remarks at National Defense University'. Available: www.gpo.gov/fdsys/pkg/DCPD-201300361/pdf/DCPD-201300361.pdf.

Obama, B. (2013h) 'Remarks at Camp Pendleton, California.' Available: www.gpo.gov/fdsys/pkg/DCPD-201300553/pdf/DCPD-201300553.pdf.

Obama, B. (2013i) 'Remarks at Knox College in Galesburg, Illinois'. Available: www.gpo.gov/fdsys/pkg/DCPD-201300520/pdf/DCPD-201300520.pdf.

Obama, B. (2013j) 'Remarks at a Democratic Congressional Campaign Committee/ Democratic Senatorial Campaign Committee Fundraiser in Beverly Hills, California'. Available: www.gpo.gov/fdsys/pkg/DCPD-201300809/pdf/DCPD-201300809.pdf.

Obama, B. (2014a) 'Address Before a Joint Session of the Congress on the State of the Union'. Available: www.gpo.gov/fdsys/pkg/DCPD-201400050/pdf/DCPD-201400050. pdf.

Obama, B. (2014b) 'The President's Weekly Address'. Available: www.gpo.gov/fdsys/ pkg/DCPD-201400687/pdf/DCPD-201400687.pdf.

Obama, B. (2014c) 'Address to the Nation on United States Strategy to Combat the Islamic State of Iraq and the Levant Terrorist Organization (ISIL)'. Available: www. gpo.gov/fdsys/pkg/DCPD-201400654/pdf/DCPD-201400654.pdf.

Obama, B. (2014d) 'The President's Weekly Address'. Available: www.gpo.gov/fdsys/ pkg/DCPD-201400662/pdf/DCPD-201400662.pdf.

Obama, B. (2014e) 'The President's Weekly Address'. Available: www.gpo.gov/fdsys/ pkg/DCPD-201400605/pdf/DCPD-201400605.pdf.

Obama, B. (2014f) 'Remarks on the Drawdown of United States Military Personnel in Afghanistan'. Available: www.gpo.gov/fdsys/pkg/DCPD-201400401/pdf/DCPD-201 400401.pdf.

Obama, B. (2014g) 'Remarks on Presenting the Medal of Honor to Sergeant Kyle J White'. Available: www.gpo.gov/fdsys/pkg/DCPD-201400359/pdf/DCPD-201400359.pdf.

Obama, B. (2014h) 'Proclamation 9162 – National Days of Prayer and Remembrance, 2014'. Available: www.gpo.gov/fdsys/pkg/DCPD-201400642/pdf/DCPD-201400642.pdf.

Perry, D. (2005) 'Ambiguities in the "War on Terror"', *Journal of Military Ethics* 4(1): 44–51.

Popescu, I. (2009) 'Strategic Theory and Practice: A Critical Analysis of the Planning Process for the Long War on Terror', *Contemporary Security Policy* 30(1): 100–24.

Ralph, J. (2006) 'America's "War on Terror": Making Sense of the "Troubling Confusion."', *The International Journal of Human Rights* 10(2): 177–91.

Roberts, A. (2005) 'The "War on Terror" in Historical Perspective', *Survival* 47(2): 101–30.

Stevenson, J. (2013) 'Demilitarising the "War on Terror"', *Survival* 48(2): 37–54.

Stevenson, J. (2014) 'The Syrian Tragedy and Precedent', *Survival* 56(3): 121–40.

Youngs, G. and Widdows, H. (2009). 'Globalization, Ethics, and the "War on Terror"', *Globalizations* 6(1): 1–6.

Zalman, A. and Clarke, J. (2009) 'The Global War on Terror: A Narrative in Need of a Rewrite', *Ethics and International Affairs* 23(2): 101–13.

5 War on terror II

Obama and the adaptive evolution of US counterterrorism

Richard Jackson and Chin-Kuei Tsui

In 2008, it was widely believed that the election of Barack Obama to the United States presidency would herald a significant shift in the country's security and counterterrorism approach, perhaps even precipitating an end to the much-maligned global 'war on terror'. However, a number of studies of his first years in office have concluded that the continuities between Bush's 'war on terror' and Obama's 'war against violent extremism' have been much greater than the noted differences, which were, in any case, comparatively minor. Moreover, the potential for a major change in policy and approach by Obama was highly circumscribed due to the institutionalization and cultural sedimentation of the war on terror discourse, the vested interests and functionality inherent in its continuation, the broader cultural acceptance and diffusion of the key terrorism narratives, the absence of a powerful change agent, and the missing structural conditions necessary for precipitating major discursive change (see Jackson 2011, 2013; McCrisken 2011, 2012).

Since then, however, some commentators have suggested that both Obama's counterterrorism discourse (see Hodges 2011) and his broader counterterrorism approach (see Stern 2015) have undergone what amounts to a significant shift which distinguishes it from the previous Bush administration. There is no question that there have been a number of observable evolutions and tactical changes in US counterterrorism since Obama's accession in 2008, as we discuss below. A key question, however, is: do these changes amount to a *significant* shift in US counterterrorism? Is Obama in the second term more willing and better able to revise US security and counterterrorism policy? How do we account for those changes we have seen in Obama's counterterrorism rhetoric and approach?

In this chapter, we examine these important questions and conclude that there is much more continuity than change in US counterterrorism policy and approach in Obama's second term, as previous research predicted (Jackson 2011, 2013). Further, we suggest that the changes which have occurred represent *adaptations* of the dominant paradigm to the evolving context in which Obama spoke, rather than substantive innovations or a transition to a whole new approach. That is, while George Bush launched the global war on terror in the immediate aftermath of the 9/11 attacks, Obama has continued the struggle against terrorism in the context of the costly ongoing occupation of Afghanistan, the broader failure of the Iraq invasion and occupation, continuing military operations across other theatres, the rise of Islamic State (IS), various scandals and bipartisan contests over issues such as torture, Guantanamo and mass surveillance, a broader sense of war weariness and scepticism, and ongoing generalized anxiety about possible terrorist attacks. In this much more complicated context, President Obama has been forced to adapt his language and policy, while maintaining the core 'war on terror' philosophy and approach enacted by Bush.

Lastly, we suggest that the necessary structural conditions for significant change in US counterterrorism discourse (see Croft 2006), lacking in the first term (see Jackson 2013), are still not present in his second term. Instead, Obama remains committed to the broad thrust of the war on terror (he is not a 'change agent'), and even if he became a change agent, no crisis or rupturing event has occurred which could provide an opening for the articulation of a new approach to counterterrorism. Consequently, we conclude that in the mode of the Hollywood movie *Groundhog Day*, the United States remains stuck in a counterterrorism loop in which the same essential approach produces the same kind of blowback, followed by the same reflexive response (see Jackson 2015a). Consequently, we predict that the US president who follows Obama will also struggle to close Guantanamo, continue to employ military force against terrorism in Iraq, the Middle East, Afghanistan–Pakistan, the Horn of Africa and elsewhere, continue to oversee a global rendition and intelligence-sharing programme, continue to engage in mass surveillance, and will most likely articulate the same central narratives, assumptions and discursive formations of the war on terror.

Continuities in Obama's counterterrorism discourse and practice

There are a great many continuities between Obama's first and second term approach to counterterrorism, and indeed, between the Obama administration's overall approach and that of his predecessor, George Bush. First, despite some minor rhetorical variations between them related to the different historical and strategic contexts (see Oddo 2014), Obama continues to articulate all the central narratives of the original 'war on terrorism' discourse (see Jackson 2005, 2011). For example, in the presidential election debates in 2012, Obama continued to state his belief that terrorism presented a major security threat to the territory and interests of the United States. Two years later, in a speech at the US Military Academy at West Point, Obama (2014e) reiterated that 'for the foreseeable future, the most direct threat to America at home and abroad remains terrorism'. Similarly, following Clinton's 'new terrorism' narrative (see Tsui 2015) and Bush's 'war on terror' discourse (see Jackson 2005), he portrays IS as a 'borderless threat' against the whole world. The notion that terrorism is a serious, existential threat to the United States is now an established, institutionally and culturally embedded feature of American politics, as the rhetoric of the presidential campaign of late 2015 and regular opinion polls also clearly illustrate.

More broadly, following Bush (and his predecessors, particularly Reagan and Clinton), Obama continues to characterize terrorism as a modern form of 'evil' with which no negotiation is possible, only forceful confrontation. In his acceptance speech for the Nobel Peace Prize, for example, he stated: 'Evil does exist in the world.... Negotiations cannot convince Al Qaida's leaders to lay down their arms' (Obama 2009d). Years later, he continued to argue that 'There can be no reasoning – no negotiation – with this brand of evil. The only language understood by killers like this is the language of force' (Obama 2014f). Directly related to this, and following Bush (see Jackson 2005), Obama's rhetoric continues to employ the medical analogy in relation to the threat of terrorism, identifying the enemy as a 'negatively moralized abstraction' (Oddo 2014: 528). For example, he describes how the 'cancer' of 'violent extremism ... has ravaged so many parts of the Muslim world' (2014f), and it will take time to 'eradicate a cancer like ISIL' (Obama 2014g). Like Reagan and Bush before him, he refers to the 'scourge of violent extremism and terrorism' (Obama 2015a), stressing that if left unchecked, it could pose a threat beyond the Middle East, including to the United States (Obama 2014a).

Like all his predecessors, particularly Bush (see Jackson 2005), Obama articulates the discourse of 'exceptionalism' in arguing that America is 'a charmed nation with a historically benevolent role in international affairs' (Oddo 2014: 526), as it has 'underwritten global security for over six decade' (Obama 2009c). Obama emphasizes that 'our cause is just', that the US is engaged in the 'noble struggle for freedom', and that unlike other empires,

> We have not sought world domination.... We do not seek to occupy other nations. We will not claim another nation's resources or target other peoples because their faith or ethnicity is different from ours. What we have fought for – what we continue to fight for – is a better future for our children and grandchildren. And we believe that their lives will be better if other people's children and grandchildren can live in freedom and access opportunity.
>
> (Obama 2009c, cited in Oddo 2014: 526)

As a final example of the continuities between administrations, despite retiring the Bush-era phrase 'war on terror' early in his first term, the language of 'war' and 'military force' continues to infuse the Obama administration's overall counterterrorism rhetoric, and affects the real-world policies and practices of US counterterrorism – such as the assertion of 'necessary force', military intervention, targeted killing, drone strikes and rendition programmes. Specifically, where change occurs it is on the margins of the principal narratives of the war on terror; most of the core features of Bush's 'war on terror' are maintained during Obama's presidency. For example, he continues to articulate that to fight against the ongoing threat of terrorism, 'military action' is indispensable (Obama 2009d), and the US remains 'at war with a specific organization – al-Qaida' (*National Strategy for Counterterrorism* 2011). The 2015 NSS indicated, in an identical mode to previous presidents, notably Bush:

The use of force ... will sometimes be the necessary choice. The United States will use military force, unilaterally and if necessary, when our enduring interests demand it: when our people are threatened; when our livelihoods are at stake; and when the security of our allies is in danger.

(*National Security Strategy* 2015: 8)

As a consequence of the similarities in language, the 'war' frame established by Bush (Jackson 2005) continues to shape the overall US approach to counterterrorism, with forceful military-based strategies continuing to dominate the Obama administration's counterterrorism response. Thus, military intervention in Afghanistan and Pakistan against the Taliban, in Iraq and Syria against IS, and against various other jihadist groups in Yemen, Libya, Somalia, Mali, the Philippines and elsewhere, continues as it had under Bush and in Obama's first term. In fact, the Obama administration has in many respects expanded Bush's war on terror to new regions and theatres. Similarly, the drone killing programme started by the Bush administration continues, and indeed, has greatly expanded under Obama (see Stern 2015), as we discuss below.

Beyond this, the Guantanamo detention camp remains open, and military tribunals for 'unlawful combatants' continue, as does the rendition and enhanced interrogation programme with US allies (see Stern 2015), mass surveillance, intelligence-led cooperation and virtually all the legal measures and security programmes initiated in the Bush era. Importantly, no *major* counterterrorism laws, programmes or institutions enacted during the Bush administration have been repealed, discontinued or disbanded by the Obama administration. In fact, the opposite has occurred: under Obama, every *major* facet of the Bush-led 'war on terror' approach has been continued, institutionalized, and in many cases, expanded and intensified. Moreover, Obama's counterterrorism approach continues with the same broad underlying concepts, narratives, frames, assumptions and philosophy.

Changes in Obama's counterterrorism discourse and practice

Despite the continuities noted above, it is important to acknowledge that Obama also promised a number of changes in counterterrorism policy, most notably ending the use of torture and closing Guantanamo. Obama's most significant policy change was announced on 1 December 2009 at the Military Academy at West Point: US troops were going to be withdrawn from Iraq, the major focus of Bush's war on terror; instead, the focus of the war would be relocated to Afghanistan and Pakistan. Obama (2009b) claimed that these countries, not Iraq, were the true 'epicenter of violent extremism practiced by Al Qaida' and that 'it is from here that the new attacks are being plotted'. Similar statements were later repeated and articulated in the 2010 *National Security Strategy* (NSS) and the 2011 *National Strategy for Counterterrorism*. Clearly, destroying Al Qaida's leadership in Afghanistan and Pakistan and weakening the organization substantially constituted the preoccupation of Obama's first-term counterterrorism policy.

Along with the decision to withdraw major forces from Iraq, the most noticeable change in the Obama administration's counterterrorism approach was a new tone and emphasis in public discourse about international security. For example, in a departure from his predecessor's frequently expressed willingness to use American supremacy to act unilaterally, Obama put much greater emphasis on multilateralism and international cooperation in counterterrorism. Thus, in a speech to a joint session of Congress in February 2009, Obama (2009a) announced: 'with our friends and allies, we will forge a new and comprehensive strategy for Afghanistan and Pakistan to defeat al Qaida and combat extremism', adding that 'to meet the challenges of the 21st century ... we will strengthen old alliances, forge new ones, and use all elements of our national power'. Even more explicitly, he stated:

> America's commitment to global security will never waver. But in a world in which threats are more diffuse and missions more complex, America cannot act alone. America alone cannot secure the peace. This is true in Afghanistan. This is true in failed states like Somalia.
>
> (Obama 2009d)

This public commitment to multilateralism was also expressed in the concept of 'burden sharing', a priority which would characterize future US engagement. For example, following the Libyan intervention, Obama stated:

> We should not be afraid to act – but the burden of action should not be America's alone. As we have in Libya, our task is instead to mobilize the international community for collective action.... American leadership is not simply a matter of going it alone and bearing all of the burden ourselves. Real leadership creates the conditions and coalitions for others to step up as well; to work with allies and partners so that they bear their share of the burden and pay their share of the costs.
>
> (Obama 2011)

Similarly, the *National Strategy for Counterterrorism* (2011: 7) stated that the US 'must join with key partners and allies to share the burdens of common security'. Moreover, this new counterterrorism approach will 'increase the engagement of America's partners', 'reduce the financial burden on the United States', and 'enhance the legitimacy of America's counterterrorism efforts by advancing its objectives without a unilateral, U.S. label'. This commitment to burden sharing has continued deep into Obama's second term, with continued rhetoric stressing that US counterterrorism strategy must 'more effectively partner with countries where terrorist networks seek a foothold' (Obama 2014e), and should be based on international consensus and cooperation among nations. The most recent *National Security Strategy* reiterates this commitment: 'we prefer to act with allies and partners.... In such cases, we will seek to mobilize allies and partners to share the burden and achieve lasting outcomes' (*National Security Strategy*, 2015: 8).

Importantly, this new rhetorical emphasis has been accompanied in practice by moves towards greater reliance on airpower and local military forces, remote warfare, particularly the use of drones, and the use of mobile special forces (see Stern 2015). For example, in September 2014, the publicly announced counter-terrorism strategy aimed at destroying IS stressed the need for 'systematic air-strikes' and a 'no boots on the ground' approach (Obama 2014g). More broadly, over the course of Obama's first and second terms, local forces in Iraq and Syria have steadily replaced US soldiers in the fight against extremists on the ground. As Obama (2014d) stated, 'the only solution that will succeed over the long term' is to use America's 'unique capabilities in support of partners on the ground so they can secure their own countries' future'. More specifically, Obama frequently stated that in the campaign against IS, the US would not fight alone; instead, it would act as 'part of a broad coalition' (2014c) and 'act with friends and partners', including Arab nations (2014b).

Similarly, in a change of tactical emphasis from the Bush era, special forces have been more frequently used by the Obama administration in the campaign against violent extremism. The most notable example is the bin Laden raid led by a small Navy SEAL team in May 2011 (Hasian 2012). In May 2015, Special Forces also targeted Abu Sayyaf, one of IS's top leaders in Syria. This is consist-ent with Obama's broader policy that US counterterrorism must be nimbler and more flexible. In the 2012 Defense Strategic Guidance (DSG), which outlines the future priorities, activities and budget requests of the Department of Defense, the Obama administration stated that 'U.S. forces will no longer be sized to conduct large-scale, prolonged stability operations' (cited in Shaw 2013: 542). Rather, they would be 'agile, flexible, and ready for the full range of contingen-cies' (Shaw 2013: 542). And, in Obama's speech to Congress requesting authori-zation to deploy force against IS, he reiterated the 'no boots on the ground' policy, saying that the United States does not intend to wage a ground war in the heart of the Middle East, although his administration would preserve the right to use military force unilaterally – in particular, its special forces – for 'unforeseen circumstances' (Obama 2015b).

Along with the greater reliance on local forces instead of US ground forces, and the greater use of special forces, the Obama administration has also come to embrace the practices of remote warfare, most notably an increased reliance on the CIA's targeted killing programme, begun during the Bush administration period (McCrisken 2013; Shaw 2013; Stern 2015; Zulaika 2012). Following 9/11, drone strikes have been widely utilized by both Bush's and Obama's administrations. According to data provided by the New America Foundation, Bush authorized approximately forty-eight drone strikes in Pakistan. In contrast, by 2013, Obama had conducted more than 300 drone strikes in that country (McCrisken 2013: 97). Overall, the Obama administration has launched as many as 450 drone attacks in counterterrorism efforts in Yemen, Somalia, Afghanistan and during the 2011 Libya crisis, killing more than 3,000 suspected terrorists and civilians (Stern 2015). Defending his drone policy, Obama (2013) argued that 'dozens of highly skilled Al Qaida commanders, trainers, bomb makers, and operatives have been taken off the battlefield. Plots have been disrupted.... These strikes have saved lives'. He further argued that, in comparison to other types of warfare, remote drone strikes are the 'least likely to result in the loss of innocent life' (2013).

Finally, the Obama administration has recently indicated a desire to focus on dealing with the root causes of terrorism, instead of simply reacting to extremist violence with force-based measures. This has resulted in financial and intellectual investment in counter-radicalisation programmes and measures (see Obama 2015a; Stern 2015), such as the White House Summit on Countering Violent Extremism held in February 2015. Here, Obama outlined a three-part plan involving: discrediting violent extremists, including through a social media campaign to counter IS propaganda; addressing the political and economic grievances which terrorist groups exploit; and improving governance in regions where groups such as IS recruit (Stern 2015).

Evaluating Obama's counterterrorism approach: evolution or adaptation?

The continuities and changes outlined above leave us with a number of important questions. For example, do the changes in Obama's language and approach outweigh the continuities and therefore indicate a *significant* evolution in counterterrorism policy, or are they more of a minor evolutionary adaptation? And how do we explain the observable changes in language and approach? More importantly, how do we explain the lack of substantive change in counterterrorism policy during Obama's second term?

We would argue, based on our analysis, as well as a series of other studies (see Jackson 2011, 2013; McCrisken 2011, 2012; Oddo 2014), that the changes in public discourse and approach between Bush and Obama do not amount to a *significant* evolutionary change, as the primary narratives, assumptions, policies, programmes and approach to responding to terrorism remain largely unchanged overall from the Bush era. That is, notwithstanding the claims of some observers (see Hodges 2011; Ivie and Giner 2009; Stern 2015), the changes amount to relatively minor differences in tone, style and emphasis, rather than a major rewriting of the long-standing war on terror narrative (Zalman and Clarke 2009). As Oddo (2014) argues, Obama rearticulates the overarching features of Bush's war on terror discourse, including its underlying foundational assumptions, primary narratives and discursive structures, but only by employing a series of micro-rhetorical strategies that create the *appearance* of change.

Analysing public remarks by Obama (2009c) in December 2009 on ways forward in Afghanistan and Pakistan, for example, Oddo concludes that Obama recontextualizes and rearticulates the main themes of the Bush discourse through varying micro-rhetorical strategies:

> For example, Obama retains – but also *amplifies* – Bush's rhetoric of 'American Heroism', increasing references to 'our' goodness in order to rally

public support for violence. Moreover, while he replicates Bush's strategy of identifying a 'savage' enemy, Obama uses qualitatively different vocabulary to name that enemy, implying a more focused mission.... Nevertheless, the variations belie overarching continuity between Obama and Bush: both presidents advocate an open-ended war against terrorists and their allies.

(2014: 522; original emphasis)

In other words, under Obama the war on terror

gets a rhetorical makeover as Obama changes the title of the campaign, renames the targeted enemy, and even re-envisions where the enemy is to be found ... to suggest a new, more modest military campaign – even as the global war is *expanded* to new continents.

(Oddo 2014: 534; original emphasis)

This is the main reason why, in practice, the basic framework of employing military force as the primary response to terrorism remains – why the US continues to employ military force against IS in Iraq, the successor to Al Qaida, and in Afghanistan, Pakistan, Syria, Somalia, Yemen and elsewhere. For example, despite Obama's publicly stated plan in February 2015 to tackle the deeper root causes of terrorism and violent extremism, little concrete progress is yet discernible, and in the White House, 'arguments in favour of more military action and aid tend to carry the day' over dealing with local political grievances (Stern 2015).

A number of explanations have been given for the lack of significant change in the course of the war on terror, despite the promise and opportunity for change represented by the election (and re-election) of Obama. McCrisken (2011: 786), for example, argues that the reason for this is that Obama is essentially a "'true believer" in the war on terrorism', and accepts its fundamental approach and rationale (see also Parmar 2011). From this perspective, the changes in approach – such as the withdrawal from Iraq and the refocus on Afghanistan and Pakistan, the emphasis on multilateralism and cooperation, and the change in language from 'war on terror' to 'war against al Qaeda and violent extremism' – relate to disagreements over specific tactics, rather than any fundamental disagreements about the overall aims, approach and strategy of the war. Moreover, he suggests that the central narrative of 'sacrifice' in presidential counterterrorism discourse, by both Bush and Obama, may have constructed a rhetorical 'sacrifice trap' in which 'staying the course' is necessary to justify previous sacrifices in lives and material (McCrisken 2012).

Related to this, Oddo (2014) argues that the reason why we see only relatively small stylistic differences between the language of Bush and Obama is the different context in which they are speaking. That is, the 'variations in Obama's rhetoric reflect substantial changes in the rhetorical situation: an increasingly skeptical public, mounting casualties abroad, political pressure to produce "change"' (2014: 522). In other words, both speakers believe in or accept the war on terror and seek to justify its continuance to their audience. However, while Bush spoke after a traumatic attack to what he perceived as a supportive audience, Obama spoke in the context of a major economic recession, a series of protracted and costly wars in Afghanistan and Iraq, continuing terrorist threats, and a number of public scandals about Guantanamo, the use of torture, mass surveillance and so on (Oddo 2014: 524). In this new context, long after the 9/11 attacks, he therefore had to modify his public rhetoric in order to justify the continued costs of the overall approach, and indeed, the expansion of the war to new theatres.

More broadly, as a great many studies of presidential and political security discourse have shown, there are longer discursive continuities and a deeper historical reflexivity in US responses to security issues such as terrorism (see Campbell 1998; Jackson 2006; Dunmire 2009; Oddo 2011; Tsui 2015; Winkler 2006). The current Bush-initiated war on terror is not the first war on terrorism (see Wills 2003), and in its primary narratives of threat and identity, and its reliance on military force and hard security measures, follows the historical pattern of previous responses to the threats posed by anarchists, Germans during the world wars, Japanese Americans during the Second World War, the so-called 'red scare', and the war on drugs. The point is that the US foreign policy establishment has a historically established, institutionally and discursively embedded reflexive response to security threats. This creates an intertextual context in which attempts by political leaders such as Obama to respond to immediate circumstances actually tend to result in reinstantiating wider existing intertextual formations (Oddo 2014: 514).

Lastly, as argued previously (see Jackson 2009, 2011, 2013), the war on terror discourse has since 9/11 been embedded as a powerful and ubiquitous narrative and discourse into the political-cultural economy of American society, thereby transforming it into a durable *social structure*; that is, it has become a hegemonic discourse and a counterterrorism 'regime of truth' (Foucault 2002). As such, the discourse has acquired a broader and deeper functionality for a variety of actors in the political-economic structures of the United States. It now functions, among other things, as an organizing policy paradigm for bureaucratic elites, a negative ideograph of national identity, a rationale and set of interests for the 'terrorism industry', and a staple media frame, and it has even played a role in mitigating the worst consequences of the financial crisis by stimulating the productivity of the security sector (see Boukalas 2015). Its functionality also extends globally to the point where it is not an exaggeration to compare it to the Cold War system. That is, as we have argued previously, the war on terror quickly became

> a productive and self-perpetuating global system in which direct economic and political benefits accrue not only to US domestic actors but also to a wide range of regimes and interest groups who collaborate in its operation and lend support to its continuation.
>
> (Jackson 2013: 84; see also Keen 2006)

Added to this, we would argue that some of the culturally and historically unique aspects of the war on terror discourse also make it particularly difficult to change. For example, as a great many observers have noted, the war on terror has been constructed as a borderless, perpetual war against a shadowy, networked and largely unknown enemy. This discursive construction means that it is impossible to imagine or articulate what kind of events or moments could signal its end, or provide the impetus for policy change. There is no surrender ceremony for the strategy of terrorism. Not even the killing of Osama bin Laden can be interpreted as the end of the war on terror; in the dominant discursive structure, such events are essentially meaningless as indicators of risk levels, increased security, or progress towards greater security (Jackson 2015c).

Moreover, this condition is magnified by what we have noted is an 'epistemological crisis' at the heart of US (and more broadly, Western) counterterrorism (Jackson 2015b; see also Zulaika 2012). That is, counterterrorism discourse and practice are today characterized by an inherent condition of 'unknowing' as its primary condition of possibility. Constructed on the central notion that it is impossible to know where, when and how the next terrorist attack will take place – that terrorism is a kind of risk that is essentially what Donald Rumsfeld famously described as an 'unknown unknown' (see Daase and Kessler 2007) – counterterrorism is forced to assume the worst and act as if terrorism remains an omnipresent threat, even if there is no evidence of future threat. As a consequence of these two aspects of the discourse – its borderless, perpetual nature and the inherent epistemological crisis – it will be impossible to know decisively or determine empirically when the threat has been eliminated or reduced to a level that could justify dismantling, or reordering, the broader discursive and institutional architecture of counterterrorism.

From this perspective, even if Obama were a genuine 'change agent' or 'norm entrepreneur' (which he is arguably not), he would face significant challenges in actually enacting significant policy changes because the structural conditions are not permissive of change at this moment. As we have argued before, and following Croft (2006), it takes 'the combination of determined agentic action and a discursive opening in the culture brought on by a crisis or rupturing event to create the conditions necessary for substantive change to what are deeply embedded social structures and political practices' (Jackson 2013). In Obama's second term, as in his first term, these conditions are not present. This is the main reason why Obama has been unable to enact some of even the modest changes he promised upon his election, such as closing Guantanamo Bay, ending torture, and so on; the current conditions and the social structure of the war on terror make such changes extremely difficult, even for a determined change agent. Even his most significant change, withdrawing from Iraq to focus on Afghanistan, is now in danger of reversal as the war against IS draws the US and other Western states deeper and deeper into the intervention, and US ground forces are deployed.

In summary, while there have been some observable changes in Obama's counterterrorism approach and public discourse, these do not amount to substantive changes in the embedded narrative of the war on terror put in place after 9/11. The war on terror, notwithstanding the retirement of the phrase itself, continues largely unabated and unchanged from its inception in October 2001. Moreover, this is not surprising or unexpected, as it has become a self-replicating, institutionally and culturally embedded social structure. In any case, Obama has proved that he is not a change agent, and even if he were, the structural conditions for significant policy change currently do not exist.

Conclusion

So what conclusions can we draw from this brief overview of Obama's second-term counterterrorism approach? Does this analysis tell us anything about the conditions of public political discourse, the current state of US counterterrorism, or what we can expect the next US president to do in response to terrorism? Most obviously, and following discourse theory (see Jackson and McDonald 2009; Oddo 2014), this review suggests that the ability of public figures to inno-vate new discourses and bring about significant policy change is circumscribed by the institutional and historical context in which they operate. In the specific context of US political culture, and the historical context of more than a decade of war on terror, Obama was constrained in his ability to challenge or rewrite the primary narratives and discursive structures of the war on terror – even if he had wanted to. Instead, he was limited to largely stylistic rhetorical adaptations and relatively minor tactical adjustments.

Related to this, we can confirm that US counterterrorism continues to be embedded and institutionalized as a self-replicating 'industry' with its own material and political interests. It now involves a plethora of government and private agencies, bureaucracies, corporations, companies, think-tanks, research centres and the like, along with lobbyists and industry financiers. The sums of money poured into, and generated by, the 'terrorism industry' are quite astro-nomical, and thus represent a powerful set of material interests for maintaining, and even expanding, the scope and activities of the war on terror.

In short, in the absence of a new crisis or rupturing event which could provide an opening for the articulation of a new approach to counterterrorism, and the emergence of a genuine change agent with the power to speak authori-tatively, we predict that US counterterrorism will remain largely unchanged in its primary form and approach for the next few years (if not decades) at least. In the mode of the popular Hollywood film *Groundhog Day*, and for the reasons outlined in this brief chapter, the United States really does remain stuck in an existential counterterrorism loop in which the same essential approach continues to be enacted over and over again, even when its most obvious result is to produce more and even worse terrorism, such as the muta-tion of Al Qaida into IS (see Jackson 2015a). Consequently, we predict that the new president who succeeds Obama, even if she or he wants to, will sim-ilarly struggle to close Guantanamo, will continue to employ military force against terrorism in Iraq, the Middle East, Afghanistan–Pakistan, the Horn of Africa and elsewhere, will continue to oversee a global rendition and intelligence-sharing programme, will continue to fund forms of mass surveil-lance, and will continue to articulate the central narratives, assumptions and discursive formations of the war on terror.

References

Boukalas, C., 2015. 'Class war-on-terror: counterterrorism, accumulation, crisis', *Critical Studies on Terrorism*, 8(1): 55–71.

Campbell, D., 1998. *Writing security: United States foreign policy and the politics of identity*, revised edition, Minneapolis: University of Minnesota Press.

Croft, S., 2006. *Culture, crisis and America's war on terror*, Cambridge: Cambridge University Press.

Daase, C. and Kessler, O., 2007. 'Knowns and unknowns in the "war on terror": uncertainty and the political construction of danger', *Security Dialogue*, 38(4): 425–6.

Dunmire, P., 2009. '"9/11 changed everything"?: An intertextual analysis of the Bush doctrine', *Discourse & Society*, 20(2): 195–222.

Foucault, M., 2002. 'Truth and power', in James Faubion, ed., *Power: essential works of Foucault, vol. 3*, translated by Robert Hurley *et al.*, London: Penguin, pp. 111–33.

Hasian, M., 2012. 'American exceptionalism and the bin Laden raid', *Third World Quarterly*, 33(10): 1803–20.

Hodges, A., 2011. *The 'war on terror' narrative: discourse and intertextuality in the construction and contestation of sociopolitical reality*, New York: Oxford University Press.

Ivie, R. and Giner, O., 2009. 'American exceptionalism in a democratic idiom: transacting the mythos of change in the 2008 presidential campaign', *Communication Studies*, 60(4): 359–75.

Jackson, R., 2005. *Writing the war on terrorism: language, politics and counter-terrorism*, Manchester: Manchester University Press.

Jackson, R., 2006. 'Genealogy, ideology, and counter-terrorism: writing wars on terrorism from Ronald Reagan to George W. Bush Jr', *Studies in Language & Capitalism*, 1: 163–93.

Jackson, R., 2009. 'The 9/11 attacks and the social construction of a national narrative', in M. Morgan, ed., *The impact of 9–11 on the media, arts and entertainment: the day that changed everything?*, New York: Palgrave Macmillan, pp. 25–35.

Jackson, R., 2011. 'Culture, identity and hegemony: continuity and (the lack of) change in US counter-terrorism policy from Bush to Obama', *International Politics*, 48(2/3): 390–411.

Jackson, R., 2013. 'Bush, Obama, Bush, Obama, Bush, Obama…: the war on terror as a durable social structure', in M. Bentley and J. Holland, eds, *Obama's foreign policy: ending the war on terror*, Abingdon: Routledge, pp. 76–90.

Jackson, R., 2015a. 'Commentary: *Groundhog Day* and the repetitive failure of Western counterterrorism policy in the Middle East', *Insight Turkey*, 17(3): 35–44.

Jackson, R., 2015b. 'The epistemological crisis of counterterrorism', *Critical Studies on Terrorism*, 8(1): 33–54.

Jackson, R., 2015c. 'Bin Laden's ghost and the epistemological crisis of counter-terrorism', in S. Jeffords and F. Al-Sumait, eds, *Covering bin Laden: global media and the world's most wanted man*, Chicago: University of Illinois Press, pp. 1–19.

Jackson, R. and McDonald, M., 2009. 'Constructivism, US foreign policy and the "war on terror"', in I. Palmer, ed., *New directions in US foreign policy*, Abingdon: Routledge, pp. 18–31.

Keen, D., 2006. 'War without end? Magic, propaganda and the hidden functions of counter-terror', *Journal of International Development*, 18: 87–104.

McCrisken, T., 2011. 'Ten years on: Obama's war on terrorism in rhetoric and practice', *International Affairs*, 87(4): 781–802.

McCrisken, T., 2012. 'Justifying sacrifice: Barack Obama and the selling and ending of the war in Afghanistan', *International Affairs*, 88(5): 993–1007.

McCrisken, T., 2013. 'Obama's drone war', *Survival*, 55(2): 97–122.

National Security Strategy, 2015. Washington, DC: The White House, available online at: http://nssarchive.us/wp-content/uploads/2015/02/2015.pdf.

National Strategy for Counterterrorism, 2011. Washington, DC: The White House, available online at: www.whitehouse.gov/sites/default/files/counterterrorism_strategy.pdf.

Obama, B., 2009a. 'Address before a joint session of the Congress', 24 February, available online at: www.gpo.gov/fdsys/pkg/PPP-2009-book1/pdf/PPP-2009-book1-Doc-pg145–2.pdf.

Obama, B., 2009b. 'Remarks at the United States Military Academy at West Point, New York', 1 December, available online at: www.gpo.gov/fdsys/pkg/PPP-2009-book2/pdf/PPP-2009-book2-Doc-pg1747–3.pdf.

Obama, B., 2009c. 'Remarks by the president in address to the nation on the way forward in Afghanistan and Pakistan', 1 December, available online at: www.whitehouse.gov/the-press-office/remarks-president-address-nation-way-forward-afghanistan-and-pakistan.

Obama, B., 2009d. 'Remarks on Accepting the Nobel Peace Prize in Oslo', 10 December, available online at: www.gpo.gov/fdsys/pkg/PPP-2009-book2/pdf/PPP-2009-book2-Doc-pg1799.pdf.

Obama, B., 2011. 'Address to the nation on the situation in Libya', 28 March, available online at: www.gpo.gov/fdsys/pkg/PPP-2011-book1/pdf/PPP-2011-book1-Doc-pg306.pdf.

Obama, B., 2013. 'Remarks at National Defense University', 23 May, available online at: www.presidency.ucsb.edu/ws/index.php?pid=103625&st=drones&st1=.

Obama, B., 2014a. 'The president's weekly address', 13 September, available online at: www.presidency.ucsb.edu/ws/index.php?pid=107492&st=ISIL&st1=.

Obama, B., 2014b. 'The president's weekly address', 20 September, available online at: www.presidency.ucsb.edu/ws/index.php?pid=107540&st=ISIL&st1=.

Obama, B., 2014c. 'The president's weekly address', 27 September, available online at: www.presidency.ucsb.edu/ws/index.php?pid=107690&st=ISIL&st1=.

Obama, B., 2014d. 'Remarks at MacDill Air Force Base, Florida', 17 September, available online at: www.presidency.ucsb.edu/ws/index.php?pid=107532&st=ISIL&st1=.

Obama, B., 2014e. 'Remarks by the president at the United States Military Academy Commencement Ceremony', 28 May, available online at: www.presidency.ucsb.edu/ws/index.php?pid=105220&st=extremism&st1=.

Obama, B., 2014f. 'Remarks to the United Nations General Assembly in New York City', 24 September, available online at: www.presidency.ucsb.edu/ws/index.php?pid=107615&st=ISIL&st1=.

Obama, B., 2014g. 'Statement by the president on ISIL', 7 September, available online at: https://www.whitehouse.gov/the-press-office/2014/09/10/statement-president-isil-1.

Obama, B., 2015a. 'Remarks at the White House Summit on countering violent extremism', 19 February, available online at: www.presidency.ucsb.edu/ws/index.php?pid=109653&st=ISIL&st1=.

Obama, B., 2015b. 'Remarks on proposed legislation submitted to the congress to authorize the use of military force against the Islamic State of Iraq and the Levant (ISIL) terrorist organization', 11 February, available online at: www.presidency.ucsb.edu/ws/index.php?pid=109385&st=ISIL&st1=.

Oddo, J., 2011. 'War legitimation discourse: representing "us" and "them" in four U.S. presidential addresses', *Discourse & Society*, 22(3): 287–314.

Oddo, J., 2014. 'Variation and continuity in intertextual rhetoric: from the "war on terror" to the "struggle against violent extremism"', *Journal of Language and Politics*, 13(3): 512–37.

Parmar, I., 2011. 'Introduction: American power and identities in the age of Obama', *International Politics*, 48(2/3): 153–63.

Shaw, I., 2013. 'Predator empire: the geopolitics of US drone warfare', *Geopolitics*, 18(3): 536–59.

Stern, J., 2015. 'Obama and terrorism: Like it or not, the war goes on', *Foreign Affairs*, September/October issue, available online at: www.foreignaffairs.com/articles/obama-and-terrorism.

Tsui, C., 2015. 'Framing the threat of catastrophic terrorism: genealogy, discourse and President Clinton's counterterrorism approach', *International Politics*, 52(1): 66–88.

Wills, D., 2003. *The first war on terrorism: counter-terrorism policy during the Reagan administration*, Lanham: Rowman & Littlefield.

Winkler, C., 2006. *In the name of terrorism: presidents on political violence in the post-World War II era*, Albany, NY: State University of New York Press.

Zalman, A. and Clarke, J., 2009. 'The global war on terror: a narrative in need of a rewrite', *Ethics & International Affairs*, 23(2): 101–13.

Zulaika, J., 2012. 'Drones, witches and other flying objects: the force of fantasy in U.S. counterterrorism', *Critical Studies on Terrorism*, 5(1): 51–68.

6 Shifting binaries

The colonial legacy of Obama's war on terror

Ben Fermor

As Barack Obama took office in January 2009, his ability to shape American foreign policy was constrained by the discursive structures already in place. Most relevant to this publication, the Bush administration's 'war on terror' had cemented a collection of understandings of how America should conduct itself in a world inhabited by Osama bin Laden, al Qaida and 'Islamic extremists' (Jackson, 2013). Other authors have demonstrated how the war on terror defined Obama as a 'war president' from the outset (Bentley, 2013; Desch, 2010), pushing him more towards continuity than change. Nevertheless, the new president seemed to want to achieve some kind of rupture from the past in asserting his own 'Obama doctrine'. The phrase 'war on terror' was dropped from official usage (McCrisken, 2013), efforts were made to close the Guantanamo Bay detention centre and to repeal the controversial USA PATRIOT Act (Pious, 2011), and the public were assured troops would be withdrawn from the long and costly war in Iraq as soon as would be practical (Aaronson, 2013). Using the phrase 'enlightened self-interest', Obama sought to achieve a legacy of multilateralism and intelligent interventionism on the basis that global stability and security would strengthen America's own national interest (Aaronson, 2013; Brooks, 2007; Obama, 2009). This chapter makes the case that this multilateralist legacy has been enabled due to a shift in the core narratives of the war on terror over the course of Obama's presidency. Where Bush relied on the core identities of 'good Americans' and 'evil terrorists' to push his unilateral approach to foreign policy (Holland, 2013; Jackson, 2005; Krebs and Lobasz, 2007; Sjostedt, 2007; Solomon, 2009), Obama manipulated this into the colonial language of 'civilisation' and 'barbarism'. As a result, the self was broadened to enable international collaboration and the other was narrowed and dehumanised, making the physical destruction of Obama's chosen targets a political necessity. The aim of this chapter is to explore how this process of broadening and narrowing the core identities of US foreign policy works, how it alters the discursive structures of the war on terror and how these strategic shifts have allowed Obama to establish a doctrine and legacy of his own.

The chapter proceeds in two parts, the first looking at post-colonial theory and examining the historical (re)production of the civilised and barbarian binary identities Obama relies upon in his discourse on terror. The second part then takes a small sample of key texts authored by Obama on the threat and occurrence of violent 'Islamist' attacks in the context of the rise of ISIL, and compares the nature of labels and qualities attached to self and other identities with those used by George Bush. For the purposes of locating strategic agency, only remarks made by the head of state are considered here. The chapter concludes in arguing that Obama has succeeded in strategically resituating the core identities underlying US foreign policy in a way that favours his preferred methods of fighting the war on terror. By widening the self-identity from America to the civilised world, Obama has manipulated the discursive structures of the war on terror to be more conducive to an international audience that can offer the US multilateral support and a burden-sharing approach to anti-terrorist intervention. By relegating the dangerous other identity from 'evil' terrorists to sub-human or 'anti-human' barbarians, he has also been able to legitimise a foreign policy doctrine that seeks to 'degrade and ultimately destroy' the enemy through relatively low-risk/low-cost aerial bombardments without resorting to more problematic methods aiming to engage, contain or detain enemy combatants. In terms of structure and agency, the president has therefore been able to take advantage of the agential power inherent in his position to manipulate the structures of the war on terror to his advantage, even if he has been unwilling or unable to dismantle them as might have been expected. It should be noted that the rise of ISIL, and the 'new threat' it represents, have undoubtedly influenced the president's choice of rhetoric. Nevertheless, the presence of a non-state jihad-inspired violent network is not objectively different from previous threats such as al Qaida to the extent that it would independently necessitate a change in core identities. Like all threats, ISIL required framing and Obama's choice of frame demonstrates the difference between his discursive legacy and that of his predecessor. This chapter argues that the choice to associate ISIL predominantly with the language of barbarism, and to oppose it to the language of civilisation, was a strategically intelligent decision. In framing the threat in these terms, Obama set the parameters of the discussion on appropriate response in a way that would resonate with his doctrine of cost-effective multilateralism. In so doing he has embedded his own doctrine into the dominant discourses of the war on terror, creating a discursive legacy which will form part of the evolving structure his successor will have to understand and manipulate in future.

Civilisation and barbarism: the continued relevance of a colonial narrative

The war on terror – named, written and dominated by Western actors and played out in the Middle East – has obvious parallels with the colonialist campaigns of the nineteenth and early twentieth centuries (Barkawi and Laffey, 2006; Gregory, 2004). The Anglo-American push for regime change in Iraq, the perceived necessity to bring Western norms to Arabic and Muslim lands (Boyle, 2011; Sjostedt, 2007, p. 233), and the general failure of occupying troops to understand the basics of local cultures (Gregory, 2004) all reflect the colonial template of a

European force attempting to structure the Orient into something that can be controlled and incorporated into a Western agenda. Add to this the wealth of natural resources in proximity to key zones of conflict – and the quick distribution of contracts to Western corporations (Halperin, 2011) – and the post-colonial critique of American foreign policy becomes difficult to dismiss out of hand. This section considers post-colonial theory in application to the core narratives of US foreign policy in the war on terror.

Edward Said wrote *Orientalism*, his seminal tome on the discursive structures of colonialism, from the basis that the 'world is made up of two unequal halves' (Said, 1995, p. 12) – the Occident and the Orient, the latter existing as the former's textual creation. The Orient has been (re)written over centuries by Western academics, authors, artists, historians and political and military actors as one of Europe's 'deepest and most recurring images of the other' (Said, 1995, p. 1). Orientalism is not just the study of 'the East' by Western scholars but a complex and continually developing structure of thought about the world that divides it into East and West, along a series of subjective fault lines. This is a process of othering that functions in the same way as George Bush's 'good Americans'/'evil terrorists' core binary, but that reaches further into the past, carrying the collected values associated with centuries of Western knowledge on the East. Crucially, each production of knowledge comes from the West and orders the East, leading Said to argue that Orientalism is an authoritarian tool used to structure the Eastern other. The language of colonialism acts as an archive of accepted knowledge and 'common sense' on Europe's other, and dictates how it exists in a world dominated by Europeans. For Said, 'the European representation of the Muslim, Ottoman or Arab was always a way of controlling the redoubtable Orient' (Said, 1995, p. 60).

Examining the core narratives and identities of Orientalism, Said argues that its language is built on a self/other binary opposition that draws an imaginary boundary between 'us' as the inhabitants of civilisation, and the 'barbarians' from the East (Said, 1995, p. 53). Said maps onto these imagined identities the basic values of 'rationality', 'virtue', 'maturity' and 'normality' for the European self and the opposing values of 'irrationality', 'depravity', 'childishness' and 'difference' for the barbarian other (Said, 1995, p. 40). With these in place, it then becomes logical that Westerners must dominate and Orientals must be dominated (Said, 1995, p. 36). The West's superior position in the hegemonic discourse on the East makes colonialism possible. Orientalism encourages a categorisation of thoughts into the binary identities of East/West, just as the war on terror encourages distinction between Americans and terrorists. Whatever thought is Western is necessarily true, rational and scientific. A Gramscian hegemony is thereby created in which the West holds power over the East, and those people who find themselves categorised as 'Oriental' are without a stake in the production of knowledge over their own reality.

The civilised/barbarian narrative is usually associated with European discourses on the East, but it has a strong presence in American cultural and political history. Three extracts of texts from key encounters with the other in

American history are taken here to demonstrate the long-standing relevance of the core colonial identities to US foreign policy. These moments are: an early encounter between Europeans and the indigenous peoples of the New World, the annexation of the Philippines at the turn of the twentieth century, and the reaction to the occupation of Kuwait by Iraq in 1990.

Starting with the arrival of Europeans on the American continent, the other as barbarian is studied by David Campbell as part of the formation of the American identity. In the discursive creation of the 'New World' following Columbus's arrival on the American continent in 1492, Campbell identifies two co-existent self/other binaries that interact in the imagery of Native Americans: the 'civilised/barbarian' and the 'Christian/Pagan' (Campbell, 1998, pp. 102–3). The author highlights the problem posed by the Native American other to the Spanish Christians, who were unsure whether they should be adopted into the Christian faith or enslaved as an inferior race. The first argument viewed the indigenes as 'culturally virgin', requiring instruction and education by enlightened Europeans (Todorov, 1984, p. 42). Campbell reasons that whilst the Christian/Pagan and civilised/barbarian identities overlapped in the Europeans' imaginations, the relative weight given to each one dictated how a Spanish foreign policy could be formulated. The Pagan could become Christian (and therefore civilised) if he was capable of using reason to perceive the 'true' faith. Conversely, following Said's portrait, a barbarian would be incapable of reasoning and so could not become either Christian or civilised.

The discursive contest is encapsulated in the 1550 Valladolid debate between Spanish philosophers Juan Ginés de Sepulveda and Bartolomé de Las Casas. The following is an extract from Sepulveda's argument in favour of the use of violence against the indigenous population and against the prohibition of their enslavement:

> The greatest philosophers declare that such wars may be undertaken by a very civilized nation against uncivilized people who are more barbarous than can be imagined.... Moreover, here is the truth of their savage life, like that of beasts: their execrable and prodigious immolations of human victims to demons; the fact of devouring human flesh; of burying alive their chieftains' wives with their dead husband and other similar crimes.
>
> (Sepulveda, cited in Campbell, 1998, p. 100)

This text highlights the historical narrative of barbarism as the other to the enlightened Christian/European. Here, the civilised self lays claim to the 'greatest philosophers' and the legitimate use of violence under the banner of the nation whilst the barbarian is savage, sub-human and only comparable to 'beasts'. Furthermore it illustrates how the experience of unusual violence, and the dehumanising narrative that gives meaning to it, can be fed into arguments in favour of violent policies at the expense of the other. The dehumanising, derationalising aspects of the barbarian label still persist in contemporary discourses on violence. After 9/11, the risk of further attacks was a prime argument in denying terrorist suspects basic human rights in Guantanamo Bay. As the war on terror continues, if members of a non-state militant group such as ISIL are labelled rebels, they may be negotiated with. If they are terrorists, negotiations are less likely but they might be imprisoned or detained. If their use of violence is so shocking as to warrant the barbarian label, the argument can be made that they are no longer human and so can only be 'degrade[ed] and ultimately destroy[ed]' (Obama, 2014b). The barbarian label opens the door for a foreign policy that seeks to bomb the enemy out of existence, rather than risk placing boots on the ground or examine the potential links between state action and radicalisation.

It is possible to view the development of this core narrative in the domestic debate on the ethics of American colonialism. The following text, taken from words attributed to President William McKinley in an interview for *The Christian Advocate*, demonstrates the use of the civilised and barbarian identities in legitimising the annexation of the Philippines. In deliberating how to deal with the formerly Spanish territories, McKinley is claimed to have come to four realisations:

1   that we could not give them back to Spain – that would be cowardly and dishonorable;
2   that we could not turn them over to France and Germany – our commercial rivals in the Orient – that would be bad business and discreditable;
3   that we could not leave them to themselves – they were unfit for self-government – and they would soon have anarchy and misrule over there worse than Spain's; and
4   that there was nothing left for us to do but to take them all, and to educate the Filipinos, and uplift and civilize and Christianize them, and by God's grace do the very best we could by them, as our fellow-men for whom Christ also died.

(Rusling, 1987)

Here, the opposing qualities of civilisation and barbarism are evident in the justification of military action. On one side of the coin, Americans take on the role of the civilisers and are attributed the traditional European qualities of honour, bravery, and the duty to bring good governance to the colonial other. On the other, the Filipinos are anarchic, unfit to rule or govern, uneducated and uncivilised. Added to this, the necessity to engage in good business demonstrates a colonial urge to restructure the lands of the other into something that can serve domestic political and economic interests. The language of barbarism is still present, though less emphasised than in Campbell's extract from Sepulveda. Instead weight is put on the inherent goodness of civilised America and its duty or manifest destiny to spread its democratic example beyond the frontier. Once again, violent action by the state is legitimised by the strategic use of the civilised/barbarian colonial narrative.

Before considering the core differences between Obama and Bush Jr.'s discourses on the threat of terrorism, it is useful to consider a more recent use of the civilised and barbarian identities. The following is taken from George Bush Sr.'s 'New World Order' address to Congress. Once again civilised values are attributed to America and its allies, and their binary opposites label Saddam Hussein and Iraq:

> At this moment, our brave servicemen and women stand watch in that distant desert and on distant seas, side by side with the forces of more than 20 other nations....
>
> This is not, as Saddam Hussein would have it, the United States against Iraq. It is Iraq against the world....
>
> Saddam Hussein is literally trying to wipe a country off the face of the Earth.... Iraq itself controls some 10 percent of the world's proven oil reserves. Iraq plus Kuwait controls twice that. An Iraq permitted to swallow Kuwait would have the economic and military power, as well as the arrogance, to intimidate and coerce its neighbors.... We cannot permit a resource so vital to be dominated by one so ruthless.
>
> (Bush, 1990)

The initial traces of colonialist discourse can be seen in the traditional imagery of the Orient as a strange and foreign land of 'distant deserts', surrounded by 'distant seas'. Looking at the core identities of the colonial narrative, the civilised self-identity has expanded, to include not only America, but 'the world' and the '20 other nations' that stand with it. Within this identity, the language of civilisation can be seen in references to bravery and the rule of law as what 'we', the civilised word, can permit. The language of barbarism is then associated to Saddam Hussein's aggression, via the colonial vocabulary of arrogance, intimidation, coercion and ruthlessness. Finally, the need for the Orient to be arranged in a way that serves the West's economic interests is shown through the importance of oil reserves to Bush's foreign policy decisions. The rhetorical devices of widening the self and narrowing and demonising the other is later reflected in Obama's language on ISIL. The broadening of the self enables a language favourable to coalition building, a condition necessary at the time to prevent Bush's allies from objecting to a US-centric solution to the problem posed by Iraq. The focusing of the barbarian identity on a specific individual in Saddam Hussein and a specific nation in Iraq balances this out by making possible and necessary a multilateral course of military action targeted against a key US enemy.

The long history of the colonial narrative and its binary identities in US foreign policy discourse offers Obama a greater wealth of historical and cultural memories to draw upon in framing the threat than the narrative predominantly used by Bush Jr. Although his discourse on the war on terror may have made use of the colonial narrative in demonising terrorism, the civilised/barbarian identities were always secondary to the more nationalistic good Americans/evil terrorists binary that Jackson (2005) argues sustains the discursive structures of the war on terror. The American/terrorist binary identities were effective for Bush Jr. in uniting Americans after 9/11 and unilaterally launching and sustaining the war on terror. However, the tradition of their juxtaposition is much younger than that of their colonial equivalents and therefore their potential to endure as the war on terror develops may be limited. Whilst Bush's binaries can be traced back before 9/11, to President Reagan's first 'war on terror' (Jackson, 2006), it was only after 2001 that their use began to resonate with the American people so powerfully. The core binaries of civilisation and barbarism meanwhile contain centuries of accumulated historical knowledge and relevance (Said, 1995), pre-date the American/terrorist narrative and give the multilateralist president a key strategic advantage in resonating with a wider international audience. The following section compares a sample of Bush's and Obama's rhetoric on the terrorist threat in order to make the case that the core identities of the war on terror have indeed shifted under Obama's presidency.

Construction of the self and other under Bush Jr. and Obama

The American identity, whatever threatening other it may be opposed to at a given time, is perhaps the most powerful narrative in US foreign policy discourse. (Re)writing what it is to be American, in terms of values, culture and responsibilities, has historically been the central theme in US foreign policy from the days of settlement, through the defining periods of the civil war, cold war and war on terror (Campbell, 1998, 2001). The tendency to oppose the American identity to the dominant contemporary perception of threat was especially prevalent under George W. Bush's presidency and in particular in his framing of the 'war on terror' doctrine. His 2006 speech on terrorism provides a good example of his use of the core American and terrorist binary identities in framing the 11 September attacks and the threat facing the nation going forward. The purpose of the analysis here is to get to the heart of the narrative Bush deploys when talking about the war on terror. This is done by seeking out the core identities within the narrative – the self, and the other which places it under threat. These core identities can be seen in the opening sentence of the speech: 'On the morning of September the 11th, 2001, our nation awoke to a nightmare attack' (Bush, 2006).

Bush first contextualises his statement by appealing to his audience's memories of 9/11, as well as the many emotions and identities that became associated with it. From there, he quickly draws himself and his audience together with the use of the possessive pronoun 'our', and attaches this to the referent of the 'nation'. Finally, the threatening other is established with the reference to the 'nightmare attack'. Two identities are therefore observable in the sentence – the (American) nation and the agents responsible for the 11 September attack, its threatening but constitutive other. This identification process allows for the deconstruction of the American identity in Bush's discourse, and enables the reader to make strange the definition of America as the opposite of what it is to inflict such an attack on the American people. Bush's language (re)writes America as the opposite of terrorism. In Campbell's (1998) theory of foreign policy, this creates a purpose for the state, which now must implement a policy to destroy terrorism.

The pattern of (re)writing America as the binary opposite of the terrorist threat is continued throughout the speech:

> We watched the twin towers collapse before our eyes....
> The attacks of September the 11th horrified our nation....
> Who had attacked us? What did they want? And what else were they planning?...
> Americans saw the destruction the terrorists had caused....
> We had to respond to the attack on our country.
>
> (Bush, 2006)

In each phrase there is a self and a corresponding other. The self, characterised as 'America', 'we' or 'our nation', is constructed through references to the dangerous other, signified by 'they', 'the attacks', 'the collapse', 'destruction' and 'the terrorists'. This is a demonstration of the use of the audience's resources (Fairclough, 2001), in throwing the memory back to the reader's knowledge of 9/11, and previous landmark speeches on the threat posed by terrorists. The language makes clear that the self is the nation, rather than alternative bodies such as the civilised world, which this chapter argues is used to a greater extent in Obama's rhetoric. Bush prioritises the American/(terrorist) other narrative to communicate his foreign policy over the more colonial civilisation/barbarian narrative that is often used elsewhere.

This deconstruction makes evident the dominant narrative in Bush's discourse. This narrative makes use of the American/(terrorist) other binary in (re)writing the national and terrorist identities. The prioritisation of the American self-identity gives an idea of both the national culture and audience to which Bush is speaking and his own understanding of the world and the events of September 11th. Whilst the American identity is hugely powerful to a national audience, its opposition to terrorism was a relatively new discursive development that achieved hegemonic status after the 9/11 attacks were framed correspondingly. Its use enabled Bush to mobilise domestic support and to take a unilateral approach to foreign policy that would endure in the years to come. When Obama's rhetoric on the war on terror is compared to his predecessor, different core identities appear to be at play. First, the self would seem to have expanded beyond America so that it applies to the entirety of the 'civilised world'. Second, the (terrorist) other appears to have been further distanced from the self through the insistent use of the colonial barbarian identity. Where the assailants behind 9/11 were 'evil' and un-American, the followers of ISIL have been further relegated in the moral hierarchy, having picked up all of the qualities of the colonial barbarian and lost any claim of belonging to the human race. This dehumanisation of the other then legitimises a foreign policy response that aims solely to destroy rather than detain, contain or otherwise deal with the latest threat to the self. The following statements are analysed to demonstrate these changes to the core identities:

> We see ISIL, a brutal, vicious death cult that, in the name of religion, carries out unspeakable acts of barbarism.
>
> (Obama, 2015a)

> ISIL has no ideology of any value to human beings ... the fact is they terror-ize their neighbors and offer them nothing but an endless slavery to their empty vision, and the collapse of any definition of civilized behavior....
>
> One thing we can all agree on is that a group like ISIL has no place in the 21st century.
>
> (Obama, 2014a)

> Its barbaric murders of so many people, including American hostages, are a desperate and revolting attempt to strike fear in the hearts of people it can never possibly win over by its ideas or its ideology....
>
> And with vile groups like this, there is only one option: With our allies and partners, we are going to degrade and ultimately destroy this terrorist group.
>
> (Obama, 2014b)

The first statement comes from the 2015 National Prayer Breakfast. ISIL is overtly labelled barbarian. The language of brutality, viciousness and 'unspeak-able acts' serves to separate the other from the self and to frame the Islamist regime as something both similar to and different from the earlier terrorists who had previously attacked America. ISIL members are not simply religious fanat-ics seeking to impose their way of life on others, they are a 'death cult' – alien not just to Americans but to every civilised group of people. This theme is con-tinued in the second extract, taken from the president's response to the execution of ISIL hostage and US citizen James Foley. ISIL is again positioned as a threat to 'civilised behaviour'. As an entity, it is discursively separated from 'human beings', said to belong in the past, and argued to have no right to exist in today's world. There is a reference to terrorism which links IS with America's previous experiences of al Qaida and Osama bin Laden, but it is constructed as a different kind of terrorism. ISIL's terrorism is barbaric, anti-human rather than anti-American, and threatens not just the US but everything that we know to be 'civi-lised'. The final quotes appear in a statement Obama made on ISIL in August 2014 that outlined US strategy in Iraq and Syria. Once again, the barbarian label is applied and this time reinforced by qualifiers of desperation and revulsion. Again, the threat is posed not necessarily to Americans but to people, whether this is the 'many people' ISIL have murdered or the people its leaders attempt to frighten into following the barbarian ideology. The self and the other identities at the heart of Obama's war on terror therefore do not exist under the same labels as they did under Bush. The self has taken on all the historic qualities of Western civilisation, and the other has degenerated from the anti-American terrorist of 9/11 into the anti-human barbarian who has been systematically opposed to civilisation and progress since Europe's first encounters with the Orient. This enables the president's closing argument for the gradual but total physical destruction of the other.

Obama still uses the good Americans/evil terrorists narrative when it can be politically advantageous in mobilising popular opinion. However, in general, the binary identities of the war on terror have been transposed onto the old colonial opposition of barbarism and civilisation. ISIL remains a 'terrorist group' in much of the president's rhetoric, and it is useful to note how this label is evoked in the final quote to justify the use of national resources to 'degrade' and 'destroy' the enemy. This would suggest that when requiring the domestic audience to support his foreign policy choices, Obama is more likely to revert to the favoured binaries of his predecessor. The reclamation of the colonial narrative, however, enables him to commit to a multinational approach by positioning America as serving the wider interests of the civilised world, and portraying ISIL as a threat to people and nations everywhere, irrespective of nationality, religion or politics. Finally, the barbarian label is crucial in dehumanising the enemy to a greater degree than was achieved by the Bush administration, and therefore making possible a foreign policy that seeks to achieve its total destruction. In a post-Iraq era where strategists are reluctant to commit boots to the ground, this enables the White House to commit to a more economical and less politically damaging campaign of aerial bombardment, in which civilian deaths can go underreported (Woods, 2014) and US military casualties can be kept to a minimum.

Whilst the previous statements were taken from remarks made on ISIL's activities within its own occupied territories, the remainder of this section considers Obama's language in reaction to the attacks in Paris on 13 November 2015. These were the most devastating attacks on European soil since the Madrid bombings of 2004 and the most severe attacks made by ISIL on 'European' territory (Henley and Chrisafis, 2015). Statements made in their immediate aftermath are examined so as to gain an understanding of how the civilised/barbarian identities were applied following a 'moment of crisis' (Croft, 2006), and how they served Obama in pursuing a multilateral response in favour of his chosen foreign policy.

As can be seen below, immediately after the Paris attacks, Obama chose to invoke different identities from what would have been expected under Bush. Instead of framing the events as an assault on America's allies in the war on terror, for example, Obama opted for the language of civilisation and human progress, in opposition to the barbarism of ISIL:

> This is an attack not just on Paris, it's an attack not just on the people of France, but this is an attack on all of humanity and the universal values that we share. . . .

Paris itself represents the timeless values of human progress.

(Obama, 2015b)

As was true with the terrible attacks that took place in Ankara, the killing of innocent people based on a twisted ideology is an attack not just on France, not just on Turkey, but it's an attack on the civilized world.

(Obama, 2015c)

ISIL is the face of evil. Our goal, as I've said many times, is to degrade and ultimately destroy this barbaric terrorist organization.

They are simply a network of killers who are brutalizing local populations.

(Obama, 2015d)

These extracts are taken from remarks made by the president in the days following 13 November. The first set of quotes comes from Obama's immediate reaction to the events on the night of the attack. The second and third are taken from remarks made by the president during the G20 summit in Turkey, two and three days later respectively. In the immediate reaction, the mass killings are framed as attacks first on a city, then on a 'people', and finally on 'humanity' and its 'universal values'. Paris is used as a metaphor for 'human progress'; the target of the attack is thereby opposed to the barbaric and historic frames used to give meaning to the perpetrators. Further on, Paris and Ankara (and America) are linked through the common self-identity of the 'civilised world'. This is an important move in legitimising US military actions against ISIL, and making possible the expansion of the 'anti-ISIL' coalition. These comments were made at a time when France and the US were conducting air strikes in Syria and were looking to solidify international support as the leaders of the most powerful nations were meeting in Turkey. By framing ISIL as a barbaric threat to 'people', 'local populations' and the 'civilised world', Obama was able to mobilise international support for multilateral intervention. The threat was located within Syria and Iraq, but was constructed as a danger to Europe and to any nation that valued civilisation and human progress. The construction of a far-reaching threat thus encourages European state elites to support action in Syria and Iraq. Finally, although the old narrative of 'evil terrorists' reappears, it is modified by the inclusion of the barbarian identity. Furthermore, the usual opposing identity of (good) Americans is left unmentioned. The text instead simply makes clear that the ultimate destruction of ISIL is now 'our' goal, with 'us' apparently meaning the G20 nations. Again, Obama is broadening the self-identity at the core of the war on terror narrative, from America(ns) to the civilised world. The strategic utility of this framing was seen soon after, as the UN Security Council unanimously adopted Resolution 2249, calling upon member states to take all necessary measures to prevent ISIL committing further attacks (UN Security Council, 2015), as France invoked the EU's Article 42.9 mutual defence clause (Traynor, 2015), and as Vladimir Putin agreed to a 'Syrian-led transition' in the country aimed at removing ISIL before holding negotiations between President Assad and the Syrian people (Murphy, 2015). Obama has strategically altered the core binaries at the heart of the discursive structures of the war on terror by broadening the self and reducing the other. In so doing, he has first made possible and necessary a foreign policy which aims to destroy ISIL from a distance rather than engage with it by other means, and second made it more difficult for potential allies to dissent from his viewpoint, thereby facilitating a doctrine of multilateralism and burden-sharing in his fight against ISIL.

Conclusion: structure, agency and Obama's legacy

The colonial narrative of opposing civilised and barbarian identities has enabled Obama to work within the existing structures of the war on terror whilst tailoring them to his strategic advantage. He has been able to use the elite agential power inherent in the presidency to alter the core identities undergirding these structures and thereby make possible and necessary his chosen foreign policy of degrading and ultimately destroying ISIL through the use of aerial bombardment in Iraq and Syria, without committing to the deployment of ground troops. The barbarian identity, with its lexicon of brutality and irrationalism, has allowed him to construct the enemy as removed from the human race and opposed to civilisation, human progress and often to human life itself. Meanwhile, the expansion of the self-identity, from 'America' to the civilised world, has enabled him to mobilise the support of an international audience, by framing any potential ISIL violence as an assault on everyone. Whilst the American/terrorist binary allowed Bush to conduct a unilateralist foreign policy and establish the war on terror as a hegemonic discourse, this was followed by a rise in anti-Americanism that often produced difficulties in garnering external support. Obama has been able to realise his doctrine of 'enlightened self-interest' or cost-effective multilateralism by using Bush's binaries where necessary for a domestic audience, but relying on the colonial narrative to sell the war on terror more generally. By expanding the self to the civilised world, Obama has created a legacy in which events such as the Paris murders will likely continue to be framed as attacks on civilisation and human progress. This framing has made it more difficult for international partners to be seen as refusing to take part in the wider struggle against terrorism, as can be seen by the rapid and unanimous passing of Security Council Resolution 2249 as well as the eventual agreement between Putin and Obama to cooperate towards a seemingly common goal in Syria. Obama therefore still remains apparently unwilling and/or unable to dismantle the discursive structures of the war on terror, but he has used his agency to strategically alter the narratives upon which these are built to his political advantage. In terms of doctrine, legacy and continuity, Obama has not been completely unable to break with the foreign policy discourses of the past, but has only sought to achieve change where it is necessary and feasible in order for him to implement his own doctrine of a post-Bush, multilateralist America. It remains to be seen whether the colonial narrative will be sufficiently embedded into the (inter)national culture to retain dominance going forward or whether, after a change of president, Bush's narrative of good Americans and evil terrorists will be reasserted as the primary theme of the war on terror. How the legacy of Obama's shift in core identities will continue to manifest itself depends largely on the extent to which this has resonated with domestic and international audiences – a question which could not be addressed in this chapter. The durability of this legacy will also likely depend on the political allegiance of Obama's successor and their vision of America's foreign policy as well as the future of ISIL. Considering Obama's tendency to revert to his predecessor's binaries when requiring domestic support, it is possible that his colonial legacy will be greater in the European and international spheres than it will domestically.

References

Aaronson, M. (2013). Interventionism in US Foreign Policy. In M. Bentley and J. Holland (eds), *Obama's Foreign Policy: Ending the War on Terror* (pp. 124–38). Abingdon: Routledge.

Barkawi, T. and Laffey, M. (2006). The Postcolonialist Moment in Security Studies. *Review of International Studies*, 32(2), 329–52.

Bentley, M. (2013). Continuity We Can Believe in: Escaping the War on Terror. In M. Bentley and J. Holland (eds), *Obama's Foreign Policy: Ending the War on Terror* (pp. 91–107). Abingdon: Routledge.

Boyle, M. J. (2011). Between Freedom and Fear: Explaining the Consensus on Terrorism and Democracy in US Foreign Policy. *International Politics*, 18(2/3), 412–33.

Brooks, D. (2007). Obama, Gospel and Verse. *New York Times*, 26 April. Retrieved 5 November 2015, from www.nytimes.com/2007/04/26/opinion/26brooks.html?_r=0.

Bush, G. H. (1990). *Address Before a Joint Session of Congress.* Retrieved 16 November 2015, from Miller Center: http://millercenter.org/president/bush/speeches/speech-3425.

Bush, G. W. (2006). *President Bush's Speech on Terrorism.* Retrieved 10 August 2015, from *New York Times*: www.nytimes.com/2006/09/06/washington/06bush_transcript.html?pagewanted=all&_r=0.

Campbell, D. (1998). *Writing Security.* Manchester: Manchester University Press.

Campbell, D. (2001). Time is Broken: The Return of The past in Response to September 11th. *Theory and Event*, 5(4), 1–11.

Croft, S. (2006). *Culture, Crisis and America's War on Terror.* Cambridge: Cambridge University Press.

Desch, M. C. (2010). The More Things Change, the More They Stay the Same: The Liberal Tradition and Obama's Counterterrorism Policy. *Political Science and Politics*, 43(3), 425–9.

Fairclough, N. (2001). *Language and Power* (2nd edn). Harlow: Pearson Education.

Gregory, D. (2004). *The Colonial Present.* Oxford: Blackwell.

Halperin, S. (2011). The Political Economy of the Anglo-American War: The Case of Iraq. *International Politics*, 48(2/3), 207–28.

Henley, J. and Chrisafis, A. (2015). *Paris Terror Attacks: Hollande says Isis Atrocity Was 'Act of War'.* Retrieved 7 December 2015, from the *Guardian*: www.theguardian.com/world/2015/nov/13/paris-attacks-shootings-explosions-hostages.

Holland, J. (2013). *Selling the War on Terror: Foreign Policy Discourses After 9/11.* Abingdon: Routledge.

Jackson, R. (2005). *Writing the War on Terror: Language, Politics and Counter-Terrorism.* Manchester: Manchester University Press.

Jackson, R. (2006). Genealogy, Ideology and Counter-Terrorism: Writing Wars on Terrorism from Ronald Reagan to George W. Bush Jr. *Studies in Language and Capitalism,* 1, 163–93.

Jackson, R. (2013). Bush, Obama, Bush, Obama, Bush, Obama … the War on Terror as Social Structure. In M. Bentley and J. Holland (eds), *Obama's Foreign Policy: Ending the War on Terror* (pp. 76–90). Abingdon: Routledge.

Krebs, R. R. and Lobasz, J. (2007). Fixing the Meaning of 9/11: Hegemony, Coercion and the Road to War in Iraq. *Security Studies,* 16(3), 409–51.

McCrisken, T. (2013). Obama's War on Terrorism in Rhetoric and Practice. In M. Bentley and J. Holland (eds), *Obama's Foreign Policy: Ending the War on Terror* (pp. 17–44). Abingdon: Routledge.

Murphy, K. (2015). *G20: Barack Obama and Vladimir Putin Agree to Syrian-led Transition.* Retrieved 23 November 2015, from the *Guardian*: www.theguardian.com/world/2015/nov/16/g20-barack-obama-and-vladimir-putin-agree-to-syrian-led-transition.

Obama, B. (2009). *Remarks by the President at the Acceptance of the Nobel Peace Prize.* Retrieved 4 December 2015, from the White House: www.whitehouse.gov/the-press-office/remarks-president-acceptance-nobel-peace-prize.

Obama, B. (2014a). *President Obama Delivers a Statement on the Murder of James Foley.* Retrieved 19 November 2015, from the White House: www.whitehouse.gov/photos-and-video/video/2014/08/20/president-obama-delivers-statement-murder-james-foley#transcript.

Obama, B. (2014b). *Statement by the President on ISIL.* Retrieved 10 August 2015, from the White House: www.whitehouse.gov/the-press-office/2014/09/10/statement-president-isil-1.

Obama, B. (2015a). *Remarks by the President at National Prayer Breakfast.* Retrieved 19 November 2015, from the White House: www.whitehouse.gov/the-press-office/2015/02/05/remarks-president-national-prayer-breakfast.

Obama, B. (2015b). *Statement by the President on the Situation in Paris.* Retrieved 16 November 2015, from the White House: www.whitehouse.gov/the-press-office/2015/11/13/statement-president-situation-paris.

Obama, B. (2015c). *Remarks by President Obama and President Tayyip Erdogan of Turkey after Bilateral Meeting.* Retrieved 19 November 2015, from the White House: www.whitehouse.gov/the-press-office/2015/11/15/remarks-president-obama-and-president-tayyip-erdogan-turkey-after.

Obama, B. (2015d). *Press Conference by President Obama – Antalya, Turkey.* Retrieved 19 November 2015, from the White House: www.whitehouse.gov/the-press-office/2015/11/16/press-conference-president-obama-antalya-turkey.

Pious, R. M. (2011). Prerogative Power in the Obama Administration: Continuity and Change in the War on Terrorism. *Presidential Studies Quarterly,* 41(2), 263–90.

Rusling, J. (1987). Remarks to Methodist Delegation, President William McKinley. In D. B. Schirmer and S. R. Shalom (eds), *The Philippines Reader: A History of Colonialism, Neo-colonialism, Dictatorship and Resistance* (pp. 22–3). Boston: South End Press.

Said, E. W. (1995). *Orientalism.* London: Penguin Group.

Sjostedt, R. (2007). The Discursive Origins of a Doctrine: Norms, Identity and Securitization under Harry S. Truman and George W. Bush. *Foreign Policy Analysis,* 3(3), 233–54.

Solomon, T. (2009). Social Logics and Normalization in the War on Terror. *Millennium: Journal of International Studies*, 38(2), 269–94.

Todorov, T. (1984). *The Conquest of America: The Question of the Other.* New York.

Traynor, I. (2015). *France Invokes EU's Article 42.7, but What Does It Mean?* Retrieved 23 November 2015, from the *Guardian*: www.theguardian.com/world/2015/nov/17/france-invokes-eu-article-427-what-does-it-mean.

UN Security Council. (2015). *Security Council Resolution 2249*. Retrieved 23 November 2015, from www.un.org/press/en/2015/sc12132.doc.htm.

Woods, C. (2014). Covert Drone Strikes and the Fiction of Zero Civilian Casualties. In M. Aaronson, W. Aslam, T. Dyson and R. Rauxloh (eds), *Precision Strike Warfare and International Intervention: Strategic, Ethico-Legal and Decisional Implications* (pp. 95–113). Abingdon: Routledge.

7 Identity, affective attachments, and US–Iranian nuclear politics

Ty Solomon

There has been a notable contrast in approach, tone, and behavior between the first and second Obama administrations with regard to Iran. Obama's first term was characterized by maintaining tough economic sanctions on Iran backed up by fairly hawkish rhetoric regarding both the supposed nature of the Iranian regime and its intentions. Upon signing into US law in 2010 the Comprehensive Iran Sanctions, Accountability, and Divestment Act, Obama stated that Iran has "violated its commitments, defied United Nations Security Council resolutions, and forged ahead with its nuclear program – all while supporting terrorist groups and suppressing the aspirations of the Iranian people" (Obama 2010). Other members of the first-term administration went further. Secretary of State Hillary Clinton – who, as a presidential candidate, claimed that the US could "totally obliterate" Iran (Morgan 2008) – suggested Iran must rethink its "dangerous" nuclear policy and that it is "moving toward a military dictatorship" (Sturcke 2010). Secretary of Defense Leon Panetta (2011) labeled Iran an "international pariah" and said that "no greater threat exists to the security and prosperity of the Middle East than a nuclear-armed Iran." However, by Obama's second term starting in early 2013, this kind of rhetoric – although still maintaining key underlining elements – began to give way to less confrontational language that more emphasized the possibility of cooperation between the two states. Iran has featured little in Obama's State of the Union addresses, and when it is mentioned little is noted other than reassurances that America will not allow Iran to develop a nuclear weapon (Obama 2012). More important is that a "peaceful resolution of this issue is still possible, and far better, and if Iran changes course and meets its obligations, it can rejoin the community of nations" (Obama 2012). In the 2015 State of the Union address, Obama (2015) emphasized that "diplomacy is at work with respect to Iran" and should therefore be allowed to continue, yet assured his audience that the "American people expect us only to go to war as a last resort, and I intend to stay true to that wisdom."

There are numerous mutually reinforcing reasons for this shift in language. One likely reflects the election of moderate Hassan Rouhani as Iranian president in 2013, which was followed by a number of friendly overtures and unprecedented meetings (since the 1979 revolution) between Iranian and US officials. Of course, this also coincides with substantially increased efforts toward sensitive negotiations with Iran over its alleged nuclear program. The "Joint Comprehensive Plan of Action," signed between Iran and the P5+1 powers (five permanent members of the UN Security Council plus Germany), was finalized in July 2015. It involves concessions from both Western powers and Iran, and is centered on three main issues: nuclear infrastructure, transparency, and sanctions. First, Iran agrees never to produce or otherwise acquire nuclear weapons, and gives assurances that its nuclear capacities (such as uranium enrichment) are solely focused on civilian energy production. Second, in return, Western powers agree to lift existing economic and financial sanctions on Iran. In addition to the US agreement to cease bilateral sanctions, the United Nations Security Council agrees to terminate all previous resolutions relating to the Iranian nuclear issue. Third, these parallel processes of peaceful nuclear capacity development and international regulatory inspections will be made transparent by international regulatory bodies. Specifically, the International Atomic Energy Agency will subject Iran to an extensive inspection regime, including maintaining a long-term presence in Iran, close monitoring of uranium development and centrifuge technology, among other issues (White House, Office of the Press Secretary, 2015).[1]

The significance of these changes – in both policy and rhetoric – mark a potentially momentous shift in US–Iran relations. Their importance should not be understated. In particular, given the Obama administration's notably harsher rhetoric toward Iran during its first term, such a comprehensive agreement with Iran on such a primary issue was far from a foregone conclusion. Yet, despite the significance of these negotiations, the discourse of the Obama administration still bears marks of the identity dynamics that have driven US policy toward Iran for the last three decades. This, in some sense, is to be expected. Decades of mistrust and tension cannot be swept away through a set of negotiations on one issue. However, even within the Obama administration's shifting discourse on Iran, an unspoken set of assumptions is subtly evident. Despite the new tone of cautious and tentative cooperation, official US discourse is marked by similar assumptions and affective undercurrents to the first Obama administration's more hawkish stance toward Iran – even if the rhetoric itself is less overtly antagonistic. This chapter helps to explain how the conditions for the agreement came about despite the harsher rhetoric of the Obama first term.

To illustrate, consider that for years US intelligence agencies have found that although Iran is developing its nuclear energy capabilities, there is no evidence that it has engaged in direct development of nuclear weapons. The 2007 US National Intelligence Estimate found that Iran ended its pursuit of nuclear weapons in 2003 and that although its uranium enrichment capabilities continued (which Iran maintains is for civilian purposes of energy generation), a military-operated weapons program likely ended (Mazzetti 2007). In 2010 and 2012, subsequent National Intelligence Estimates maintained that although Iran had hastened its uranium enrichment, "there is no hard evidence that Iran has decided to build a nuclear bomb" (Risen and Mazzetti 2012). Despite the lack of evidence of a weapons program, US foreign policy elites – including the Obama administration – nevertheless evidently *believe* that Iran desires nuclear weapons. This disconnect between evidence and belief could potentially be explained via recourse to psychological theories of misperception (Jervis 1976). Yet the individual level-of-analysis focus of most political psychology frameworks (McDermott 2004) often neglects the multiple intersubjective factors at play. Mistrust no doubt has a role here, too, as both sides readily admit. However, what is often missing – somewhat surprisingly – from scholarship are the affective and emotional politics involved in US–Iranian relations. This display of belief in spite of evidence points toward what Mercer (2010) terms "emotional beliefs." That is, "feeling is believing because people use emotion as evidence" (Mercer 2010: 1). Building upon these insights, this chapter draws on Slavoj Žižek's social psychoanalytical framework to contend that the intersections of identities and affect are central to unraveling this empirical puzzle posed by the nuclear politics between Iran and the US. Dynamics of affect and emotion are, this chapter argues, key to a more comprehensive understanding of the politics between the US and Iran regarding the latter's nuclear program. Specifically, Žižek's approach helps to account for the peculiar dynamics of beliefs and evidence in contemporary US–Iranian nuclear politics, and points to the overlapping roles of rhetoric and affect in the social construction of identity.

The chapter proceeds as follows. First, it briefly reviews existing arguments regarding US–Iranian relations, and finds that most work has neglected affective factors. Both realist and constructivist analyses rightly focus on the geostrategic concerns and socially constructed perceptions involved. However, these studies tend to neglect the affective dimensions involved in the social construction of identity. The chapter suggests instead that the affective underpinnings involved in the intersubjective process of identity construction are key to understanding the disjuncture between evidence and belief here, and thus offer a more comprehensive understanding of the case. Second, the chapter turns to Žižek's (1993, 1997) social-psychoanalytical framework, which is concerned, among other issues, with how affect is involved in the social construction of identity. For him, identity is constructed with reference to an other, in line with most IR constructivist frameworks (Wendt 1999). However, where he departs from IR views is in the contention that affective aspects of desire and enjoyment are deeply involved in the particular type of "otherness" for a particular identity. Third, applying these concepts to elite US discourses on Iran takes a step beyond (yet complements) existing analyses and argues that desire and enjoyment not only help to account for discrepancies between empirical evidence and perceptions, but also begin to capture some of the key affective underpinnings of American constructions of Iran as the "other" of US identity.

Extant arguments: self-interests and identities in US–Iran relations

Most IR analyses of the Iranian nuclear issue focus on the conflicting geopolitical interests of the US and Iran. As structural realism argues that states are most concerned about their security and the balance of power (Waltz 1979), many analyses take American and Iranian interests as pre-given and materially based. As Mearsheimer (1995: 91) contends, "the distribution of material capabilities among states is the key factor for understanding world politics." Through this lens, Iranian and US interests will naturally be at odds – Iran will strive toward regional hegemony to ensure its security, and the US will aim to keep access to a strategic area as a major resource base. Along these lines, Kroenig (2009) suggests that states' nuclear proliferation decisions are based largely on their geostrategic position. Several scholars find that states' policies toward Iran stem from similar material interests, such as the strategic value of oil (Talmadge 2008; Wagner and Onderco 2014), potential payoffs in rational bargaining outcomes (Sebenius and Singh 2012), or strategic reactions to Iran's latent nuclear capability and "hedging" (Bowen and Moran 2015). For Sanati (2014: 126), most of the US' and Iran's behavior toward each other "stems from the interplay and ultimate collision of their core national interests, posited in the shifting power changes in contemporary history." Stephen Walt (2013) succinctly offers a realist perspective, and argues that

> [T]he real issue isn't whether Iran gets close to a bomb; the real issue is the long-term balance of power in the Persian Gulf and Middle East…. If Iran ever escapes the shackles of international sanctions and puts some competent people in charge of its economy, it's going to loom much larger in regional affairs over time.

From a constructivist perspective, other scholars have emphasized the role of socially constructed identities and perceptions in producing US–Iranian tension. Taking a step beyond realism, constructivism argues that interests are not materially based, but rather coalesce through processes of social interaction via language, norms, and practices (Wendt 1999). Interests are not themselves "objective" or pre-given, but are filtered through self-images and identity. Through this lens, antagonistic US–Iranian relations are less material facts than they are products of a particular shared history, normative ideas, and identities that have developed in contingent ways. For example, Tirman (2009: 536) emphasizes the role that narratives play, in that "perpetual distrust [is] deeply rooted in the two national narratives and [is] reinforced by the actual actions" of both Iran and the US. Similarly, Fayyaz and Shirazi (2013) demonstrate that representations of Iran in American media overwhelmingly portray an "enemy" image that defines the production of knowledge and meanings given to Iran within US culture. Adib-Moghaddam (2007, 2009) further shows how US–Iranian relations are not merely the conflicts of material national interests, but rather have deeper roots in discursive contexts and symbolic politics that produce antagonistic identities. For him (2009: 512), a key task is to explore "representations of Iran and the United States, and how the fundamental friend–enemy distinction setting the two countries apart has come about." More specifically, in American politics Iran holds a particularly central position within neoconservative discourses. Iran occupies a "prominent place in the imagination of influential neoconservative strategists with direct links to the decision-making process in Washington and immense resources to influence public discourse in the USA" (Adib-Moghaddam 2007: 636). A key theme of these studies, then, is that US–Iranian relations are not so much the product of naturally opposed material interests but instead are socially produced through narratives that shape shared understandings of the relationship in particular ways.

Both accounts are useful in illuminating competing geostrategic interests and in uncovering the socially constructed identities constituting the antagonistic politics. Yet each account suffers from a few weaknesses. What accounts for the prominence of the US obsession with Iran despite the fact that it poses little material threat to the US? As constructivists have long noted, realist conceptualizations of interests and threats as materially based and pre-given do not grant adequate explanatory weight to the power of narratives to shape shared understandings, and to explain how interests and perceptions of threat can change over time (Thrall and Cramer 2009). While constructivism, in this sense, remedies some of realism's shortcomings, it also has trouble explaining several issues. For example, constructivism's contention that identities (and therefore interests) are socially constructed helps to explain the variability of threat perceptions. Yet constructivism has trouble explaining how some narratives prevail while others do not. Why do some narratives "win" over others? While constructivist research has recently begun to engage with emotions (Ross 2014), this chapter argues that there is a distinctive affective aspect to how narratives of identity are efficacious. In other words, *given* that identities and narratives are historically contingent constructs, what accounts for the visceral emotional "grip" of narratives beyond their mere social-constructedness (Glynos 2001: 195)? Both realism and constructivism neglect the role of affect and emotion in the intersubjective processes of identity construction. It is precisely in this process that Žižek's framework of desire and enjoyment can help.

Desire and enjoyment in national identity

Žižek's analysis of identity has similar starting points to many in IR who have emphasized the role of language in the social construction process. Žižek's Lacanian-inspired framework shares many of the assumptions about ontology and epistemology underlying discourse approaches in IR, and starts from the notion that agents do not have access to reality outside of narratives, which can be understood as "framings of meaning and lenses of interpretation, rather than objective, historical truths" (Hansen 2006: 7). Subjects and their identities are produced in and through language, and since language has no firm foundation in biology or "objective" material facts, identities themselves have no firm rooting in such material factors (Campbell 1998: 12).

However, to argue that identities have no firm foundation outside of language is not to suggest that they are endlessly fluid or infinitely variable. Many instances of discourse exhibit considerable power of stability and efficacy. For

Žižek, this relative stability can be understood through two linked concepts – desire and enjoyment – that aim to account for the visceral "grip" (Glynos 2001) of narratives of identity, beyond the fact of their social constructed-ness.

For Žižek (1997), a key question that constructivist approaches overlook is: if identities are never fully rooted or pinned down (even if they exhibit some temporary stability), why do subjects keep trying to fulfill the image of a pure, "whole" identity in the face of constant frustrations? This is where the concept of desire enters. As agents' identities are socially constructed through narratives – and yet as narratives never really produce the imagined "essences" that agents nevertheless believe in – subjects' desire for such stability is elicited. Desire here is understood not in a conventional or sexual sense, but rather in the sense of desire for ontological stability, an imagined stable, fixed, or whole identity. Moreover, as language and narrative are fluid systems, never able to fully deliver the pure identity they seem to promise, desire always exists as long as a subject remains a subject within discourse. This situation leaves the subject in a bind: she desires to attach herself to and invest in a narrative that she feels is her own, that fully represents her, yet no narrative ever fully delivers on this promise. The subject is thus left as desiring, desire remains unsatisfied, and the subject is driven to continue its identification practices (Solomon 2015: 29).

Although a key factor in social construction processes, desire functions alongside enjoyment in the production of subjectivity. Since language cannot fully bring the stability that the subject seeks, Žižek contends that the subject's incompleteness also plays a key role in the feelings of "wholeness" that it aspires to. While desire is oriented toward the promise of enjoyment, enjoyment itself is never quite reached. "Enjoyment" thus refers to this always aspired to, and desired for, state of anticipated "wholeness" that is ultimately unattainable. This is because language itself (a lacking and unfixed system) produces lacking subjects (Žižek 1997). There is a continual frustration in relation to wholeness precisely because it is never attained and is impossible to reach. The subject's incompleteness therefore produces the condition of both possibility and impossibility of enjoyment. Language creates the possibility of the subject to pursue enjoyment (through identification with narratives), but the enjoyment that the subject seeks is a retroactively created fiction produced only by the subject's use of language to articulate its desires. Yet precisely because enjoyment "itself" cannot be captured in language (since it is illusory), subjects can never quite articulate or pin down what *exactly* attracts them to a discourse, yet it is this visceral attraction that binds them as subjects to the discourse. Žižek offers the example of the enjoyment underlying religious devotion. When a believer describes his spiritual experience to a skeptic and cries:

> "You don't really understand it at all! There's more to it, something words cannot express!" he is the victim of a kind of perspective illusion: the precious *agalma* perceived by him as the unique ineffable kernel which cannot be shared by others (non-believers) is precisely *jouissance* [enjoyment].
>
> (Žižek 1997: 50)

A more explicitly political example – and one that bears directly on US constructions of Iran – is Žižek's analysis of nationalism. He argues that national identity cannot be understood through constructivist approaches alone. That is, the fact that nations are socially constructed does not adequately capture the visceral, affective pull of nationalist identity discourses. Rather, the pull of the enjoyment seemingly promised through such discourses is what elicits such strong identification. One could list the markers of national identity that seemingly define what it is (for instance in the US, the flag, Fourth of July, founding fathers, etc.), yet there is always something *else*, beyond such features, that *really* pulls us to identify with a group. This unnameable, inexpressible *thing* is enjoyment. As Žižek (1993: 201) notes, if:

> [W]e are asked how we can recognize the presence of this Thing, the only consistent answer is that the Thing is present in that elusive entity called "our way of life." All we can do is enumerate disconnected fragments of the way our community organizes its feasts, its rituals of mating, its initiation ceremonies, in short, all the details by which is made visible the unique way a community *organizes its enjoyment.*

The national "thing" – enjoyment that exceeds attempts to capture it in discourse – is also paradoxical, and it is this paradoxical aspect that draws it into nationalist discourses of threats from the "other." Žižek (1993: 201) notes that our imagined national enjoyment – *our thing* – appears to us

> as something accessible only to us, as something "they," the others, cannot grasp; nonetheless it is something constantly menaced by "them." It appears as what gives plenitude and vivacity to our life, and yet the only way we can determine it is by resorting to different versions of the same empty tautology.

Think of recent discourses producing migrants as people who are usually weak and desperate yet who are "marauding" "our" countries and who threaten our "standard of living" (Perraudin 2015). "The national Thing exists as long as members of the community believe in it; it is literally an effect of this belief in itself" (Žižek 1993: 202). What is at stake in nationalist discourses and conflict, then, is the "possession" of the national "thing" (Žižek 1993: 202). "We always impute to the other an excessive enjoyment: he wants to steal our enjoyment (by ruining our way of life) and/or he has access to some secret, perverse enjoyment" (Žižek 1993: 202). Yet key here is the notion that enjoyment is something that is never attainable (nationalist discourses promising to do so notwithstanding). "What we conceal by imputing to the Other the theft of enjoyment is the traumatic fact that *we never possessed what was allegedly stolen from us*" (Žižek 1993: 203), since what is perceived to have been stolen (our essence, "way of life," and so on) is nothing other than the retrospective presumption that we once "had" it. Such presumed origins or "essences" are illusory, but the promise of their delivery through nationalist discourses is what helps elicit audiences' affective identifications with such discourses.

As Kingsbury (2008) discusses, the notion of enjoyment offers some novel insights into the politics of affect. For example, enjoyment suggests an answer to the question of:

> How do the painful yet thrilling emotional lures of enjoyment that irrupt in the social antagonisms of, for example, racial, nationalist, and ethnic enmities trump the lures of pleasures that can only be acquired in times of peace and material prosperity?
>
> (Kingsbury 2008: 51)

In other words, why do people sometimes seem to strongly desire conflict (ethnic, nationalist, or otherwise) when it will immediately result in their harm? The role of enjoyment in nationalism suggests one answer – that audiences become so viscerally attached to their modes of enjoyment that violence (at least partially) brought about through this politics of othering becomes a struggle over the very indefinable *thing* that forms the core of the affective investment in the nation. The politics of enjoyment thus suggests "a difficult truth: when people and groups are locked in conflict, they are – beyond their immediate interest in securing sovereignty over another land or people – *already* experiencing intangible gains" (Lane 1998: 5 quoted in Kingsbury 2008: 51).

As the following section suggests, incorporating desire and enjoyment – more specifically, the "theft" of enjoyment – into identity arguments can shed some light on some of the heretofore unexamined affective identity politics surrounding the US–Iranian nuclear issue.

"Stealing our enjoyment": the affective co-constitution of US and Iranian identity

As of this writing, US–Iranian relations seem to be undergoing some substantial changes as represented by direct dialogue between the two (through the P5+1 group) regarding Iran's alleged nuclear program. The scope of these shifts should not be understated. Yet even alongside the changes brought about during the second Obama administration, there are some notable underlying discursive similarities between the first and second Obama administrations regarding Iran. Some of these underlying similarities stretch back to characterizations during the George W. Bush administration, where Iran was included in the "axis of evil" and the administration not only criticized Tehran's alleged pursuit of a nuclear weapon, but also frequently emphasized Iranian influence throughout the region as a threat in itself. A notable 2007 speech by Vice-President Dick Cheney reveals some of these concerns: "Operating largely in the shadows, Iran attempts to hide its hands" in using violence to spread its influence; Iran's

> efforts to destabilize the Middle East and to gain hegemonic power is a matter of record.... Given the nature of Iran's rulers, the declarations of the Iranian president, and the trouble the regime is causing throughout the

region ... our country and the entire international community cannot stand by as a terror-supporting state fulfills its most aggressive ambitions.

(Cheney 2007)

Concerns over Iranian influence would go on to form a key element of the Obama administration's discourse.

Obama's first-term discourse on Iran was marked by both diplomatic overtures and castigation of threats. While Obama's steps toward a "new beginning" with Iran (Black 2009) garnered much attention, this was often matched by more hawkish discourse by him and administration officials. For example, in an early first-term speech Obama (2009) stated that:

> Iran's nuclear and ballistic missile activity poses a real threat, not just to the United States, but to Iran's neighbors and our allies.... As long as the threat from Iran persists, we will go forward with a missile defense system that is cost-effective and proven.

Former first-term Secretary of State Hillary Clinton recently suggested in even stronger terms the threat of Iranian influence:

> A lot of this is weakness [from the Arab Spring uprisings] that Iran takes advantage of, and you know, in this world, you can be mad at somebody taking advantage of you. But at the end of the day, that's your fault. That you haven't figured out how to defend yourself, and how to protect yourself, and how to fend off external interests, and how to treat your own people in a way that they will not look outside your borders. That's part of what's been going on, as you know, and the Iranians have been incredibly focused on exploiting any opening.

(Maloney 2014)

The discourse of Obama's second-term administration displays a notable change in tone from some of the more hawkish first-term rhetoric. This is likely due to at least two factors: the 2013 election of moderate Hassan Rouhani as Iranian president, and the intensive nuclear negotiations throughout 2013–2015. While much of the second-term discourse has been more restrained, many of the same themes are on display regarding the concern about broader Iranian influence in the Middle East. Second-term Secretary of Defense Chuck Hagel noted that "while Iran's nuclear program is a critical worry, its other missile threats, terrorism links and occasional provocative maritime behavior also greatly concern the US and the region. And those threats are not addressed by the nuclear agreement" (Associated Press 2013). Elsewhere he assured Congress that he'll "focus intently on countering Iran's malign influence" (Capaccio 2013). More recently, Secretary of State John Kerry, who has played a pivotal role in the nuclear negotiations, tried to reassure Gulf allies that the US was prepared to "push back" against Iranian influence in the region (Reuters 2015). Similarly, Secretary of

Defense Ashton Carter promised that the US would combat Iran's "malign influence" despite the nuclear deal (Cooper 2015). In a strategic sense, much of this discourse regarding Iranian "influence" is aimed at allaying US regional allies concerned that a nuclear deal may lessen the US's stance toward what many Gulf states view as a common foe.

However, in a broader sense, the Obama administration's concern about not only potential Iranian weapons but "malign influence" directly echoes themes that stretch back at least thirty years in US foreign policy history. As Andrew Bacevich (2005) has discussed, US policy toward the Middle East has been largely aimed at retaining dominant influence in the region. Although from the end of World War II to 1979, the US sought to ensure political stability and access to oil in ways that minimized overt American involvement, the Iranian revolution and the Soviet invasion of Afghanistan prompted the US to become much more deeply involved. Dealing with these crises, President Jimmy Carter believed that the Middle East needed to take center stage in US foreign policy. "A great contest for control of that region had been joined, one that Iran's Ayatollah Khomeini had made unmistakably clear was not simply an offshoot of the already existing East–West competition" (Bacevich 2005: 181). The following year he articulated what became known as the Carter Doctrine, which stated that the US would play a central role in the region's politics. "Any attempt," Carter boldly declared, "by any outside force to gain control of the Persian Gulf region will be regarded as an assault on the vital interests of the United States of America, and such an assault will be repelled by any means necessary, including military force" (quoted in Bacevich 2005: 181). Bacevich argues that this basic tenet has guided US foreign policy toward the Middle East ever since. "As a consequence, each of President Carter's successors has expanded the level of US military involvement and operations in the region" (Bacevich 2005: 181). American identity, in this sense, has long been constructed with reference to the Iranian "other."

Of note here are the near mirror images of American and Iranian ambitions in the region. Despite the shifted tone and more cautiously optimistic discourse on Iran, much of the Obama administration's second-term discourse nevertheless continues many of the same core themes of US foreign policy developed over the past thirty years. In one sense this is expected – although Obama has drawn down American forces in Iraq and Afghanistan during his tenure, a wholesale shift in American foreign policy toward either Iran or the Middle East was not expected. However, what often gets neglected in both realist and constructivist analyses of US–Iranian relations is what this mirroring reveals. While Iran is the enemy, it curiously seems to embody all the traits that America *should* be with regard to Middle East politics. The image of an ambitious Islamic competitor suggests that while this reinforces American desires to be the promoter of stability in the region, there nevertheless seems to be something to *admire* in Iranian assertiveness. Iranian influence throughout the region, prominent and now growing, has long been a common trope in American foreign policy discourse, and Obama's second-term rhetoric – despite a shift in tone regarding nuclear negotiations – remains largely unchanged in this respect. Moreover, something about "their" ambition in spreading their influence reinforces *our* notions of who we *should* be during this competition. Each mention of Iranian ambition and influence by American officials is usually matched by the suggestion that the US has fallen behind and that it must step up similar efforts. These discourses subtly illustrate some of the notions of enjoyment discussed above.

In nationalistic tensions it is often not merely a fear of the other for fear's sake but a fear that the other might steal our national "thing" – our enjoyment. Žižek (1993: 203) observes,

> We always impute to the "other" an excessive enjoyment: he wants to steal our enjoyment (by ruining our way of life) and/or he has access to some secret, perverse enjoyment.... The basic paradox is that our Thing is conceived as something inaccessible to the other and at the same time threatened by him.

In American discourses on Iran, the mutual construction of self and other occurs not only on a discursive level, but also through a perceived "theft of enjoyment." The representations of Iranian influence, and concerns over the Iranian nuclear program, in American discourse are in a sense a mirror of what American behavior *should* be. The US should not only keep Iran from developing nuclear weapons, but should also work to counter Iranian influence across the region. Deeply rooted in American objectives since at least the Carter presidency, American discourse on Iran displays a concern that Iran is enjoying precisely what America *should be* enjoying – growing influence, ambition, and assertiveness in a vital region. American identity has long been constructed in relation to the Iranian other (Adib-Moghaddam 2009). Yet a key factor in the social construction of identity is the affective dynamics of desire and enjoyment. While realist and constructivist lenses point to the strategic and socially produced aspects of US identity vis-à-vis Iran, they say little about the role of affect and desire. Although Iran poses little material threat to the US, and despite the fact that American identity is socially constructed by "othering" Iran, the politics of enjoyment offer a new insight into the relationship. That is, not merely is American identity constructed against the Iranian "other," but the politics of enjoyment shed light on how these particular narratives have gained affective currency with American audiences. Iran is seen to be enjoying growing dominance in Middle East politics – precisely the element that American identity is seen as lacking in relation to Iran. Iran is "stealing" American enjoyment of political hegemony of Middle East politics, and it is this affective pull that helps to (in part) account for the American obsession with Iran despite a lack of material threat.

In this sense, the affective links between discourse, desire, and enjoyment help to account for the discursive conditions under which the Obama administration heavily pushed for a robust nuclear agreement with Iran. Despite little to no evidence that Iran is actually developing nuclear weapons (according to successive US National Intelligence estimates), the Obama administration (and many prominent elite voices in the US across the political spectrum) nevertheless evidently believes that Iran wishes to develop them. Although political psychological approaches (McDermott 2004) would well analyze the individual traits and variables that might account for elite diplomatic behaviors during the agreement negotiations, such approaches would be less able to capture the broader, intersubjective collective understandings and affective movements that produce the *conditions of possibility* for the negotiations and agreements in the first place. Following a range of discourse-based research (Doty 1996; Hansen 2006), this chapter contends that examining the discursive production of conditions of possibility is a key move in foreign policy analysis. Following Doty (1996), this chapter asks how it became possible – or commonsensical – that an Iranian nuclear agreement was necessary and desirable from the perspective of American national interests. The affective investments of desire and enjoyment in particular representations of Iranian identity have helped to bring about a particular "common sense" in the US about Iran regarding its alleged nuclear ambitions. However, the prevailing American "common sense" regarding Iran is neither neutral nor pre-given. Rather, it is the result of ongoing series of representations that elicit American identifications that are underpinned by affective investments of desire and enjoyment. Consequently, the discursive conditions of possibility for the nuclear agreement between the US and Iran are in an important part shaped by the desires for enjoyment represented in American images of Iranian identity, and resultant American desires to pursue fantasies of control in the Middle East.

Conclusion

Although there are notable contrasts in the way the Obama administration's discourse on Iran has shifted from his first to second terms, much of the official language carries with it many of the same themes that have characterized US rhetoric on Iran for thirty years. Obama's second-term discourse has often been much more muted in tone due to the sensitive nature of the nuclear negotiations. However, alongside these more diplomatic openings are continued concerns of Iran's perceived increasing influence in the region. Harking back to US foreign policy themes that stretch back to at least the Carter administration's definition of US interests as political and military hegemony in the Middle East, the Obama administration's concern over both Iranian nuclear weapons and influence marks a continuation of American perceptions and policy. This chapter argues that in order more fully to understand the identity politics behind American obsessions with Iran – despite little material threat – analyses should consider how the politics of affect is entangled with identity. Drawing upon Žižek's concepts of desire and enjoyment – notions that capture aspects of the affective construction of identity – the chapter suggests that the Obama administration's second-term rhetoric displays some of the same affective underpinnings as prior US discourses. While it does not claim that enjoyment (or more accurately, the perceived "theft" of enjoyment) is not the only affect or emotion involved here, it does aver that the US–Iranian relationship is ripe for further work on the mutually entangled roles of affect, identity, and security.

Note

1 See full text of the agreement at www.state.gov/e/eb/tfs/spi/iran/jcpoa/.

References

Adib-Moghaddam, A. (2007) "Manufacturing War: Iran in the Neoconservative Imagination" *Third World Quarterly* 28(3): 635–653.

Adib-Moghaddam, A. (2009) "Discourse and Violence: The Friend–Enemy Conjunction in Contemporary Iranian–American Relations" *Critical Studies on Terrorism* 2(3): 512–526.

Associated Press (2013) "Chuck Hagel Reassures Gulf Nations Iran Deal Will Not Stop Flow of US Arms" *Guardian*, December 7, www.theguardian.com/world/2013/dec/07/chuck-hagel-gulf-iran-deal-weapons.

Bacevich, A. (2005) *The New American Militarism*. Oxford and New York: Oxford University Press.

Black, I. (2009) "Barack Obama Offers Iran 'New Beginning' with Video Message" *Guardian*, March 20, www.theguardian.com/world/2009/mar/20/barack-obama-video-iran.

Bowen, W. and Moran, M. (2015) "Living with Nuclear Hedging: The Implications of Iran's Nuclear Strategy" *International Affairs* 91(4): 687–707.

Campbell, O. (1998) *Writing Security: United States Foreign Policy and the Politics of Identity*. Minneapolis: University of Minnesota Press.

Capaccio, A. (2013) "Hagel Vows Pentagon to Help Combat Iran's 'Malign' Role" *Bloomberg Business* March 4, www.bloomberg.com/news/articles/2013–03–04/hagel-vows-pentagon-to-help-combat-iran-s-malign-role.

Cheney, R. (2007) Address to the Washington Institute's Weinberg Founders Conference. October 21. www.washingtoninstitute.org/policy-analysis/view/vice-president-cheney-address-to-the-washington-institutes-weinberg-founder.

Cooper, H. (2015) "US Defense Secretary Visits Israel to Soothe Ally after Iran Nuclear Deal" *New York Times*, July 20, www.nytimes.com/2015/07/21/world/middleeast/in-visit-to-israel-defense-secretary-vows-vigilance-in-fighting-irans-influence.html.

Doty, R. (1996) *Imperial Encounters: the Politics of Representation in North–South Relations*. Minneapolis: University of Minnesota Press.

Fayyaz, S. and Shirazi, R. (2013) "Good Iranian, Bad Iranian: Representations of Iran and Iranians in *Time* and *Newsweek* (1998–2009)" *Iranian Studies* 46(1), 53–72.

Glynos, J. (2001) "The Grip of Ideology: A Lacanian Approach to the Theory of Ideology" *Journal of Political Ideologies* 6(2): 191–214.

Hansen, L. (2006) *Security as Practice: Discourse Analysis and the Bosnian War*. New York and London: Routledge.

Jervis, R. (1976) *Perception and Misperception in International Politics*. Princeton, NJ: Princeton University Press.

Kingsbury, P. (2008) "Did Somebody Say Jouissance? On Slavoj Žižek, Consumption, and Nationalism" *Emotion, Space, and Society* 1: 48–55.

Kroenig, M. (2009) "Exporting the Bomb: Why States Provide Sensitive Nuclear Assistance" *American Political Science Review* 103(1): 113–133.

Lane, C. (1998) "The Psychoanalysis of Race: an Introduction." In: Lane, C. (ed.), *The Psychoanalysis of Race*. New York: Columbia University Press, pp. 1–37.

McDermott, R. (2004) *Political Psychology in International Relations*. Ann Arbor: University of Michigan Press.

Maloney, S. (2014) "Addressing America's Challenge in the Middle East, Hillary Clinton Backs Diplomacy with Iran" Brookings Institution, December 7, www.brookings.edu/blogs/markaz/posts/2014/12/06-hillary-clinton-saban-israel-iran-nuclear.

Mazzetti, M. (2007) "US Says Iran Ended Atomic Arms Work" *New York Times*, December 3.

Mearsheimer, J. J. (1995) "A Realist Reply" *International Security* 20: 82–93.

Mercer, J. (2010) "Emotional Beliefs" *International Organization* 64(1): 1–31.

Morgan, D. (2008) "Clinton Says US Could 'Totally Obliterate' Iran" *Reuters*, April 22.

Obama, B. (2009) Remarks by President Barack Obama in Prague as Delivered, April 5, www.whitehouse.gov/the-press-office/remarks-president-barack-obama-prague-delivered.

Obama, B. (2010) Remarks by the President at Signing of the Iran Sanctions Act, www.whitehouse.gov/the-press-office/remarks-president-signing-iran-sanctions-act.

Obama, B. (2012) Remarks by the President in State of the Union Address, www.whitehouse.gov/the-press-office/2012/01/24/remarks-president-state-union-address.

Obama, B. (2015) Remarks by the President in State of the Union Address, www.whitehouse.gov/the-press-office/2015/01/20/remarks-president-state-union-address-january-20–2015.

Panetta, L. (2011) Remarks by Secretary of Defense Leon E. Panetta at the Saban Center, December 2, www.defense.gov/transcripts/transcript.aspx?transcriptid=4937.

Perraudin, F. (2015) "'Marauding' Migrants Threaten Standard of Living, Says Foreign Secretary" *Guardian*, August 10, www.theguardian.com/uk-news/2015/aug/09/african-migrants-threaten-eu-standard-living-philip-hammond.

Reuters (2015) "Kerry to Visit Gulf Arab States, Vows to 'Push Back' Against Iran" July 22, www.reuters.com/article/2015/07/22/us-iran-nuclear-kerry-idUSKCN0PW0CZ20150722.

Risen, J. and Mazzetti, M. (2012) "US Agencies See No Move by Iran to Build Bomb" *New York Times*, February 24.

Ross, A. (2014) *Mixed Emotions: Beyond Fear and Hatred in International Conflict.* Chicago and London: University of Chicago Press.

Sanati, R. (2014) "Beyond the Domestic Picture: The Geopolitical Factors that have Formed Contemporary Iran–US Relations" *Global Change, Peace & Security* 26(2): 125–140.

Sebenius, J. and Singh, M. (2012) "Is a Nuclear Deal with Iran Possible? An Analytical Framework for the Iran Nuclear Negotiations" *International Security* 37(3), 52–91.

Solomon, T. (2015) *The Politics of Subjectivity in American Foreign Policy Discourses.* Ann Arbor: University of Michigan Press.

Sturcke, J. (2010) "Hillary Clinton: 'Iran Is Moving towards a Military Dictatorship'" *Guardian*, February 15, www.theguardian.com/world/2010/feb/15/hilary-clinton-iran-military-dictatorship.

Talmadge, C. (2008) "Closing Time: Assessing the Iranian Nuclear Threat to the Straight of Hormuz" *International Security* 33(1): 82–117.

Thrall, T. and Cramer, J. (2009) *American Foreign Policy and the Politics of Fear: Threat Inflation after 9/11.* London and New York: Routledge.

Tirman, J. (2009) "Diplomacy, Terrorism, and National Narratives in the United States–Iran Relationship" *Critical Studies on Terrorism* 2(3): 527–539.

Wagner, W. and Onderco, M. (2014) "Accommodation or Confrontation? Explaining Differences in Policies Toward Iran" *International Studies Quarterly* 58: 717–728.

Walt, S. M. "What's Really at Stake in the Iranian Nuclear Deal" *Foreign Policy Blog*, November 25, http://foreignpolicy.com/2013/11/25/whats-really-at-stake-in-the-iranian-nuclear-deal.

Waltz, K. N. (1979) *Theory of International Politics*. Boston: Addison-Wesley.

Wendt, A. (1999) *Social Theory of International Politics*. Cambridge: Cambridge University Press.

White House, Office of the Press Secretary (2015) "Key Excerpts of the Joint Comprehensive Plan of Action (JCPOA)," www.whitehouse.gov/the-press-office/2015/07/14/key-excerpts-joint-comprehensive-plan-action-jcpoa.

Žižek, S. (1993) *Tarrying with the Negative*. Durham, NC: Duke University Press.

Žižek, S. (1997) *The Plague of Fantasies*. London: Verso.

Part III
Obama's major challenges

8 Plus ça change?

Reflecting on Obama's nuclear agenda and legacy

Jason Douglas and Andrew Futter

Introduction: time for a change?

The election of Barack Obama in late 2008 was seen by many as a vote for change in US foreign policy, and perhaps nowhere was this feeling more strongly held than in the realm of nuclear weapons. Indeed, even before the much vaunted April 2009 Prague speech (Obama, 2009), then President-elect Obama had been vocal about his commitment to nuclear reductions and to the ultimate goal of nuclear disarmament. In an interview with *Arms Control Today* published in December 2008, he remarked:

> As President, I will set a new direction in nuclear weapons policy and show the world that America believes in its existing commitment under the nuclear Nonproliferation Treaty [NPT] to work to ultimately eliminate all nuclear weapons ... and I will make the goal of eliminating nuclear weapons a central element of US nuclear policy.
>
> (Obama, 2008)

While Obama did temper expectations slightly by making it clear that the US would not disarm unilaterally (Obama, 2008), many felt that the world was on the cusp of a new era in global nuclear politics (Mooney, 2008). Obama was the first president for a generation to breathe life back into the goal of a world free from nuclear weapons and was awarded the prestigious Nobel Peace Prize in 2009 (at least in part) for his re-engagement with the disarmament issue (Erlanger and Stolberg, 2009).

The centrepiece of Obama's nuclear agenda would be a new strategic arms reduction agreement with Russia to replace the expiring Strategic Arms Reduction Treaty (START) and Strategic Offensive Reductions Treaty (SORT) (and particularly the START verification regime), but this would be augmented by concurrent moves to reduce the role of nuclear weapons in US security; make amendments to US nuclear posture; seek agreements with Iran and North Korea over their disputed nuclear ambitions; strengthen and reaffirm the US commitment to the NPT; and pursue Senate ratification of the Comprehensive Test Ban Treaty (CTBT); as well as raising the profile of nuclear security. Taken together,

Obama's extensive nuclear portfolio suggested a marked change from the nuclear thinking and policies of his predecessor, George W. Bush, and perhaps even the beginning of a truly transformative period in US and global nuclear politics. Given the complex and multi-faceted nature of these issues, however, it was clear that Obama had set himself an enormous challenge and it is therefore unsurprising (indeed, understandable) that many of them remain largely unchanged as the next presidential election campaign gathers momentum.

As we come to look back over eight years of Obama in office, progress has certainly been made on a number of these issues: the New START nuclear arms reductions treaty signed with Russia in 2010; a diversification in US deterrence thinking and capabilities away from singular reliance on nuclear retaliation; a tentative agreement with Iran over its disputed nuclear programme reached in 2015; and the creation and augmentation of new international fora and networks to combat the threat of nuclear terrorism. However, and while these achievements are certainly significant and should not be downplayed, this is perhaps not the progress or transformation in US and global nuclear politics that many people had hoped for and some believed possible. In fact, the general trends in nuclear policy over the past few years are perhaps best thought of as a continuation of what had gone before – with some subtle changes in tack – and an evolution in US nuclear thinking rather than something closer to a revolution (Futter, 2013). While it would perhaps be unfair to criticise Obama for not meeting the myriad nuclear challenges set at the start of his presidency, it may well be that some will look back on these years as a period of missed opportunities, where a greater and sustained political commitment to certain nuclear goals, and perhaps a more discrete and focused nuclear agenda could have delivered more durable and lasting results. As Sarah Tully (2014) puts it: 'President Obama has long talked the talk of reducing the dangers of nuclear weapons, but the administration has been slow to walk the walk in terms of nuclear weapons reductions in recent years.'

That said, it may be that the greatest legacy and change driven by Obama has been the shift in contours of the global nuclear debate and the re-emergence of nuclear disarmament as a genuine, albeit aspirational, political goal. In this way, Obama's greatest nuclear legacy might be how his administration laid the foundations for future changes to global nuclear orthodoxy that might otherwise prove impossible.

In order to review the various successes and failures of the Obama administration's nuclear agenda, and therefore consider its legacy, this chapter looks at and reviews four key objectives in turn: (1) the first section looks at how Obama sought to reduce the role of nuclear weapons in US national security, make changes to nuclear doctrine, and re-engage with the global disarmament movement; (2) the second evaluates Obama's attempts to reignite the nuclear arms reduction process with Russia, notably by the 2010 New START treaty, and considers the prospects for future 'deep' cuts; (3) the third section looks at how the Obama administration has sought to address nuclear proliferation challenges – namely North Korea and Iran – and its wider (re-)engagement with the NPT regime; (4) while the fourth looks at the new measures designed to combat the threat of nuclear terrorism and to enhance global nuclear security. The conclusion brings this all together, reflects on Obama's nuclear achievements and missed opportunities over the past two terms, and begins to consider his nuclear legacy.

Reduce US reliance on nuclear weapons and alter nuclear posture

The primary component of Obama's nuclear agenda was to reduce reliance on nuclear weapons for US national security and deterrence, and attempt to move US posture away from a stance increasingly seen as an anachronistic hangover from the Cold War. The idea was that US nuclear forces could be augmented and even possibly replaced by advanced conventional weaponry, while at the same time moves could be made to relax nuclear use guidelines and reduce nuclear alert status. Taken together, Obama believed these changes would help to 'finally put an end to Cold War thinking' (2009), and set the stage for his wider suite of international nuclear initiatives. This was most clearly outlined in the 2010 'Nuclear Posture Review' (NPR):

> Fundamental changes in the international security environment in recent years – including the growth of unrivalled US conventional military capabilities, major improvements in missile defences ... enable us to fulfil ... objectives at significantly lower nuclear force levels and with reduced reliance on nuclear weapons ... without jeopardizing our traditional deterrence and reassurance goals.
>
> (US Department of Defense, 2010b: v)

However, by seeking to roll out an effective and multi-layered missile defence system domestically as well as in Europe and East Asia, while also seeking advanced conventional capabilities which strategic competitors consider first-strike weapons, Obama's ambitious plan was conceptually flawed. As Andrew Futter and Ben Zala (2013: 108) explain:

> The central problem is that US superiority in advanced conventional weaponry makes its very difficult for any US rival to agree to work toward a nuclear free world when such a move – already made difficult by existing conventional balances – will magnify US power. More specifically, the close link between nuclear reductions and increases in conventional capabilities essentially works to decrease US vulnerability in a nuclear disarmed world, while at the same time increasing the vulnerability of its current or future rivals and adversaries.

In essence, US plans were more likely to see rivals further embrace nuclear weapons as central components of their respective national security strategies than to marginalise them. Rivals regarded this as a US push for strategic superiority by deploying both a *sword* and a *shield*: missile defences would essentially render the US invulnerable to attack while it could then use its offensive forces (nuclear but more likely conventional) with relative impunity and they have made their feelings on this issue abundantly clear.

The second strand of Obama's domestic nuclear agenda was to update, relax and modify US nuclear posture and the guidelines underpinning nuclear use. According to the 2010 NPR, the 'fundamental' as opposed to the 'sole' role of US nuclear weapons is to deter attack on both the United States and its allies (US Department of Defense, 2010b: viii). As such, nuclear weapons might be used to deter or respond to threats other than those posed by nuclear weapons. The NPR also revived the US security assurances to allies and potential rivals:

> For the first time, the United States is explicitly committing not to use nuclear weapons against nonnuclear states that are in compliance with the Nuclear Nonproliferation Treaty, even if they attacked the United States with biological or chemical weapons or launched a crippling cyberattack.
>
> (Sanger and Baker, 2010)

The Union of Concerned Scientists has called for Obama to

> declare that the sole purpose of US nuclear weapons is to deter a nuclear attack on the United States and its allies, and to respond to such an attack if necessary ... giving nuclear weapons roles beyond deterring nuclear attack is both unnecessary and counterproductive.
>
> (Union of Concerned Scientists, 2015: 4)

Likewise, the Obama administration has also shied away from adopting a No-First Use (NFU) posture, meaning that, potentially, the US reserves the right to introduce nuclear weapons first in a crisis (Gerson, 2010). In addition to this, at the time of writing many hundreds of US Intercontinental Ballistic Missiles (ICBMs) remain on hair-trigger alert ready to be fired within minutes of receiving the order – a posture seen by many as a dangerous hangover from the dark days of the Cold War (Global Zero Commission, 2015).

Obama's attempts to revitalise and reorient US nuclear posture – and to move beyond Cold War thinking – have met with some success. Advanced conventional forces are beginning to play a greater role in deterrence by augmenting (though not replacing) nuclear options, and US nuclear use doctrine has been constricted. Moves toward a more nuanced deterrence capability, however, are a double-edged sword (as will be explained in greater detail below), and the US still retains hundreds of heavily armed nuclear weapons on hair-trigger alert, with the option to use them first in a crisis.

Reignite the nuclear arms reduction process

Perhaps the most prominent component of Obama's nuclear agenda was to re-engage Russia in nuclear arms control and reduction talks, seek a new agreement to replace the expiring 1991 START and 2002 SORT treaties, and set the stage for future – possibly multilateral – deep nuclear cuts. As then President-elect Obama explained in late 2008:

> The United States and Russia should seek real, verifiable reductions in all US and Russian nuclear weapons ... I am committed to working with Russia and other nuclear weapons states to make deep cuts in global stockpiles by the end of my first term.

> (Obama, 2008)

This would be part of a broader re-set of East–West relations designed to repair the damage Obama believed had been caused under his predecessor George W. Bush (Simes, 2007). It would also become a central plank in his 'Prague Agenda' (Obama, 2009).

There were several compelling reasons for a new arms control treaty. First, conditions had improved between the former Cold War rivals to such an extent that an agreement could further reduce the number of weapons as well as tensions that existed between the two. Second, reducing global nuclear arsenals (however incrementally) was in keeping with the spirit of the NPT, an endeavour Obama strongly supported. Finally, and perhaps most crucially, the original START, concluded between them in 1991, was on the verge of lapsing and a successor to that treaty was required, if only for the stringent verification measures the original treaty mandated. The resulting New START, signed and ratified in 2010, was a tough sell domestically for the Obama administration. Although it passed through the Senate it did so with many expensive strings attached. Most notably, in return for Republican acquiescence, the administration was required to devote significantly more resources to the nuclear weapons complex (Wilson, 2011). As a result, the United States is now committed to a programme of extensive nuclear modernisation (Wolfsthal *et al.*, 2014).

There were also grave concerns within the Republican camp that the treaty would impede or prohibit the future deployment of US missile defence systems, a criticism the administration emphatically denied. The Preamble of the treaty, agreed by both parties, affirmed the growing link between offensive and defensive armaments, acknowledging:

> [T]he existence of the interrelationship between strategic offensive arms and strategic defensive arms, that this interrelationship will become more important as strategic nuclear arms are reduced, and that current strategic defensive arms do not undermine the viability and effectiveness of the strategic offensive arms of the parties.

> (US Department of State, 2010)

It was interpreted by Moscow as a means of withdrawing from the treaty should US missile defences be seen to impair Russia's offensive capability. This section, in particular, was a source of contention for Republicans who viewed the linkage between offence and defence as unacceptable.

Notwithstanding these seemingly insurmountable obstacles, the US has repeatedly stressed its desire for further negotiated arms cuts with Moscow. This desire formed the basis of Obama's 2013 Berlin speech which, while underlining his continued commitment to the Prague Agenda, also called for nuclear arms reductions of 'up to one third' between the US and Russia. Such sweeping cuts, if enacted, would be a hugely significant step and would be the largest nuclear reductions to take place between the two in the post-Cold War era since the conclusion of START in 1991 (Obama, 2013). The drive for further cuts was marred somewhat, however, by Obama's insistence that the US continue to adhere to a counterforce nuclear doctrine, a strategy which places a premium on fast, accurate and powerful nuclear weapons to be deployed against enemy military targets in the event of a crisis; a strategy perceived as aggressive and threatening by others and one which evidently runs counter to the idea of nuclear reductions. In any case, domestic political opposition to further cuts has presented a seemingly redoubtable obstacle. Republicans, while lending their tacit approval to New START, 'did not consent to a goal of [nuclear] disarmament' and have made their hostility to further cuts known (Sessions, 2011). Although the Obama administration had raised the possibility of circumventing Congressional opposition by not seeking a negotiated treaty with Russia, it was largely overtaken by events. While political opposition stood in the way of further arms reductions, international conditions appeared to present considerable impediments of their own. Russia's 2014 annexation of Crimea, as well as US accusations that Moscow had violated the 1987 Intermediate Nuclear Forces (INF) Treaty (Sokov and Pomper, 2014), made progress in arms control extremely difficult (if not impossible) for the Obama administration to achieve. According to Gary Samore, former White House Coordinator for Arms Control and Weapons of Mass Destruction, '[t]he most fundamental game changer is Putin's invasion of Ukraine.... That has made any measure to reduce the stockpile unilaterally politically impossible' (quoted in Broad and Sanger, 2014). It has also likely stymied any chance of removing US tactical nuclear weapons based in Europe (Vartabedian and Hennigan, 2014). Nevertheless, New START continues to be implemented in a 'business-like' fashion, and there have been calls for the US to accelerate the cuts required ahead of the 2018 deadline (Kimball, 2015).

At the time of writing, prospects for further nuclear cuts look dismal, and one scholar has even suggest that we may have reached the 'end of history for nuclear arms control' (Arbatov, 2015). It is also interesting to note that despite the fanfare that accompanied the re-set and the successful signing of New START, Obama has actually made the least cuts of all post-Cold War presidents (Broad, 2014). While this appears to be at odds with his disarmament vision, it may well be the case that Obama is preparing the ground for further nuclear cuts in the future.

Re-engage with the NPT and address nuclear proliferation challenges

As Obama stated in his Prague speech, the basic compact of the NPT remained 'sound':

> Countries with nuclear weapons will move towards disarmament, countries without nuclear weapons will not acquire them, and all countries can access peaceful nuclear energy. To strengthen the treaty, we should embrace several principles. We need more resources and authority to strengthen international inspections. We need real and immediate consequences for countries caught breaking the rules or trying to leave the treaty without cause.

> (Obama, 2009)

Indeed, Obama was the first president for a generation to breathe life back into the goal of a world free from nuclear weapons.

Obama entered office committed to diplomacy and dialogue with Iran, whose nuclear activities had been suspect for a number of years. Iran was a pressing case which had flouted international norms and was known for its human rights violations and sponsorship of terrorism as well as its apparent pursuit of a rudimentary nuclear capability (Einhorn, 2015). A nuclear Iran would be enormously damaging to both regional and international stability as well as presenting a setback to the global non-proliferation regime which Obama had pledged to bolster during his time in office. While diplomacy was the preferred option, Obama reserved the right to use military means to prevent a nuclear Iran. Having applied a programme of economic sanctions against Iran, the P5+1/E3+3 and Tehran entered negotiations surrounding the latter's nascent nuclear programme. An agreement was reached between the parties in mid-July 2015 which would see sanctions relief for Iran in return for a strict curtailment of its nuclear programme (Einhorn, 2015). The deal concluded is a hugely positive step for the Obama administration and will effectively prevent a new case of horizontal nuclear proliferation. Legislation concluded earlier in the year, however, ensured that Congress had a sixty-day window in which to review the deal. Though the costs of rejection appeared to outweigh the benefits, the deal continues to face strong opposition from Republicans (Cirincione, 2015). It still remains for the Obama administration to convince critics of the merits of the agreement and in doing so strengthen his nuclear legacy (Phillips, 2015).

Like Iran, Obama had, prior to his election as president, signalled his intention to extend an olive branch to outlier states like North Korea. The death of Kim Jong-Il in 2011 seemed to signal a new departure for the isolated regime. Unfortunately, his son Kim Jong-Un who succeeded him has followed a similar path to his father's. As Nahal Toosi has noted, 'President Barack Obama may be racing to secure a nuclear deal with Iran, but his nonproliferation legacy could ultimately hinge on a country further to the east – one that already has nuclear weapons and is led by an unpredictable 30-something' (Toosi, 2015). A series of provocations have alerted the international community to the dangers North Korea poses, particularly as it is already known to be in possession of a rudimentary nuclear capability. Pyongyang has not shied away from rattling its nuclear sabre in recent years and has launched a number of missile tests which have caused concern for neighbouring states, particularly South Korea and Japan. Despite a willingness to negotiate, Obama has made very limited progress with North Korea. Pyongyang conducted three nuclear tests during Obama's presidency and it is entirely possible that it might seek to test again in the near future (FlorCruz, 2015).

Another facet of Obama's overall nuclear agenda was the pursuit of CTBT ratification. The CTBT was signed by the United States in 1996 but has yet to be ratified. There are also seven other outliers, collectively known as Annex 2 states, that are yet to ratify. By outlawing 'any nuclear weapon test explosion or any other nuclear explosion', the CTBT aims to prevent both horizontal and vertical nuclear proliferation. US opponents of ratification (the vast majority of them Republicans) see it as a potential ligature which could bind US freedom of action in an uncertain and complex security environment, while proponents regard scientific and computerised modelling as an effective means of testing without an actual nuclear detonation. Technical and verification measures are also in place to ensure the compliance of other nuclear states. As of September 2015, the treaty continues to languish at committee stage in the US Senate and is unlikely to be examined seriously before the end of Obama's term, particularly as Republicans control both the House and the Senate. The administration position is currently one of 'education', and they have been loath to 'rush anything through' (Taheran, 2014). Ultimately, however, Obama will undoubtedly be held responsible for a lack of progress towards CTBT ratification, but its fortunes have unquestionably been tied to the political balance during his time in office.

As Kingston Reif has remarked, 'For all the well-justified praise US President Barack Obama has received for his efforts to roll back the Iranian nuclear threat, the rest of his nuclear security agenda has stalled' (2014). While this may be a somewhat overly pessimistic assessment of the Obama record, it undoubtedly contains some truth. In a similar vein, while the US decided to attend the third meeting of the Humanitarian Initiative in Vienna in December 2014 – having decided not to participate in the earlier ones – it is unlikely to support the nuclear weapons ban called for by the participants (Squassoni, 2015).

Raise the importance of nuclear security and combat the threat of nuclear terrorism

In the realm of nuclear security, Obama embraced several of the precepts of Bush's nuclear security strategy, notably the Proliferation Security Initiative (PSI) and the Global Initiative to Combat Nuclear Terrorism (GICNT). The PSI which was launched in 2003, was adopted as a key policy instrument by the

Obama administration. Its purpose was, according to the 2010 'National Security Strategy':

> To detect and intercept nuclear materials ·in transit, and to stop the illicit trade in these technologies, we will work to turn programs such as the Proliferation Security Initiative and the Global Initiative to Combat Nuclear Terrorism into durable international efforts. And we will sustain broad-based co-operation with other nations and international institutions to ensure the continued improvements necessary to protect nuclear materials from evolving threats.
>
> (Obama, 2010: 24)

Clearly, this initiative fit well with the Prague Agenda in that it sought to prevent nuclear material from falling into the hands of terrorist organisations and non-state actors, the most pressing international threat to the United States. America faces 'no greater or more urgent danger', according to one policy document (Obama, 2010: 23). The issue of nuclear security was foremost in the minds of administration officials and was seen as imperative in maintaining effective nuclear deterrence as well as US national security more broadly. In fact, the overarching security threat to the United States was perceived by the Obama administration to be the danger of nuclear materials or weapons falling into the hands of terrorist groups. Despite the complexities involved, terrorist acquisition of a nuclear weapon was seen as an improbable, though not impossible, scenario (see Levi, 2009). Preventive measures were thus required and to that end Obama convened a summit to challenge international leaders to join the global effort. Gathering in Washington DC in April 2010, the summit was the largest meeting of world leaders since 1945. That said, 'Despite the gains made to date on nuclear material security', according to Kingston Reif, 'it is unclear whether the administration has crafted a strategy to build on its achievements' (2014).

The 2012 National Security Summit was convened in Seoul, South Korea, with all attending states pledging to fully pursue and strengthen their efforts in fulfilling the goals laid out in Washington two years previously. The security of fissile materials remained the uppermost concern, but the 2012 summit was criticised for merely reaffirming the goals put forward in 2010 as opposed to introducing tangible initiatives of its own. The 2012 communiqué did, however, place an emphasis on the security of Highly Enriched Uranium (HEU) and urged all states, by the end of 2013, to secure all stocks of this fissile material and reduce their reliance on it as much as possible (US Department of State, 2012). As Steven Pifer (2015: 108) notes:

> The summits succeeded in drawing high-level attention to the need to secure highly enriched uranium as well as separated plutonium and in encouraging states to take steps to do so, even if all participants did not agree to implement all steps.

A minor incident at the 2012 Nuclear Security Summit in Seoul seemed to suggest that a limitation of some form might be placed on US missile defences. A conversation between Obama and outgoing Russian President Dmitri Medvedev was picked up by a journalist in which the former was recorded as saying that, following the November presidential elections (and provided he won), there would be room for greater 'flexibility' on missile defences.

Obama also pledged to pursue the Fissile Material Cut-off Treaty (FMCT) as a matter of course. This was seen as a logical component of US nuclear strategy as well as of Obama's wider Prague Agenda (Pecquet, 2013). In order to forestall nuclear proliferation, fissile materials need to be secured and as such the FMCT is regarded as essential to that endeavour. While Obama can, of course, be lauded for his enthusiasm in pursuing such an agreement, significant obstacles remain. Any such treaty will need to be negotiated under the auspices of the Conference on Disarmament (CD) which rules on a consensus basis. The treaty also lacks traction in that it appears unready to launch formal discussions between the parties. Thus far, there has been no substantive discussion on any such treaty, with an impasse between all nuclear states (both recognised and non-recognised) on the issue since the early 1990s. As a means of overcoming the deadlock various other fora have been suggested, given the serious doubts about the viability of pursuing the treaty through the CD though the CD is still preferred by the Obama administration.

Meanwhile the future of the Nunn–Lugar Co-operative Threat Reduction (CTR) programme seems uncertain after Russia refused further US help to secure its nuclear stockpiles (Bender, 2015). The CTR, co-sponsored by former Senator's Sam Nunn and Richard Lugar, was designed to provide insurance against, and ultimately neutralise, the problem of 'loose nukes' in the former Soviet Union. It was initiated in 1991 following the end of the Cold War, a time when the former Soviet republics were in ferment and the prospect of nuclear weapons and materials being sold on the black market appeared a likely scenario (Allison *et al.*, 1999). The CTR provided funds to destroy both nuclear weapons and their associated infrastructure and delivery vehicles. Russia unilaterally withdrew from the process in January 2015 and its future – particularly in light of recent Russian aggression – appears unclear. 'The order of the day', according to Michael Krepon, 'is to maintain as much security cooperation as possible with Russia while contesting its actions in Ukraine, developing patterns of security cooperation with China, and reaching a constraining nuclear accord with Iran' (2015).

While questions remain about the future of the Nunn–Lugar initiative and the nuclear security summits, Obama clearly has made notable progress in addressing the threat of nuclear terrorism and creating and establishing international fora to deal with these challenges. While much of this builds upon what went before, notably the PSI, GICNT and UN Resolution 1540 (Khripunov, 2014), Obama has undoubtedly institutionalised nuclear security as a central international objective. Whether future administrations will capitalise on these gains remains to be seen.

Conclusion: Obama's nuclear legacy

It is perhaps fair to say that Obama was never likely to live up to the hype and fulfil the expectation that emerged around his nuclear agenda in 2009 and 2010, or to please those who saw him as the figurehead of a move to thoroughly revisit, revise and perhaps transform not just US nuclear strategy but the central tenets of global nuclear order more broadly. That is not to say that Obama has not been successful in his nuclear agenda: the New START was a hard-fought and worthwhile endeavour; a new triad of strategic forces is slowly augmenting the traditional role of nuclear weapons in deterrence; a lasting deal with Iran over its disputed nuclear programmes looks possible; and the issue of nuclear security and nuclear terrorism is now at the centre of the international nuclear debate. At the same time, however, the New START deal appears to be based on a shaky foundation, not least due to expanding US (and NATO) ballistic missile defence plans, Russian nuclear posturing and possible violations of the INF treaty. Likewise, Russian activities in Ukraine, coupled with the vicissitudes of US domestic politics, make the chances of further nuclear arms cuts very slim; the capricious nature of the North Korean regime remains a constant nuclear concern, and it is unclear how durable the Iran deal will be; the CTBT remains in the US political wilderness, while the failure of the 2015 NPT review conference to reach consensus raises serious concerns about the future of the international non-proliferation regime. Obama's pledge to modernise all three legs of the strategic triad and to invest heavily in the US nuclear weapons complex also leaves open the possibility that the nuclear arsenal may be expanded under a different president in the future.

It is easy to be critical of Obama's nuclear score-sheet given the herculean tasks he appeared to set himself and the comprehensive range of nuclear issues he vowed to address, but this is as much a product of the hype and belief that surrounded his election victory as it is a sober judgement of his achievement. Indeed, it is unlikely that any president would have been able to make progress or solve all of these complex issues, even with a supportive Congress and a productive relationship with Russia. His approach may be best summed up as 'Lord make me chaste, but not yet', a quote commonly attributed to St Augustine; Obama would like to make major moves towards disarmament but circumstances compel him to adopt a more considered strategy. Or as Steven Pifer has noted, Obama was stymied by the '3 R's': Russians, Republicans and reluctance (2015: 101).

But this is perhaps missing what is arguably the central contribution of the Obama years – and likely to be his greatest legacy – which is that he has changed the way in which we think about the nuclear debate and the context of nuclear orthodoxy. In this way it is important not just to focus on the explicit headline-catching initiatives but also to consider the wider normative dynamics that frame the debate and discussion around nuclear issues. While Kingston Reif is right to suggest that '[l]egacies are defined by actions ... not words' (2014), it may well be that Obama *has* changed the nuclear debate in a significant way, and in doing so *could* provide the impetus and initiative for further, more substantial moves in the future. While he still has some six months left until he departs the White House, ultimately it would be unfair at this remove to judge Obama's nuclear legacy too harshly until we see what comes next.

References

Allison, G., Cote, O., Miller, S. and Falkenrath, R. (1999) *Avoiding nuclear anarchy: containing the threat of loose Russian nuclear weapons and fissile material* (Cambridge, MA: MIT Press).

Arbatov, A. (2015) 'An unnoticed crisis: the end of history for nuclear arms control?', Carnegie Moscow Center, 16 June, http://carnegie.ru/2015/06/16/unnoticed-crisis-end-of-history-for-nuclear-arms-control/ians.

Bender, B. (2015) 'Russia US nuclear security alliance', *Boston Globe*, 19 January, www.bostonglobe.com/news/nation/2015/01/19/after-two-decades-russia-nuclear-security-cooperation-becomes-casualty-deteriorating-relations/5nh8NbtjitUE8UqVWFIooL/story.html.

Broad, W. (2014) 'Which president cut the most nukes?', *New York Times*, 1 November, www.nytimes.com/2014/11/02/sunday-review/which-president-cut-the-most-nukes.html?_r=0.

Broad, W. and Sanger, D. (2014) 'US ramping up major renewal in nuclear arms', *New York Times*, 21 September, www.nytimes.com/2014/09/22/us/us-ramping-up-major-renewal-in-nuclear-arms.html.

Cirincione, J. (2015) 'What happens if the Senate rejects the Iran deal?', *Los Angeles Times*, 23 August, www.latimes.com/opinion/op-ed/la-oe-cirincione-iran-deal-scenarios-20150823-story.html.

Einhorn, R. (2015) 'Debating the Iran nuclear deal', Brookings Institution, August, www.brookings.edu/research/reports2/2015/08/iran-nuclear-deal-battleground-issues-einhorn?utm_source=Arms+Control+Association+E-Updates&utm_campaign=33f36fb347-The_P5_1_and_Iran_Nuclear_Deal_Alert_Aug_20&utm_medium=email&utm_term=0_0bf155a1a2-33f36fb347-79431113.

Erlanger, S. and Stolberg, S. (2009) 'Surprise Nobel for Obama stirs praise and doubts', *New York Times*, 9 October, www.nytimes.com/2009/10/10/world/10nobel.html.

FlorCruz, M. (2015) 'Under Kim Jon Un, North Korea may launch new nuclear test in October', *International Business Times*, 17 July, www.ibtimes.com/under-kim-jong-un-north-korea-may-launch-new-nuclear-test-october-2013393.

Futter, A. (2013) 'US nuclear weapons policy after the War on Terror: from primacy to sufficiency', in Michelle Bentley and Jack Holland (eds), *Obama's foreign policy: ending the War on Terror* (London: Routledge).

Futter, A. and Zala, B. (2013) 'Advanced US conventional weapons and nuclear abolition: why the Obama plan won't work', *The Nonproliferation Review*, 20:1, pp. 107–122.

Gerson, M. (2010) 'No first use: the next step for US nuclear policy', *International Security*, 35:2, pp. 7–47.

Global Zero Commission on Nuclear Risk Reduction (2015) 'De-alerting and stabilizing the world's nuclear force postures', April, www.globalzero.org/files/global_zero_commission_on_nuclear_risk_reduction_report0.pdf.

Khripunov, I. (2014) 'A work in progress: UN Security Resolution 1540 after 10 years', *Arms Control Today*, May, www.armscontrol.org/act/2014_05/A-Work-in-Progress-UN-Security-Resolution-1540-After-10-Years.

Kimball, D. (2015) 'New pathways to disarmament', *Arms Control Today*, May, www. armscontrol.org/print/6941.

Krepon, M. (2015) 'Nunn–Lugar, R.I.P.', *Arms Control Wonk*, 27 January, http://krepon. armscontrolwonk.com/archive/4458/nunn-lugar-r-i-p.

Levi, M. (2009) *Inside nuclear terrorism* (Cambridge MA: Harvard University Press).

Mooney, A. (2008) 'Obama says time to rid world of nuclear weapons', *CNN*, 16 July, http://edition.cnn.com/2008/POLITICS/07/16/obama.speech/.

Obama, B. (2008) '2008 Presidential Q & A: President-elect Barack Obama', *Arms Control Today*, December, www.armscontrol.org/system/files/Obama_QA_FINAL_ Dec10_2008.pdf.

Obama, B. (2009) 'Remarks by President Barack Obama, Hradčany Square, Prague, Czech Republic', White House Office of the Press Secretary, 5 April, www.white-house.gov/the-press-office/remarks-president-barack-obama-prague-delivered.

Obama, B. (2010) 'National Security Strategy', White House, Washington DC, May, www. whitehouse.gov/sites/default/files/rss_viewer/national_security_strategy.pdf.

Obama, B. (2013) 'Remarks by President Obama at the Brandenburg Gate, Berlin, Germany', White House Office of the Press Secretary, 19 June, www.whitehouse.gov/ the-press-office/2013/06/19/remarks-president-obama-brandenburg-gate-berlin-germany.

Pecquet, J. (2013) 'Obama to push for nuclear treaty', *The Hill*, 2 September, http://thehill. com/policy/international/282051-obama-to-push-for-nuclear-treaty-in-second-term.

Phillips, A. (2015) 'Why the Iran deal is so huge for Obama's legacy', *Washington Post*, 31 July, www.washingtonpost.com/news/the-fix/wp/2015/07/31/why-the-iran-deal-is-huge-for-obamas-legacy/.

Pifer, S. (2015) 'Obama's faltering nuclear legacy: the 3 R's', *The Washington Quarterly*, 38:2, pp. 101–118.

Reif, K. (2014) 'Obama's nuclear legacy on the line', *Bulletin of the Atomic Scientists*, 28 February, http://thebulletin.org/obamas-nuclear-legacy-line.

Sanger, D. and Baker, P. (2010) 'Obama limits when US would use nuclear arms', *New York Times*, 5 April, www.nytimes.com/2010/04/06/world/06arms.html?pagewanted= all&_r=0.

Sessions, J. (2011) 'Implementation of the New Strategic Arms Reduction Treaty (START) and plans for future reductions in nuclear warheads and delivery systems post-New START', Hearing before the Subcommittee on Strategic Forces of the Committee on Armed Services, United States Senate, 4 May, http://fas.org/irp/congress/2011_hr/news-tart.pdf.

Simes, D. (2007) 'Losing Russia: the costs of renewed confrontation', *Foreign Affairs*, 86:6, pp. 36–52.

Sokov, N. and Pomper, M. (2014) 'Is Russia violating the INF Treaty?', *The National Interest*, 11 February, http://nationalinterest.org/commentary/russia-violating-the-inf-treaty-9859.

Squassoni, S. (2015) 'Talk is cheap: Washington attends the humanitarian initiative on nuclear weapons impacts', *Bulletin of the Atomic Scientists*, 12 May, http://thebulletin. org/talk-cheap-washington-attends-humanitarian-initiative-nuclear-weapons-impacts7844.

Taheran, S. (2014) 'US officials reaffirm support for CTBT', *Arms Control Today*, October, www.armscontrol.org/ACT/2014_10/News/US-Officials-Reaffirm-Support-for-CTBT.

Toosi, N. (2015) 'Barack Obama's true nuclear test: North Korea', *Politico*, 5 June, www. politico.com/story/2015/05/barack-obamas-true-nuclear-test-north-korea-117651.html.

Tully, S. (2014) 'Obama hasn't fulfilled his promises on nuclear weapons reduction', *Business Insider*, 29 October, www.businessinsider.com/obama-hasnt-fulfilled-his-promises-on-nuclear-reduction-2014–10?IR=T.

Union of Concerned Scientists (2015) 'What will President Obama's nuclear legacy be?', *Fact Sheet*, www.ucsusa.org/nuclear-weapons/us-nuclear-weapons-policy/obamas-nuclearlegacy#.VdM2q3hN3zI.

United States Department of Defense (2010a) 'Ballistic Missile Defence Review', February, http://archive.defense.gov/bmdr/docs/BMDR%20as%20of%2026JAN10%200630_for%20web.pdf.

United States Department of Defense (2010b) 'Nuclear Posture Review', April, http://archive.defense.gov/npr/docs/2010%20Nuclear%20Posture%20Review%20Report.pdf.

United States Department of State (2010) 'Treaty between the United States of America and the Russian Federation on measures for the further reduction and limitation of strategic offensive arms', www.state.gov/documents/organization/140035.pdf.

United States Department of State (2012) 'Key facts on the 2012 Seoul Nuclear Security Summit', Bureau of International Narcotics and Law Enforcement Affairs, 28 March, www.state.gov/t/isn/rls/fs/187208.htm.

Vartabedian, R. and Hennigan, W. (2014) 'NATO nuclear drawdown now seems unlikely', *Los Angeles Times*, 19 September, www.latimes.com/nation/la-na-europe-nukes-20140920-story.html.

Wilson, C. (2011) 'Republicans want nukes modernization', *Reuters*, 9 May, www.reuters.com/article/2011/05/09/us-nuclear-usa-modernizationidUSTRE7485S420110509.

Wolfsthal, J., Lewis, J. and Quint, M. (2014) 'The trillion dollar nuclear triad', James Martin Center for Nonproliferation Studies, Monterey, CA, January, http://cns.miis.edu/opapers/pdfs/140107_trillion_dollar_nuclear_triad.pdf

9   The assassin in chief

Obama's drone legacy

Christopher Fuller

It is a mark of the importance aerial bombing has played in the implementation of America's foreign policy that the legacies of numerous presidents have been shaped by how they have utilised America's airborne superiority. Furthermore, it is an indication of the controversy the recourse to aerial domination frequently generates that these legacies are fiercely debated by scholars. Truman's presidency was intractably defined by his decision to drop two atom bombs upon Japan – and the degree to which this was a calculated act of atomic diplomacy in the face of perceived Soviet expansionism. Nixon's apparent willingness to employ massive bombardments against the North Vietnamese saw him portrayed as the 'Mad Bomber', whilst later accounts argued that this violent image was part of a premeditated strategy to force negotiations and hasten the end of the war. Bush Sr's presidency is synonymous with footage, played nightly by cable news networks, of 'smart munitions' destroying targets with previously unseen levels of accuracy during the first Gulf War – images seen by America's advocates as evidence of their ability to secure a 'New World Order', and its detractors as confirmation of rampant US militarism in the post-Cold War world. Bill Clinton intended his use of cruise missiles to destroy al-Qaeda-linked training camps in Afghanistan to be a warning to the terrorist group of America's 'infinite reach', the name given to the operation. Yet those seeking the president's impeachment at the time likened the strikes to the events in the Hollywood caper movie *Wag the Dog*, a manufactured distraction for the beleaguered Commander in Chief. Obama's personal connection to more than 500 drone strikes and an estimated 5,000 casualties places him firmly amongst his bombing contemporaries, with similar contention.

This chapter considers how Barack Obama came to adopt drone warfare as the centrepiece of his counterterrorism policy, and discusses the legacy it leaves for both his presidency and that of his successors. It does this through the examination of three distinct aspects of America's drone campaign: first, the counterterrorism legacy left by two terms of unmanned warfare; second, the broad infrastructural legacy, specifically the physical network of bases and the costs associated with their maintenance; third, the legal architecture which underwrites the drone programme, deliberating the constitutional implications this has for the presidency going forward. The chapter concludes by arguing that in the short term Obama's legacy is the establishment of an Executive dangerously empowered with the seductive ability to undertake lethal actions in a seemingly cost-free manner across the globe, whilst in the longer term his tenure has dramatically lowered the political, legal and moral threshold for the United States to employ autonomous weapons in the future.

Background – drone evolution, not revolution

When asked by *New York* magazine in late 2014 to share his thoughts on the likely historical legacy of Barack Obama's presidency, the Pulitzer Prize-winning historian Gordon Wood warned such an exercise was 'a fool's errand'. 'We live in a fog', Wood observed (quoted in *New York* 2015). Obama's legacy could only be determined by historians decades removed from current events, able to look back through the noise and tumult of daily political life with the benefit of hindsight, to tell their society what had *actually* happened during the forty-fourth president's tenure in the White House. Of course, Wood is correct – there is far too much uncertainty regarding how many of the policies implemented by the Obama administration will play out in the long term to make accurate predictions on the legacy he will leave. Yet, despite the discomfort historians feel when dealing with the ambiguity of the present, there are certain aspects of a president's tenure one can confidently identify as legacy-defining before the passage of time. The institutionalisation of drone warfare is most certainly one such legacy. Of the 53 historians who engaged with *New York*'s task, 17 specifically identified Obama's connection to lethal drones as integral to how he will be remembered. Historian Alfred McCoy (2015) summed up the view most succinctly, noting that the president 'will be remembered as the progenitor of drone warfare'. However, whilst Obama's leadership has certainly played a key role in institutionalising the use of drones for targeted killing, it is inaccurate to speak of him as the originator of this approach, and the context within which he came to adopt unmanned warfare must be clarified in order to enable an accurate judgement of his legacy.

As early as 1984 the US government sought a clandestine capability for the 'pre-emptive neutralization of anti-American terrorist groups ... and terrorist leaders' overseas (National Security Decision Directive 138; see National Security Council 1984). Responsibility for overseeing this mission was handed to the Central Intelligence Agency's (CIA) newly formed Counterterrorism Center (CTC) in February 1986 (National Security Council 1986), which promptly initiated the Eagle Program, a drone prototype designed to fulfil the pre-emptive neutralisation role (Clarridge with Diehl 1997: 339). Despite stuttering development, by September 2000 the CTC was flying a Predator drone – the technological descendant of the Eagle – over Afghanistan in search of Osama bin Laden, with Richard Clarke, Clinton's counterterrorism adviser, requesting an armed variant be built to provide a 'see it/shoot it' option (Clarke 2000: 7). Although the missile-equipped Predator was not deployed by the time Clinton left office, following 9/11 the CTC adopted the armed drone in its war against al-Qaeda's core leadership in the Afghanistan/Pakistan (AfPak) region, hastily establishing outposts, temporary relay stations and teams of informants to provide intelligence for strikes (Woodward 2010: 6). Therefore, Obama's contribution to drone warfare, while important, is better regarded as an incremental step as opposed to the revolution observers have commonly presented it as – the formal institutionalisation of an approach his predecessors had been developing over the past three decades.

Counterterrorism legacy

The Obama administration may have rejected the phrase 'War on Terror' (Bentley 2014: 91), but it had little choice but to continue the battles associated with George W. Bush's expansive conflict. The situation Obama inherited was dire. America was mired in two increasingly costly and unpopular wars in Afghanistan and Iraq, with no clear victories in sight and its primary opponent, al-Qaeda, resurgent after transforming itself into a global franchise operation. Determined not to hand a similar legacy on to his successor, Obama set himself the task of ending the two wars responsibly, whilst dramatically narrowing the War on Terror from an open-ended conflict to a focused campaign intended to 'disrupt, degrade, dismantle and ultimately defeat' al-Qaeda, its affiliates and adherents (White House 2011b: 8). To achieve this, the president sought a strategy which would enable the United States to pursue the terrorist organisation into the safe havens of the AfPak region, the failed state of Somalia, and Yemen's unpoliced deserts, while simultaneously reducing its military footprint, scaling back the unilateralism and perceived brutality of the Bush administration, and adapting to the new constraints of a much-weakened economy following 2008's economic crash.

Obama selected John Brennan as the man to develop this challenging counterterrorist strategy, appointing him assistant to the president for homeland security and counterterrorism. A former CIA analyst with an impressive CV, Brennan had advised then-Senator Obama on intelligence matters during his 2008 election campaign, building an extremely close rapport with the victorious candidate. During Obama's first term, Brennan used this close relationship to take what Gregory D. Johnson (2015) describes as the 'raw infrastructure the Bush administration had left behind' and 'mold[ed] it into an institution that would survive'. Drawing upon his extensive experience as lead analyst in the CTC from 1990 to 1992, chief of the CIA's newly founded Terrorist Threat Integration Center (TTIC) from 2003 to 2004, and interim director of the newly-established National Counterterrorism Center (NCC) from 2004 to 2005, Brennan transformed the way the United States hunted terrorists. Working so closely with Obama that colleagues in the White House and Pentagon began to refer to him as 'deputy president' (Cherlin 2013), the former CIA analyst drew upon multiple levers of American power to create a new, data-driven approach to targeted killing.

Brennan took advantage of what, in technological terms, is referred to as connectedness – the sudden conjunction of a range of technologies which had developed independently of one another. Advances in drone technology had seen the introduction of the Reaper in 2007. The successor to the Predator was capable of carrying fifteen times the ordinance and flying at three times the speed – transforming the unmanned aircraft into what the Department of Defense (DoD) labelled a 'true hunter-killer' (DoD 2006). At the same time, improved missile technology saw the manufacture of cheaper and more precise variants of the Hellfire, the primary munition used in drone strikes; new digital techniques were utilised by the National Geospatial Agency to map out the physically inaccessible territory utilised by America's enemies; the Air Force improved its global positioning system (GPS) guidance; and third-party advances in laser and infrared sensor technology, coupled with the increased feed quality from drone cameras, further enhanced the precision US drones could promise. Finally, machine-learning algorithms, increased computing power and near infinite data storage capacity combined to allow the National Security Agency to conduct surveillance on a hitherto unknown scale, capturing massive amounts of data which could be used to build a picture of known and suspected terrorists' patterns of life (Ball 2013).

As director of the NCC in 2004, Brennan had overseen the creation of a clearinghouse for all of the government's various terrorist databases. Congruently, Obama's 2008 election campaign had relied heavily upon voter targeting through spreadsheets built up via data-mining and microtargeting (Scola 2013). Consequently, both men entered the White House with a firm understanding of the potential these technological developments offered to create a new, data-driven approach to tracking and targeting America's enemies. Drones seemed to offer a way to balance the proportionality and adherence to the laws of 'just war' Obama had reiterated as American ideals during his Nobel Peace Prize acceptance speech (2009), whilst still enabling America to undertake the pre-emptive neutralisation of its terrorist enemies it had sought since the Reagan administration. The Disposition Matrix (Miller 2012) was born – a next-generation kill list populated with thousands of names, biographies and biometric data acquired by the US intelligence community, and with it, the institutionalisation of the post-9/11 national security state, a recognition that the United States would continue hunting targets around the globe with lethal force indefinitely.

With the Disposition Matrix and accompanying drone strikes – the 'kinetic piece' of what an anonymous CTC official described as 'an enormously long chain of collection and analysis' (Miller and Tate 2011) – Obama passes on a counterterrorism legacy where the drone strike is no longer a tool for counterterrorism strategy, but *is* counterterrorism strategy. '[T]he entire apparatus of the United States government has been bent toward the process of targeted killing over the past decade', observes the Bureau of Investigative Journalism's (BIJ) Chris Woods (2015). 'This isn't the CIA,' Woods concludes, 'this is the US in its greatest sense that is responsible for this.' By institutionalising targeted killing via drone, Obama leaves a dangerously seductive legacy for his successors. When President Ford banned the CIA from engaging in acts of assassination through Executive Order 11905 in 1976, he explained the decision was as much about protecting future presidents from the temptation to use covert killing as a perceived quick fix as it was about protecting agents and their potential targets (Mazzetti 2014: 46). Drones have reintroduced this quick fix temptation to the Oval Office. As Patrick Porter (2015: 206) observes, they offer a seemingly 'clinical, detached, and relatively cost-free way of projecting power'. The problem this poses, Porter warns, is that this combination of factors lowers the inhibitions, making policy makers more likely to resort to drone killings in situations where they might not otherwise have applied force at all.

The apparent greater freedom to act offered by drones may also, ironically, have the opposite impact upon future occupants of the White House, instead creating a kind of political stasis as drones consistently offer an immediate but short-term solution to threats facing the United States. Despite his initial efforts to change the dynamics of America's conflict with radical Islam, for example his 'New Beginning' speech in Cairo (White House 2009b), Obama's adoption of drone warfare created a culture whereby his administration came to rely upon the high-tech, low-risk quick fix to threats, with too little consideration for the long-term consequences of this response. Current research (Jordan 2014) suggests targeted killing will only ever be a short-term solution to the danger posed by large, bureaucratic groups such as al-Qaeda and the Islamic State, disrupting the organisation but never tackling the root causes necessary to remove the threat entirely. Yet the ability to promptly eliminate a suspected threat, combined with the American public's demand for complete security (Cronin 2013: 194), means it will be difficult for future presidents to break out of what Colonel Mark Maxwell (2012) has dubbed the 'whack-a-mole' cycle. Obama's successors will most certainly be wise enough to know that the resistance of groups like al-Qaeda and the Islamic State does not disappear as leaders such as Osama bin Laden or Abu Bakr al-Baghdadi are eliminated, rather these leaders are themselves products of more deep-seated forces. 'Those men', Herbert Hoover (Hoover and Gibson 1943: 10) observed in his text on the challenges of bringing peace, 'only light the match to a train of powder which has been laid over the years before'. America's unflinching support for the Israeli government regardless of its treatment of the Palestinian people, close relations with corrupt and oppressive Middle Eastern regimes, and the impact of the environmental damage caused by exploitative energy policies have all been cited (Scheuer 2007: 11–14) as motivating factors which drive individuals to join anti-Western jihads. When faced with challenging these inherent issues it is easy to see why, regardless of the questionable long-term efficacy of the strategy, America's leaders are likely to continue to support targeted killings with drones as the United States' counterterrorism tool of choice – a troubling policy legacy for a president who campaigned on changing the status quo.

The more immediate legacy of Obama's drone war against al-Qaeda and its affiliates is, at best, mixed. With regard to the AfPak region, a leaked CIA report (2009) revealed that Obama's authorisation of over 350 strikes had the primary aim of degrading the Taliban's insurgency to a level which would allow Afghan security forces to maintain stability once NATO's combat operation ceased at the end of 2014. Data from the BIJ (2015) suggests the campaign was very effective at locating and killing Taliban militants, with an estimated 2,006 to 3,309 casualties between 2009 and NATO's withdrawal. Behind this apparent success, however, a wide gap exists between the US government's assessment of the number of civilians counted among those casualties, and non-governmental reports, casting doubt on the administration's claims of precision. The divergence is partially explained by the differing methodologies of counting the dead (Becker and Shane 2012), with the Obama administration having adopted the practice of classing all military-age males killed in a strike zone as 'militants' unless evidence to the contrary is provided posthumously, an approach which exposes a dangerous erosion of the distinction between civilian and combatant. Furthermore, despite the body count, the Obama administration was forced to negotiate the retention of 10,000 US combat troops in Afghanistan (Ministry Foreign Affairs 2014) for up to a decade following the official withdrawal, and has continued sporadic unmanned strikes in the region, suggesting that even after two terms of intensive drone warfare, the Taliban remain a legitimate threat.

In the case of al-Qaeda, Obama informed Congress two years into his drone campaign that his forces had 'taken out more than half of al-Qa'ida's leadership' (White House 2011c). The group's own sources reiterated this message, with a report from a senior commander lamenting 'so many brave commanders have been snatched away ... by the planes that are unheard, unseen and unknown' (Al-Libi 2009). Leon Panetta, speaking as Secretary of Defense (Alexander 2012), but also as the Director of Central Intelligence who oversaw the Agency's escalation of drone warfare, struck a similar encouraging tone, reporting that the United States had 'decimated core al-Qaeda'. However, exposing the limitations of the campaign, Panetta cautioned that 'even with these gains, the threat from al Qaeda has not been eliminated'. Whilst the United States may have 'slowed the primary cancer', Panetta warned that it had 'metastasized to other parts of the global body', beyond the reach of America's drones. This has been particularly evident in Iraq. Already in a chaotic state before Obama assumed power, the complete withdrawal of American forces, combined with the instability wrought by the Arab Spring and Syrian civil war, enabled the former affiliate al-Qaeda in Iraq to grow into a self-declared Islamic State (ISIS). With huge swathes of territory under its control, tens of thousands of fighters and billions of dollars of stolen military equipment, the group proved beyond the means of Obama's drone strategy. The president was forced to launch Operation Inherent Resolve on 10 September 2014, which marked a return to the more conventional combat operations of his predecessor, with aircraft from US carriers and allies such as Britain and Jordan flying thousands of sorties, at a cost of billions of dollars, in support of ground forces drawn from American-trained Iraqi forces and Iranian militias (DoD 2015).

Following 9/11, George W. Bush kept a copy of the FBI's Most Wanted List of twenty-two anti-American terrorists in the drawer of his Oval Office desk, crossing off the names as each was reported captured or killed, 'his own personal scorecard for the war' (Woodward 2003: 224). By the time Obama entered the office, there were fourteen names left on Bush's original list, although the War on Terror had long since bolstered al-Qaeda's ranks. Obama's successor does not inherit a paper list, but a digital grid, containing not dozens but thousands of names. Two terms of drone warfare have exposed remote targeted killing as an effective tactic for killing militants, but an insufficient strategy for actually ending America's ongoing conflict.

Infrastructural legacy

As well as forging the disparate collection of counterterrorism tactics introduced during Bush's two terms into a White House-centric strategy, the Obama administration also formalised and expanded the loose physical infrastructure which had sprung up to support the burgeoning drone programme under his predecessor, transforming a series of dusty outposts into what Ian Shaw (2013) has dubbed a 'Predator Empire'. Serving as a map of the frontiers of American influence, Obama established a network of bases from which the CIA, Air Force and Joint Special Operations Command operate their drones. This criss-crossing system of runways, hangars and relay stations provides the US with lily pads of coverage over the territory of anti-American forces and terrorist safe havens. This network ranges from airbases within the territory of NATO allies such as Turkey, to military compounds left in the wake of America's Afghan occupation, such as Jalalabad airbase. The Arabian Peninsula is patrolled from bases in the midst of the Saudi desert, the United Arab Emirates and Qatar, whilst American installations across North and East Africa ensure overwatch of hotspots such as Libya and Somalia. The Obama administration's efforts to keep the existence of many of these bases secret, for example pressuring the *New York Times* and *Washington Post* to withhold information (Sullivan 2013) which would expose the existence of the Saudi Arabian facility, coupled with the intensive diplomacy required to persuade compliant nations to host drones, reveal the substantial political and financial capital Obama invested in building and maintaining this infrastructure.

The most noteworthy expansion of the drone network under Obama came about through his authorisation to escalate America's unmanned war into the new fronts of Yemen and Somalia shortly after he assumed office in 2009. Not only did this significantly increase the range and tempo of drone strikes, with estimates ranging from 105 to 230 operations resulting in 473 to 1,227 fatalities across the two countries, but it also dramatically expanded the infrastructure supporting drone operations (BIJ 2015). Following Obama's order to expand, the DoD discovered a gap in its satellite coverage over the new frontiers of the Predator Empire, so placed what the commercial satellite provider Intelsat described as 'an urgent call from the Pentagon's Joint staff' (DoD 2009), requesting the redeployment of the company's Galaxy-26 satellite from its orbit over North America to the Indian Ocean. 'The repositioned Intelsat satellite', noted the company's press release (DoD 2009), would support 'launch and flight operations of Unmanned Aerial Vehicles (UAVs) ... in an area reaching from

Germany to Southeast Asia' by allowing US pilots using the relay station at Ramstein Air Base, Germany, to connect with the unmanned aircraft. The base had served as a temporary drone operations centre, made up of trailers and porta-potties and functioning without the German government's knowledge, since the last years of the Clinton administration (Whittle 2014: 155–156).

Obama's institutionalisation of drone use as a permanent fixture of US policy was confirmed in February 2010 by a United States Air Force (USAF) construction request to upgrade the Ramstein relay hub (Department of the Air Force 2010). The $10 million project was intended to 'satisfy the long-term SATCOM Relay requirements for Predator, Reaper and Global Hawk [drones], eliminating current temporary set-ups'. Time-lapsed satellite imagery of the American base from Google Earth reveals its extensive expansion under the Obama administration, transforming its drone support from temporary trailers into a relay station capable of supporting 'squadron level', 'multi-theatre-wide operations' across Europe, Africa and the Middle East. The extent to which the Obama administration embedded unmanned systems was further emphasised in February 2011, when the Air Force requested an additional $15 million for the construction of a second relay station, based in Sigonella, southern Italy, to carry 'half of the UAS [unmanned aerial system] transmissions', as well as acting as a 'back-up system to the Ramstein site' to avoid what the Air Force described as the risk of a 'single point of failure' (2011).

The popular perception of the drone is one of a tool which enables America to project lethal force while a handful of personnel remain safely encased in air-conditioned trailers in the US. In reality, the expanded drone network Obama leaves behind requires substantial manpower and the maintenance of a global presence. In order to maximise flight time and connectivity over specific countries, geographically dispersed local bases are required from which on-site pilots, unimpeded by the lag of long-distance remote control, execute take-offs and landings (Whittle 2014: 151–152). Obama's expansion of drone operations into Somalia and Yemen required the establishment of bases in the Seychelles and Ethiopia (Whitlock 2011) – a diplomatically sensitive process which took four years of high-level government negotiations (Barnes 2011; US State Department 2009). Additionally a large maintenance crew of 168 people – known as a 'launch recovery element' – is required to keep the fragile Predator drone armed, fuelled and in the skies (Zenko 2012). Furthermore, teams of informants must be recruited to operate on the ground, without whom drones are little more than 'flying high-resolution video cameras armed with missiles' (Woodward 2010: 6). To this end the CIA maintains Counterterrorist Pursuit Teams numbering in the thousands to keep its AfPak drone campaign operational. Additionally, as the need for the supplementary relay station suggests, the drone network is extremely data-heavy to run. Huge quantities of information flow on a daily basis through the National Security Agency (NSA) servers in Fort Meade, the CTC at Langley and even the White House's Situation Room, meaning in addition to pilots and sensor operators, the drones require thousands of surveillance analysts and targeters to process the intelligence which informs the strikes. After years of sustained warfare, this human element of the drone network is showing serious signs of mental stress and fatigue. The myth that the detachment from the warzone produces a 'Playstation mentality' among drone operators has been largely debunked, with research revealing that the distance does not remove those involved from the psychological consequences of engaging in warfare (Gettinger 2014). Despite being more widely known for his second term restraint in refusing to commit American infantry on the ground in Libya, Syria or Iraq, Obama still leaves a legacy of battle-hardened, and in some cases battle-damaged, personnel, with the real psychological cost on veterans and wider American society of America's remote war only likely to reveal fully itself in the looming future.

Although his administration bore the upfront costs of institutionalising the drone network, Obama's successors will need to consider the price of its maintenance. As the intricacies of America's secretive web of bases have become more exposed, so too have its political and economic costs. Public backlash caused the US to lose its bases in Iraq and Pakistan in 2011, and the political sensitivities of hosting drone operations were further highlighted when the German government faced legal action over its apparent complicity in the deaths of civilians allegedly killed in American drone strikes in Yemen (Connolly 2015). Growing instability across the Middle East has increased both American costs of keeping its facilities secure, and the threat to those allied governments which allow lethal strikes to be launched from their territory, with the likes of the Islamic State utilising their effective propaganda machine to call for 'lone wolf' attacks upon governments they deem guilty of collaboration (ISIS 2015). Furthermore, human rights campaigners and non-governmental organisations, opposed to what they see as unrestrained US imperialism and an excessive use of lethal force, demand an end to America's drone warfare, from the streets of Islamabad, Pakistan, to the gates of RAF Waddington, to the Senate floor in Washington DC itself (Masood and Mehsud 2013; Press Association 2013; Paul 2013). Although global opposition to drone strikes does not match the critical levels of anti-Americanism prompted by the Bush administration's programme of detention and 'Enhanced Interrogation', Obama's drone legacy raises the ire of many around the world, suggesting policy makers will need to consider the balance between the national security benefits drones provide, and the hostility towards the United States they provoke.

Legal architecture

It is a sign of the legal complexities which surround the deployment of unmanned lethal force that the bases which make up the drone network are home not just to pilots, technicians and targeters, but to lawyers too. At Al-Udeid Air Force Base in Qatar, for example, the Pentagon retains three Judge Advocate Generals (JAGs), ready to sign off on potential strikes at a moment's notice (Hastings 2012). These JAGs have an extensive body of presidential findings, legal memos and precedent to draw upon to justify the targeted killings the drones undertake. Like with the practice of targeted killing and the bases themselves, much of this legal architecture was inherited from the Bush administration, with legal scholar Robert Chesney observing the 'remarkable degree' of 'consistency of policy' regarding the application of lethal force between the two administrations (Chesney 2013: 163). Over his two terms, Obama refined rather than challenged the legal remit of drone warfare. At its core is the Authorization for Use of Military Force Against Terrorists (2001 (AUMF)), passed by Congress in the emotional days following 9/11 granting the president the right to use 'all necessary and appropriate force' against any individual, group or nation connected to al-Qaeda (United States Congress 2001). Whilst some supporters hoped Obama would repeal the expansive statute, his administration continued to utilise it, stretching the AUMF's boundaries by expanding America's drone campaign to engage affiliates which had no connection to al-Qaeda at the time of the bill's passing. Obama used the AUMF to justify strikes against the Yemenbased al-Qaeda in the Arabian Peninsula (AQAP), a group formed in 2009, almost a decade after 9/11, and the Islamic State in both Iraq and Syria, a rival offshoot rather than affiliate of the terror group. This exploitation of the terms of the authorisation relies upon the wilful cross-branch, cross-party ignorance of the majority of lawmakers, posing significant questions with regard to the drone campaign's actual constitutional authority (Fair 2014: 210). Despite its hardened physical infrastructure, the drone network's legal architecture is therefore built upon unstable legal foundations and the legislature's corroboration – something future presidents may not always be able to count upon.

One strike in particular, sanctioned under the AUMF and signed off personally by Obama, has had far-reaching consequences for the conduct of US counterterrorism, especially in view of the increased flow of foreign fighters to the so-called Islamic State – namely the killing of the American citizen Anwar al-Awlaki in September 2011. When it was revealed that Awlaki – a senior Yemen-based AQAP member known for delivering fiery anti-American sermons via the Internet – was on the Obama administration's kill list, the *New York Times* (Shane 2010) observed that 'it is extremely rare, if not unprecedented, for an American to be approved for targeted killing.' Following the successful strike, critics of Obama's drone war, such as the investigative journalist Glenn Greenwald (2011), decried the action as having denied the extremist cleric the due process he was entitled to under the Constitution. After two years of legal challenges demanding the administration publish documentary evidence pertaining to the judicial reasoning behind the strike, Obama's attorney general, Eric Holder, was forced to release the Justice Department memos used to justify the targeting of foreigners and Americans in drone strikes. In a letter written to Patrick J. Leahy, chairman of the US Senate Judiciary Committee, which accompanied the release of the memos, the attorney general answered the administration's critics, clarifying that the president had not just drawn upon the AUMF, but was acting on 'generations-old legal principles and Supreme Court decisions handed down during World War II' which established that 'United States citizenship alone does not make such individuals immune from being targeted' (Holder 2013).

The focus upon Awlaki's citizenship distracted attention from the more significant revelation exposed through the publication of the Justice Department memos. Setting out the administration's criteria to justify drone strikes, the memo (Holder 2010) revealed that if capture was 'not feasible' at the time, and available intelligence warned the suspect posed an 'imminent' and 'continued' threat to United States persons, then targeted killing 'would constitute the lawful conduct of war'. The Obama administration replaced Bush's large-scale extraordinary rendition and detention with a policy whereby suspicion of a threat, based upon evidence not necessarily rigorous enough to stand up in a US court of law, became enough to justify the suspect's execution. The addition of a 'continued' threat, along with the elastic quality of the measure 'imminent', revealed the perpetual nature of the drone warfare Obama had institutionalised. Since clarified in a 'US Policy Standards and Procedures' document (White House 2013), the Obama administration drew upon the policy of pre-emption formalised as part of the Bush Doctrine, but shifted its focus from nation states to individual terror suspects. This shift has granted the president an unprecedented degree of legal authority to order the killing of any terror suspect sheltering in any country deemed unwilling or unable to facilitate their capture. Such power, while used with a degree of moderation under Obama, opens up the risk of serious abuse and misuse in the future, likely testing Obama's successor's self-restraint, especially when combined with the confidentiality attached to drone use.

The culture of secrecy Obama has created around the application of lethal force via drones poses an interesting question for his successors. Should they continue to wage remote warfare from the shadows of classification, or seek to bring drone strikes into the light though greater transparency? Obama's association with covert action is a legacy many did not anticipate upon his entry to the White House. The day after his inauguration Obama promised to run the 'most transparent' administration in US history (White House 2009a), pledging an 'unprecedented level of openness'. Ultimately, however, the CIA's desire for maximal latitude in its AfPak drone campaign, combined with Brennan's push for the 'judicious use of drones anyplace where al-Qaeda and its associates travel', overcame Obama's instincts for accessibility (Sanger 2013: 256). 'The CIA gets what it wants', the president told his national security team in an early Situation Room meeting in 2009 (Klaidman 2012: 121). In the case of drones, this meant total secrecy. The Obama administration opted to withhold all official data from the US public and majority of Congress on national security grounds, thus significantly limiting oversight. Such secrecy prompted numerous legal and political challenges aimed at forcing America's lethal drone use into the open to enable greater political and public scrutiny.

Obama's national security team was able to control the flow of information relating to drone strikes by blurring the legal division between the civilian CIA, whose analysts and targeters provide the data which drive the strikes, and the military Air Force, whose pilots conduct the operations. By classing drone warfare as taking place under the auspices of the CIA, the administration utilised the Agency's authority to undertake covert action without needing to publicly acknowledge its foreign activities under Title 50 of the US Code (Cornell Law

School n.d.). This enabled the application of the sort of secrecy and deniability usually reserved for America's civilian spies to the Air Force's lethal actions, whilst limiting Congressional exposure to that of the highly classified briefings of the Intelligence Oversight committees. This manipulation of the system has led to calls for responsibility for drone strikes to be officially transferred from the CIA to the US military, where, due to the DoD's requirement to operate under Title 10 of the US code (Cornell Law School n.d.), the programme would be more transparent, thus limiting the president's freedom to unilaterally employ drone strikes with minimal oversight and scrutiny – an option future occupants of the Oval Office are likely to be reluctant to surrender.

Further to limiting Congressional oversight, Obama's use of drones has significantly eroded Congress's authority to dictate when the United States should engage in war or even undertake military actions which may lead to war. The War Powers Resolution, passed in November 1973 following the exposure of Nixon's decision to secretly bomb Cambodia, was intended to prevent future presidents from waging war unilaterally by requiring that the Commander in Chief notify Congress within forty-eight hours of ordering armed forces to undertake military action. The resolution also forbid those forces from remaining engaged for more than sixty days without Congressional authorisation or a formal declaration of war (United States Congress 1973). The remote nature of drone warfare enabled Obama to bypass this resolution when undertaking Operation Unified Protector, the 2011 NATO campaign to oust Muammar Gaddafi in the wake of an Arab Spring-inspired popular uprising in Libya. Obama received heavy criticism from political opponents for what one of his advisers described as 'leading from behind' (Lizza 2011) during the mission – a position detractors argued made the president look weak on the international stage. Yet through his actions Obama dramatically increased the Commander in Chief's power. His administration argued that the president did not require Congressional authorisation to continue the bombing campaign – which went well beyond the sixty-day threshold – because US operations did not 'involve the presence of US ground troops, US casualties or the serious threat thereof, or any significant chance of escalation into a conflict characterized by these factors' (White House 2011a). According to Obama's interpretation, the lack of direct physical threat through combat to American service personnel enabled the president to bypass the need for Congressional authority to wage war, an interpretation of the law which significantly lowers the threshold for future presidents to launch sustained military action using drones. Combined with the malleable use of the AUMF, Obama has overseen what Yale Professor of Law Bruce Ackerman (2011) has described as 'a decisive break in the American constitutional tradition'. As such, his successors inherit greater presidential authority to unilaterally bomb targets than any previous Commander in Chief.

The precedent set by the Obama administration over Libya poses fundamental questions about America's future conduct of warfare. Whilst the use of lethal unmanned systems is currently limited to human-piloted drones, the United States was the first country in the world to publish an official policy statement on autonomous weapons. On 21 November 2012, the DoD released Directive

3000.09, setting out guidelines for autonomy in weapons systems. The document revealed a level of sensitivity towards the thorniest issue of lethal robotics – the possibility of autonomous machines targeting humans – by clarifying that any autonomous (AWS) or semi-autonomous system (SAWS) 'shall be designed to allow commanders and operators to exercise appropriate levels of human judgement over the use of force' (DoD 2012: 2). In other words, humans should remain in the loop, dictating when robots can employ lethal force – a minimal requirement demanded by the likes of Human Rights Watch to satisfy the core principles of distinction and proportionality under international humanitarian law (Human Rights Watch 2012). But such criteria would not require the human to be present where the weapon system was functioning, introducing the very real prospect of unmanned ground units to accompany airborne drones in the near future. Under the precedent set by Obama, future presidents would not need Congress's permission to deploy remotely controlled ground units, as any conflict involving AWS or SAWS would technically not involve the presence of US ground troops or the direct risk of American casualties.

Critically, the Obama administration's efforts over the past two terms to convince American citizens that drones are legal, ethical and wise has won the programme significant public support from a nation tired of seeing its citizens killed or maimed on foreign battlefields, but equally unwilling to adopt a non-interventionist foreign policy. Reflecting this attitude, a Pew Research Center (2011) poll revealed that 68 per cent of the public approved of drone strikes. Even more emphatically, a *Washington Post*/ABC News poll (2012) the following year found 83 per cent of Americans approved of drone strikes against suspected terrorists overseas, and similarly, a March 2013 poll found 65 per cent of Americans supported lethal drones (Brown and Newport 2013). Although increased debate around the controversies of drone use appears to have reduced support, with a July 2014 poll (Fuller 2014) showing support having dropped to 52 per cent, the majority of Americans' still favour the use of drones to unleash lethal force against suspected terrorists on foreign soil. Americans comfort with remote warfare, their current aversion to sending US troops to fight abroad, and the growing evidence of the limitations of the United States' ability to shape events on the ground with airstrikes alone, combine to create a unique demand for robot ground forces. As future leaders build upon the foundations set by Obama, it is likely only a matter of time before an American president has the capability to unilaterally deploy mechanical boots on the ground to complement the remote aerial presence, a military revolution 2009's Nobel Peace Prize-winning president will have played a significant role in ushering in.

Conclusion

The later decades of the Cold War saw both Congress and the Executive itself try to limit the power of the president, which had swelled over the course of the decades-long conflict. Ford's assassination ban and Congress's War Powers Act were both introduced to curtail the president's ability to act unilaterally in a clandestine manner, for the sake of both the country and future occupants of the Oval Office. The Church Committee's 1975–76 investigation into the government's use, or abuse, of the CIA pointed out that, for all the Agency's questionable activities during its early decades, it was always the White House that encouraged reckless operations such as assassination attempts against foreign leaders. The CIA seemed to offer a quick fix to complex policy problems, wrapped in a clandestine cloak of deniability, a seductive combination. As Senator Church wrote in his committee's final report (United States Senate 1976: 564), 'once the capability for covert activity is established, the pressures brought to bear on the President to use it are immense'.

The first decades of the twenty-first century have seen the limits placed upon the Commander in Chief bypassed or overridden completely for the sake of expediency in America's War on Terror, with the perpetual nature of the fight once more engorging Executive power. Upon entering the Oval Office, Obama inherited a remote targeted killing programme in its embryonic stage. He leaves his successor a formalised and embedded global drone network. Classified and protected by a complex legal architecture, and pursuing targets drawn from an immense digital database, pilots send commands along fibre optic cables from their air base in Nevada to relay stations across Western Europe, which broadcast them to specifically tasked orbiting satellites and onto patrolling drones below, operating out of a network of bases ranging across Asia, Africa and the Middle East. Data flows back from the drones simultaneously to the NSA, CTC and the Situation Room of the White House itself, placing the next president at the heart of the most complex global killing machine ever constructed.

How this legacy will come to be seen – as technological utopianism, balancing America's national security interests with its liberal values, removing American soldiers from harm's way and sparing civilians through ever greater precision, or as part of a dystopian normalisation of expansive presidential authority, global targeted killings and omnipotent American power – will rest heavily upon how Obama's successors decide to utilise the network he leaves them. As such, it is impossible to predict what perspective future historians will bring to Obama's actions for, as Wood rightly warned (*New York* 2015), we live in the fog of the present. What is already clear, however, is that Obama's drone legacy reflects a new American approach to war, where conflict is not distinguished by battlefield wins and losses, where territorial control and nation building come second after the relentless hunting and killing of suspected militants, and where the Commander in Chief is also the assassin in chief, eliminating America's enemies one by one with specifically targeted strikes.

References

Ackerman, B. (2011) 'Obama's Betrayal of the Constitution', *New York Times*, 11 September. Available online at www.nytimes.com/2014/09/12/opinion/obamas-betrayal-of-the-constitution.html (accessed 28 May 2015).

Al-Libi, A. (2009) *Guide to the Law Regarding Muslim Spies*, June. Available online from Middle East Research Institute, *Jihad and Terrorism Threat Monitor*, Report No. 2438, 9

July. Available online at www.memrijttm.org/content/en/report.htm?report=3403& param=GJN (accessed 10 June 2014).

Alexander, D. (2012) 'US Has Decimated al Qaeda Chiefs but Must Persist in Fight: Panetta', Reuters, 20 November. Available online at www.reuters.com/article/2012/11/21/ us-usa-qaeda-panetta-idUSBRE8AK03R20121121 (accessed 4 December 2014).

Ball, J. (2013) 'NSA Stores Metadata of Millions of Web Users for up to a Year, Secret Files Show', *Guardian*, 30 September. Available online at www.theguardian.com/ world/2013/sep/30/nsa-americans-metadata-year-documents (accessed 7 July 2015).

Barnes, J.E. (2011) 'US Expands Drone Flights to Take Aim at East Africa', *Wall Street Journal*, 21 September. Available online at www.wsj.com/news/articles/SB10001424053 111904106704576583012923076634?mg=reno64-wsj&url=http%3A%2F%2Fonline. wsj.com%2Farticle%2FSB10001424053111904106704576583012923076634.html (accessed 8 June 2015).

Becker, J. and Shane, S. (2012) 'Secret "Kill-List" Proves a Test of Obama's Principles and Will', *New York Times*, 29 May. Available online at www.nytimes.com/2012/05/29/ world/obamas-leadership-in-war-on-al-qaeda.html (accessed 8 June 2015).

Bentley, M. (2014) 'Continuity We Can Believe in: Escaping the War on Terror', in Bentley M. and Holland J. (2014), *Obama's Foreign Policy: Ending the War on Terror*. Abingdon: Routledge.

Brown, A. and Newport, F. (2013) 'In US, 65% Support Drone Attacks on Terrorists Abroad', Gallup, 25 March www.gallup.com/poll/161474/support-drone-attacks-terrorists-abroad.aspx (accessed 8 June 2015).

Bureau of Investigative Journalism (BIJ) (2015) 'Drone Wars'. Available online at www. thebureauinvestigates.com/category/projects/drones/drones-graphs/ (accessed 7 July 2015).

Chesney, R.M. (2013) 'Beyond the Battlefield, Beyond al-Qaeda: The Destabilizing Legal Architecture of Counterterrorism', *Michigan Law Review*, 112(163): 163–224.

Church Committee Final Report (1975). Available online at US Senate Select Committee on Intelligence, www.intelligence.senate.gov/sites/default/files/94755_I.pdf (accessed 5 June 2015).

CIA (2009) 'Best Practices in Counterinsurgency: Making High-Value Targeting Operations an Effective Counterinsurgency Tool', 7 July. Available online at https://wikileaks.org/ cia-hvt-counterinsurgency/WikiLeaks_Secret_CIA_review_of_HVT_Operations.pdf (accessed 7 July 2015).

Clarke, R. (2000) *Strategy for Eliminating the Threat from the Jihadist Networks of al-Qida*. Available online at www2.gwu.edu/~nsarchiv/NSAEBB/NSAEBB147/clarke%20 attachment.pdf (accessed 20 May 2015).

Clarridge, D with Diehl, D. (1997) *A Spy for All Seasons: My Life in the CIA*. New York: Scibner.

Coll, S. (2005) *Ghost Wars: The Secret History of the CIA, Afghanistan and Bin Laden*. New York: Penguin.

Connolly, K. (2015) 'Court Dismisses Claim of German Complicity in Yemeni Drone Killing', *Guardian*, 27 May. Available online at www.theguardian.com/world/2015/ may/27/court-dismisses-yemeni-claim-german-complicity-drone-killings (accessed 2 June 2015).

Cornell Law School (n.d.) US Code, 'Title 50, 3093, Presidential Approval and Reporting of Covert Actions.' Available online at Cornell Law School, www.law.cornell.edu/ uscode/text/50/3093 (accessed 12 February 2015).

Cronin, A. (2013) 'The "War on Terrorism": What Does it Mean to Win?', *Journal of Strategic Studies* 37(2): 174–197.

Department of the Air Force (2010) 'FY 2011 Military Construction Project Data: Ramstein Air Base, Germany', February. Available online at www.ndr.de/geheimer_krieg/satcom101.pdf%20 (accessed 27 May 2015).

Department of the Air Force (2011) 'Military Construction Program Fiscal Year 2012 Budget Estimates', February. Available online at Air Force Financial Management & Comptroller, www.saffm.hq.af.mil/shared/media/document/AFD-110210–037 (accessed 27 May 2015).

Department of Defense (DoD) (2006) '"Reaper" Moniker Given to MQ-9 Unmanned Aerial Vehicle', 14 September. Available online at www.defense.gov/transformation/articles/2006–09/ta091406a.html (accessed 29 May 2015).

Department of Defense (DoD) (2009) 'Intelsat Repositions Satellite to Serve Military Units in Asia & Mideast', 24 March. Available online at www.intelsat.com/news/intelsat-repositions-satellite-to-serve-military-units-in-asia-mideast/ (accessed 26 May 2015).

Department of Defense (DoD) (2012) 'Autonomy in Weapon Systems Directive 3000.09', 21 November. Available online from Defense Technical Information Center, www.dtic.mil/whs/directives/corres/pdf/300009p.pdf (accessed 28 May 2015).

Department of Defense (DoD) (2015) 'Operation Inherit Resolve: Targeted Operations Against ISIL Terrorists.' Available online at www.defense.gov/home/features/2014/0814_iraq/ (accessed 10 June 2015).

DeYoung, K. (2014) 'A CIA Veteran Transforms US Counterterrorism Policy', *Washington Post*, 29 May. Available online at www.washingtonpost.com/world/national-security/cia-veteran-john-brennan-has-transformed-us-counterterrorism-policy/2012/10/24/318b8eec-1c7c-11e2-ad90-ba5920e56eb3_story.html (accessed 29 May 2015).

Fair, C.C. (2014) 'Drones, Spies, Terrorists, and Second-Class Citizenship in Pakistan', *Small Wars and Insurgencies* 25(1): 205–235.

Fuller, J. (2014) 'Americans Are Fine with Drone Strikes. The Rest of the World? Not so Much', *Washington Post*, 15 July. Available online at www.washingtonpost.com/blogs/the-fix/wp/2014/07/15/americans-are-fine-with-drone-strikes-everyone-else-in-the-world-not-so-much/ (accessed 3 June 2015).

Gettinger, D. (2014) 'Burdens of War: PTSD and Drone Crews', 21 April. Available online at Bard Drone Center, http://dronecenter.bard.edu/burdens-war-crews-drone-aircraft/ (accessed 2 June 2015).

Greenwald, G. (2011) 'The Due-Process-Free Assassination of US Citizens Is Now a Reality', *Salon*, 30 September. Available online at www.salon.com/2011/09/30/awlaki_6/ (accessed 28 May 2015).

Hastings, M. (2012) 'The Rise of the Killer Drones: How America Goes to War in Secret', *Rolling Stone*, 16 April. Available online at www.rollingstone.com/politics/news/the-rise-of-the-killer-drones-how-america-goes-to-war-in-secret-20120416?page=2 (accessed 3 June 2015).

Holder, E. (2010) 'Memorandum of the Attorney General Re: Applicability of Federal Criminal Laws and the Constitution to Contemplated Lethal Operations Against Shaykh Anwar al-Aulaqi', 16 July. Available online at US Department of Justice www.nytimes.com/interactive/2014/06/23/us/23awlaki-memo.html (accessed 28 May 2015).

Holder, E. (2013) 'Letter to Patrick J. Leahy, Chairman US Senate Judiciary Committee', 22 May. Available online at US Department of Justice, www.justice.gov/slideshow/AG-letter-5–22–13.pdf (accessed 28 May 2015).

Hoover, H. and Gibson, H (1943) *The Problems of Lasting Peace.* New York: Doubleday, Doran.

Human Rights Watch (2012) *Losing Humanity: The Case Against Killer Robots*, 19 November. Available online at www.hrw.org/reports/2012/11/19/losing-humanity-0 (accessed 28 May 2015).

ISIS (2015) 'Jordanian Pilot Kaseasbeh Burned Alive by Islamic State', 4 February. Available online at http://leaksource.info/2015/02/04/jordanian-pilot-kaseasbeh-burned-alive-by-islamic-state-jordan-executes-is-requested-prisoner-rishawi-in-response/ (accessed 11 June 2015).

Johnson, G.D. (2015) 'The Untouchable John Brennan', *Buzzfeed*, 24 April. Available online at www.buzzfeed.com/gregorydjohnsen/how-cia-director-john-brennan-became-americas-spy-and-obamas?utm_source=Sailthru&utm_medium=email&utm_term=%2ASituation%20Report&utm_campaign=2014_Situation%20Report#.se9YwE8L9 (accessed 10 May 2015).

Jordan, J. (2014) 'Attacking the Leader, Missing the Mark: Why Terrorist Groups Survive Decapitation Strikes', *International Security* 38(4), 7–38.

Klaidman, D. (2012) *Kill or Capture: The War on Terror and the Soul of the Obama Presidency*. New York: Houghton Mifflin Harcourt.

Lizza, R. (2011) 'The Consequentialist: How the Arab Spring remade Obama's Foreign Policy', *New Yorker*, 2 May. Available online at www.newyorker.com/magazine/2011/05/02/the-consequentialist (accessed 28 May 2015).

Masood, S. and Mehsud, I.T. (2013) 'Thousands in Pakistan Protest American Drone Strikes', *New York Times*, 23 November. Available online at www.nytimes.com/2013/11/24/world/asia/in-pakistan-rally-protests-drone-strikes.html (accessed 2 June 2015).

Maxwell, M. (2012) 'Rebutting the Civilian Presumption: Playing Whack-A-Mole Without a Mallet', in Finkelstein C., Ohlin, J.D. and Altman, A. (eds), *Targeted Killings: Law and Morality in an Asymmetrical World*. Oxford: Oxford University Press.

Mazzetti, M. (2014) *The Way of the Knife: The CIA, a Secret Army, and a War at the Ends of the Earth*. New York: Penguin.

McCoy, A. (2015) '53 Historians Weigh In on Barak Obama's Legacy', *New York*, 11 January. Available online at http://nymag.com/news/politics/obama-history-project/alfred-mccoy/ (accessed 28 April 2015).

Ministry of Foreign Affairs (2014) 'Security and Defense Agreement', 30 September. Available online at Ministry of Foreign Affairs, Islamic Republic of Afghanistan, http://mfa.gov.af/en/news/text-of-security-and-defense-cooperation-agreement-between-the-islamic-republic-of-afghanistan-and-the-united-states-of-America (accessed 7 December 2014).

National Security Council (1984) 'National Security Decision Directive 138', 3 April. Available online at Reagan Presidential Archive, www.reagan.utexas.edu/archives/reference/Scanned%20NSDDS/NSDD138.pdf (accessed 25 January 2015).

National Security Council (1986) 'National Security Decision Directive 207', 20 January. Available online at National Security Archive, www.gwu.edu/~nsarchiv/NSAEBB/NSAEBB55/nsdd207.pdf (accessed 28 May 2015).

New York (2015) '53 Historians Weigh In on Barak Obama's Legacy', *New York*, 11 January. Available online at http://nymag.com/daily/intelligencer/2015/01/53-historians-on-obamas-legacy.html (accessed 28 April 2015).

Obama, B. (2009) 'Remarks by the President at the Acceptance of the Nobel Peace Prize', 10 December. Available online at www.whitehouse.gov/the-press-office/remarks-president-acceptance-nobel-peace-prize (accessed 8 June 2015).

Obama, B. (2013) 'Remarks by the President at the National Defense University', May 2013. Available online at www.whitehouse.gov/the-press-office/2013/05/23/remarks-president-national-defense-university (accessed 8 June 2015).

Paul, R. (2013) Senate Filibuster, 6 March. Available online at www.c-span.org/video/?c4373357/senator-rand-paul-filibuster (accessed 2 June 2015).

Cherlin, R. (2013) 'Obama's Drone-Master', *GQ*, 17 June. Available online at www.gq.com/news-politics/big-issues/201306/john-brennan-cia-director-interview-drone-program (accessed 29 May 2015).

Pew Research Center (2011) 'War and Sacrifice in the Post-9/11 Era', 5 October. Available online at www.pewsocialtrends.org/2011/10/05/war-and-sacrifice-in-the-post-911-era/ (accessed 5 June 2015).

Porter P. (2015) *The Global Village Myth: Distance, War, and the Limits of Power.* London: Hurst.

Press Association (2013) 'Hundreds of Anti-drone Protesters March against UK Flight-control Centre', 27 April. Available online at www.theguardian.com/world/2013/apr/27/anti-drone-protestors-march-uk (accessed 2 June 2015).

Sanger, D.E. (2013) *Confront and Conceal: Obama's Secret Wars and Surprising Use of American Power.* New York: Random House.

Scahill, J. (2015) 'Germany is the Tell-tale Heart of America's Drone War', *The Intercept*, 17 April. Available online at https://firstlook.org/theintercept/2015/04/17/ramstein/ (accessed 2 May 2015).

Scheuer, M. (2007) *Imperial Hubris: Why the West is Losing the War on Terror.* Washington DC: Potomac Books.

Scola, N. (2013) 'Obama, the "Big Data" President', *Washington Post*, 14 June. www.washingtonpost.com/opinions/obama-the-big-data-president/2013/06/14/1d71fe2e-d391-11e2-b05f-3ea3f0e7bb5a_story.html (accessed 4 June 2015).

Shane, S. (2010) 'US Approves Targeted Killing of American Cleric', *New York Times*, 6 April. Available online at www.nytimes.com/2010/04/07/world/middleeast/07yemen.html?hp (accessed 28 May 2015).

Shaw, Ian G.R. (2013) 'Predator Empire: The Geopolitics of US Drone Warfare', *Geopolitics*, 18(3): 536–559.

Spiegel Staff (2015) 'A War Waged from German Soil: US Ramstein Base Key in Drone Attacks', *Spiegel*, 22 April. Available online at www.spiegel.de/international/germany/ramstein-base-in-germany-a-key-center-in-us-drone-war-a-1029279.html (accessed 8 June 2015).

Sullivan, M. (2013) 'The Times Was Right to Report – at Last – on a Secret Drone Base', *New York Times*, 6 February. Available online at http://publiceditor.blogs.nytimes.com/2013/02/06/the-times-was-right-to-report-at-last-on-a-secret-drone-base/?_r=0 (accessed 2 June 2015).

United States Congress (1973) 'War Powers Resolution', 7 November. Available online at Government Accountability Office, https://bulk.resource.org/gao.gov/93–148/00005E54.pdf (accessed 8 June 2015).

United States Congress (2001) 'Authorization for Use of Military Force Against Terrorists [AUMF]', 18 September. Available online at Government Printing Office, http://frwebgate.access.gpo.gov/cgi-bin/getdoc.cgi?dbname=107_cong_public_laws&docid=f:publ040.107 (accessed 8 June 2015).

United States Senate (1976) 'Final Report of the Select Committee to Study Governmental Operations with Respect to Intelligence Activities', 26 April. Available online US Senate Select Committee on Intelligence, www.intelligence.senate.gov/sites/default/files/94755_I.pdf (accessed 7 July 2015).

United States State Department (2009) Cable, Embassy Port Louis, 'Seychelles: Ocean Look Tops Agenda During Presidential Meeting', 22 September. Available online at https://cablegatesearch.wikileaks.org/cable.php?id=09PORTLOUIS292 (accessed 7 July 2015).

Washington Post/ABC News Poll (2012) 4 February. Available online at www.washingtonpost.com/wp-srv/politics/polls/postabcpoll_020412.html (accessed 2 June 2015).

White House (2009a) 'Open Government Initiative.' Available online at www.whitehouse.gov/open (accessed 27 May 2015).

White House (2009b) 'Remarks by the President at Cairo University', 4 June. Available online at www.whitehouse.gov/the-press-office/remarks-president-cairo-university-6-04-09 (accessed 3 June 2015).

White House (2011a) 'United States Activities in Libya', 15 June. Available online at Federation of American Scientists, http://fas.org/man/eprint/wh-libya.pdf (accessed 28 May, 2015).

White House (2011b) *United States National Strategy for Counterterrorism*, June. Available online at White House, www.whitehouse.gov/sites/default/files/counterterrorism_strategy.pdf (accessed 29 May 2015).

White House (2011c) 'Quarterly Report on Afghanistan and Pakistan', September. Available online at www.scribd.com/doc/66998459/WH-Report-on-Afghanistan-and-Pakistan-September-2011 (accessed 17 December 2014).

White House (2013) 'US Policy Standards and Procedures', 23 May. Available online at www.whitehouse.gov/sites/default/files/uploads/2013.05.23_fact_sheet_on_ppg.pdf (accessed 3 June 2015).

Whitlock, C. (2011) 'US Drone Base in Ethiopia is Operational', *Washington Post*, 27 October. Available online at www.washingtonpost.com/world/national-security/us-drone-base-in-ethiopia-is-operational/2011/10/27/gIQAznKwMM_print.html (accessed 8 June 2015).

Whittle, R. (2014) *Predator: The Secret Origins of the Drone Revolution*. New York: Henry Holt.

Woods, C. (2015) Quoted in *Drone* (documentary directed by Tonje Hessen Schei). Spectrum [on DVD].

Woodward, B. (2010) *Obama's Wars*. New York: Simon & Schuster.

Woodward, B. (2003) *Bush at War*. New York: Pocket Books.

Zenko, M. (2012) 'Ten Things You Didn't Know About Drones', *Foreign Policy*, 27 February. Available online at http://foreignpolicy.com/2012/02/27/10-things-you-didnt-know-about-drones/ (accessed 2 June 2015).

Zenko, M. and Welch, E. (2012) 'Where the Drones Are', *Foreign Policy*, 29 May. Available online at http://foreignpolicy.com/2012/05/29/where-the-drones-are/ (accessed 2 June 2015).

10 Hard choices in democracy promotion

Obama and Egypt

Nicolas Bouchet

The beliefs and personality of presidents are central to how US democracy promotion plays out. Given how concentrated in the White House the foreign policy process has been under Barack Obama (Rothkopf, 2014), and the fact that most of his administration's democracy advocates have been on the White House staff rather than in the State Department and agencies, his character and views may matter even more than did those of his predecessors. There has been a growing consensus as Obama's presidency has unfolded that he is a realist (Kaplan, 2014; Zakaria, 2009). This is reinforced by his relativist views on American exceptionalism, which make him less given than most US political leaders to wrap his talk of democracy in the banner of America's special or even divine mission as champion of freedom. The realist portrait can be overdone, however. While Obama's analysis of international issues and of what the United States can and cannot do in the world is usually realist, he also expresses very liberal understandings and prescriptions, including concerning the importance of democracy and human rights (Betts, 2015; Bouchet, 2013; Dueck, 2011; Rose, 2015; Smith, 2013). In fact, he has shown a mix of realism and liberalism in his worldview – and this is how he sees himself (Lizza, 2011; Mann 2012) – while in his actions (and inaction) he has been above all pragmatic and cautious. This makes him more a temperamentally realistic president than a purely intellectually realist one. There does appear, though, to have been a shift to greater realism, and maybe pessimism, in Obama's views with regard to democracy promotion, at least in the Middle East and North Africa (MENA) as result of the outcomes of the Arab Spring and the conflicts that have erupted in the region since (Traub, 2013).

Obama's personality and mix of realism and liberalism have set the broad lines within which his administration's democracy promotion has developed. This has been shaped by his understanding of the limits of US power and agency. Hence his pursuit of a grand strategy of retrenchment through a strong prioritization of issues, regions and countries, and a willingness to cut losses (Sestanovich, 2014). Obama has also deployed considerable public frankness over why America puts other interests above democracy. What is more, over the course of his presidency he and his aides have shifted from the boilerplate rhetoric of a false choice between interests and values to one that stresses having to make hard or imperfect choices, especially with regard to the MENA in the context of the growing prioritization of the security agenda that the administration has framed as 'countering violent extremism' (CVE). Obama's traits and mindset have also encouraged the emergence of a more long-term, developmental view of democracy promotion. While these moves have been welcomed as correctives to some of the shortcomings of US democracy promotion, carried too far they could also justify a retreat into passivity – especially when coupled with the president's repeated assertion about the inevitability of democracy. Already they have made it too easy for the Obama administration to fall back on the traditional choice of security over democracy and of tolerance of autocrats in return for security cooperation, particularly in the MENA.

Each president's democracy promotion comes to be defined by one emblematic case, usually that of a country that is strategically important in general or at a particular juncture. For Ronald Reagan, this case was Poland, for Bill Clinton, Russia, and for George W. Bush, Iraq. Egypt is Obama's emblematic case. Democracy promotion towards any one country also plays out in different contexts that are shaped by how that country combines different characteristics: whether it is strategically important, whether it is a US ally, its domestic and/or international security situation, its degree (e.g. full autocracy, authoritarian, hybrid regime) and type (e.g. personalistic, military, party, monarchic, radical or conservative, theocratic) of 'non-democracy', and whether it is experiencing internal democratization or counter-democratization pressures. The experience of Obama's administration is unusual for having been faced in Egypt with effectively five contexts. They are:

- in relations with a long-entrenched allied autocratic regime under President Hosni Mubarak (2009–10);
- in reaction to a 'pro-democracy' crisis during the revolution (early 2011);
- in supporting an attempted transition under the military and then President Mohammed Morsi (early 2011 to mid-2013);
- in reacting to an 'anti-democracy' crisis around the coup against Morsi (mid-2013); and
- in relations with an autocratic ally under Abdul Fatah al-Sisi following a transition breakdown (mid-2013 to date).

Thus Egypt offers a multiple case study of how Obama has confronted some fundamental issues in democracy promotion and of the degree of continuity and change in democracy promotion under him, not just in relation to George W. Bush, but also in a longer historical perspective. It also raises important questions regarding the possible future of US democracy promotion under Obama's successors.

The long game and hard choices

With regard to democracy promotion, some key themes stand out as resulting from Obama's mindset and temperament, and these have been clearly in evidence in policy towards the MENA in general and Egypt in particular. Most important is the recognition and acceptance of the limits of US agency in the political development of other countries. There has been a consistent stress in the administration's democracy promotion talk and practice on the impossibility of the external imposition of norms and institutions. While this has long been part of US rhetoric on the subject, under Obama it has been given more than lip service, which has led critics to accuse him of timidity in advocating democratic values. Democracy promotion has also been shaped by Obama's overall retrenchment strategy and his wish to avoid too costly commitments abroad, especially in the MENA, reinforced by the decision to undertake a strategic rebalancing to Asia. The ebb and flow of Obama's democracy and Egypt policies must therefore be seen not just in the context of their respective salience in MENA policy, but also in the context of the relative importance of the region among Obama's wider foreign policy concerns. Just as retrenchment has led to a strong attempt at prioritization among regions, issues and countries in foreign policy, so within democracy promotion, which has been demoted in places like Egypt when it began to look like an investment with limited near-term returns. Prioritization was also evident in Obama's second-term with the tighter focus in MENA policy on Iran, Syria, Islamic State and counterterrorism, and the relegation of countries like Egypt and issues like democracy to the second rank. From the start, the Obama administration showed willingness to assess situations realistically and to change policy tack where it saw that its wishes regarding democracy were not so easily realizable, as well as to admit frankly and publicly that the United States' actions sometimes would not accord with its proclaimed ideals. This was a positive development in view of the sometimes utopian language of previous administrations, but in Obama's second term explanations as to why the United States occasionally (usually, critics say) relegates its promotion of democracy in the interest of security in the MENA began to sound more like a regurgitation of the old 'friendly tyrants' argument than refreshing candour.

One consequence of Obama's pragmatism has been talk that US democracy promotion should be more opportunistic and select targets where results can be achieved as and when they present themselves. This analysis is correct inasmuch as it matches the reality of the new global environment that is far less hospitable for democracy promotion than in the previous two decades, but pragmatic opportunism could easily turn into reactivity, passivity or even inactivity, providing excuses to wait for something to happen in countries rather than trying to support democratization processes and actors in very poor situations. Another consequence has been that taking a long-term view – the 'long game' – is a growing central feature of the administration's democracy promotion discourse, focusing on more organic, gradual and developmental change, as well as making policy less interventionist and respectful of other countries' paths and choices. This move has taken place alongside the consolidation of a narrative in relation to the MENA that transitions were hijacked by extremists – and that elected governments also have to govern justly to be considered democratic – but that, even though the situation in most countries looks bad now, democracy will be achieved in the long term. As with the desire for more opportunism, the combination of these two developments carries the risk that the long game can morph into a wait-and-see approach in which the United States need not do much at any given moment to move things along towards democracy if it is eventually inevitable.

Under Obama, the United States has increasingly recognized the threat that the 'closing space' – i.e. systematic attempts by governments to curtail the freedom of civil society and to cut it off from outside sources of support – poses to democracy and democracy promotion. His administration has gradually placed more emphasis on combating this trend and created funds and institutional structures to that end. As well as reacting to a global anti-democratic phenomenon that predates the Obama presidency, this focus on defending civil society actors and reaffirming their right to receive transnational support is a logical component of the view of democratization as an organic process that must be 'owned' locally, with external actors in a background supportive role. The Obama administration's pushback against the closing space has also displayed the hallmarks of its overall inclination to seek multilateral solutions to international problems. This can be seen, for example, in the creation of the multi-donor Lifeline Embattled CSO Assistance Fund and the multi-stakeholder Open Government Partnership, as well as the renewed US engagement with the Community of Democracies. While, compared to his immediate predecessors, Obama may not leave behind an expanded bureaucratic base for democracy promotion within the US government (in part because this cannot be expanded endlessly and over time there is less scope to do so), his presidency has seen real institutional progress in the multilateralization of this policy field.

In Obama's first term, he and his aides regularly indulged in the American traditional rhetoric proclaiming the pursuit of democratic ideals or other goals in foreign policy to be a false choice, while at the same time, as noted above, being frank about sometimes having to choose other interests over democracy. This was more an evolution from rather than a sharp break from overoptimistic pronouncements after the end of the Cold War about the ease of jointly promoting democracy and security and economic interests. In Obama's second term, though, there has been an incipient shift to a rhetoric of being faced with hard or imperfect choices, not just in the traditional security–democracy dilemma but also as part of the increasingly dominant CVE agenda, which is mostly directed at the MENA. The difference in emphasis may be slight but it is significant. Obama and others argue that democracy and human rights are a necessary part of the policy response to violent extremism, which is in continuation of the earlier inclusion of democratization as a remedy for the causes of terrorism, but they do so while also stressing more that the United States finds itself forced to make imperfect choices. So far the administration's choices relating to CVE across the region have usually fallen on the security side rather than the democracy side. Looking at the case of Egypt in detail makes this very clear.

From Mubarak to Morsi to Sisi

Democracy promotion has been on the US foreign policy agenda to some degree in most regions of the world since the 1980s. The exception for a long time was the MENA, where security interests led successive administrations to rule out upsetting the regional order by addressing – beyond token rhetoric – popular dissatisfaction with deeply autocratic regimes. Not only did the United States abstain from backing democratic change, it actively supported the status quo since most rulers followed its foreign policy line whereas alternative leaders more responsive to domestic public opinion would likely not (Lynch, 2013b). That was long true of Egypt where various US security interests required autocracy (Brownlee, 2012). That is not to say that democracy was entirely absent from the US policy debate. Some argued that ignoring demands for political change would lead to instability that would threaten US interests. However, this only led to minimal attempts at nudging allies towards superficial reforms and to essentially unthreatening assistance to civil society and political parties (Bouchet, 2015; Hamid, 2011; Lynch, 2013b). The George W. Bush presidency saw the first real break with the MENA exception in democracy promotion. For a couple of years in the mid-2000s there were genuine diplomatic efforts to encourage reform in Egypt as well as increased support for more politically substantive civil society. But Bush was ultimately unwilling to challenge Mubarak as repression was stepped up again, just as he was unwilling to recognize the electoral mandate of Islamists in the Palestinian territories. After 2006, funding of democracy assistance continued but not diplomatic pressure. Washington reverted to the non-confrontational approach of encouraging economic reforms that might in the long term create the preconditions for democratic progress (Hassan, 2012).

In Obama's first year, there was a deliberate downplaying of democracy in official rhetoric and to some extent in practice, intended to move away from Bush's controversial legacy on this issue. Given Bush's focus on the region, this was more striking in relation to the MENA. Yet Obama's initial policy toward Egypt was in fact in continuity with Bush's much toned-down one of 2006–8. Furthermore, this continuity between them was itself in continuity with US policy of decades. Obama tried to restore relations with Mubarak, which had been hurt by Bush's brief democracy promotion, by downgrading the issue. Attention was refocused on partnership over the Palestinian–Israeli peace process and counterterrorism. Democracy assistance was revised, with the US Agency for International Development reverting to funding only government-registered NGOs, which it had stopped doing in 2002. With Egyptian politics dominated by whether Mubarak would stand again in 2011 or arrange succession by his son, the administration appeared to take a long view as to when the moment might turn propitious for engaging in support of reforms. Nonetheless, there was a gradual shift to democracy. Obama included it as a central element of engagement with the Arab world in his 2009 Cairo speech. The speech did not directly challenge the region's autocrats, but it was the latest example of trying to nudge them into reforming. At the same time, there was not much of an effort to support Egypt's civil society and only limited criticism of Mubarak for muzzling it or for rigging the 2010 elections (Bouchet, 2011). One observer described the latter as perhaps the most rigged in the country's history (Hamid, 2011). Critics said that there had been no follow-up to the speech and that non-confrontational engagement with the regime was not achieving anything. In the second half of 2010 the administration undertook a review of MENA policy and of how much to push for political reforms. This reportedly concluded that regimes would respond to popular pressure for change with repression and that transitions were unlikely under the current generation of rulers (Sanger, 2012: 282–3). Yet, by questioning long-held assumptions, the review seems to have spurred a small increase in the democracy rhetoric aimed at Mubarak in late 2010. This, and perhaps also a sense that private advice to rulers was being ignored, led Secretary of State Hillary Clinton to address more directly and openly the need for reform in the Arab world in a speech in Qatar, days before the Egyptian revolution began (Clinton, 2011).

The Egyptian revolution of 2011 was Obama's greatest democracy crisis management test. His handling of it was above all pragmatic, trying to preserve US interests vested in the relationship with Mubarak and the military while attempting to push him into an 'orderly transition' once it became clear he could not survive (Bouchet, 2011). Obama's initial hesitancy may also have been influenced by the repression of the 2009 protests in Iran. The administration also used its long-standing military-to-military ties to discourage the use of force against protesters. Confronted with a democracy crisis in a strategically important country, Obama gave up the traditional US preference for nudging an ally to reform and also the second-best option of a regime-managed transition (Bouchet, 2013). The latter was in line with the equally traditional view that gradual democratization is less destabilizing, not least for US interests. A managed transition was also attractive given the constitutional requirement of an election, which Islamists would likely win, should Mubarak resign (Lizza, 2011). During these weeks of rapid change, the administration was criticized for reacting slowly and having constantly to catch up with events. But in a wider historical perspective its gear-change was fast, from silence over fraudulent elections in November–December 2010 to calling on Mubarak to step down at the start of February 2011, with the final decision taken within a handful of days (Bouchet, 2013) (all the while under pressure from allies in the region to stand by Mubarak). Trying to engineer an orderly transition made sense in that this would reconcile protecting US interests and aligning with demands for change. But that was not a realistic option almost from the start of the protests – there would be either repression or revolution, and the administration realized quickly that its preferred outcome was not possible. By most accounts, the change was down to Obama. After attempting a balancing act, and positioned between advisers who urged caution or siding with the protesters, he appears to have been the decisive factor in a major break in policy towards Egypt and the region by coming to the conclusion that a choice had to be made in favour of democratization forces (Lizza, 2011; Sanger, 2012: 296).

Following the revolution, Egypt went through two years of intensifying political turmoil as the military, the Muslim Brotherhood, and other secular and Islamist forces confronted one another over a new constitution and political institutions as well as parliamentary and presidential elections, while civil unrest grew. The military worked throughout to entrench its power and clashed with the Brotherhood and its elected president. From 2011 to 2013, the Obama administration tried to support the transition under the Supreme Council of the Armed Forces (SCAF) and then President Morsi. It increased its public statements on democracy and supported holding elections for transferring power to a legitimate parliament and president (Carothers, 2014; Hawthorne, 2013). In May 2011, Obama announced that it would 'be the policy of the United States to support reform across the region, and to support transitions to democracy', backed by economic support and democracy assistance (Obama, 2011). This was rightly praised at the time as a landmark statement of intent by a US president on the side of democracy in the MENA. After electoral successes for the Muslim Brotherhood, the administration also broke new ground in its acceptance of the results (as it did in Tunisia and Libya) and willingness to work with long-feared actors. There was a genuine and unprecedented effort to build ties with elected Islamists (Lynch, 2015). US engagement also matched the Brotherhood's initial broadly democratic path (Carothers and Brown, 2013).

Yet 2011–13 also saw the military and Brotherhood trying to entrench their political power in undemocratic ways. The military did not want a real transition, imposing constitutional arrangements to insulate its power from elected politicians. It waged a 'relentless campaign' for a counter-revolution (Dunne, 2012). The underlying political order from which the military and its allies benefited remained intact after Mubarak's ousting (Cook, 2015b). This was helped by Morsi and the Brotherhood trying to avoid direct confrontation with the military. As foreign democracy NGOs moved to capitalize on the revolution's opening, the authorities cracked down on them with unprecedented force, starting under the SCAF and continuing under Morsi. The arrest, trial and conviction of their employees, including Americans, was a stark counterpoint to the administration's engagement with the SCAF and Brotherhood. Once elected, the Brotherhood tried to impose its political vision, in the eyes of critics in a majoritarian way going beyond its electoral mandate, and it continued Mubarak-era authoritarian practices (Carothers and Brown, 2013; Dunne, 2014b). This was most evident in Morsi's November 2012 decree effectively asserting absolute presidential power until a new constitution was adopted (Brown, 2013).

While the Obama administration made real efforts to help the transition, this did not erase the primacy of security interests. Thus it did not react much to the SCAF's neutering of the transition or to Morsi's authoritarian moves. Even the prosecution of American NGO workers did not lead to an emphatic public response. Morsi's decree may have ended the honeymoon in the US–Brotherhood relationship, but as with Mubarak the administration did not condemn his behaviour since he did not challenge US foreign policy (Carothers, 2014; Dunne, 2014a). By the start of 2013, the administration was under growing fire for not doing enough to support liberal and secular democratic actors. Despite evidence to the contrary, it clung to the narrative of a democratically well-intentioned Brotherhood (Carothers and Brown, 2013). There was nonetheless rising US frustration and slowly an increase in criticism, though this remained mostly in broad terms and by lower-level officials. As the situation deteriorated further, officials tried in private to push the Brotherhood into compromising with its opponents and opening up the political process (Dunne, 2014a). But since the administration's support for the government was not conditional on democratic progress, its private or even occasional public appeals were easily ignored (Hawthorne, 2013).

From late 2012, the political conflict in Egypt intensified and violent protests increased. The Obama administration appeared slow in grasping the scale of the crisis and in responding. This may be because it had become too invested in the relationship with Morsi and in using private channels to influence him to realize early the scale of opposition to him (Hawthorne, 2013). When a coup appeared imminent, officials including Secretary of Defense Chuck Hagel and Chairman of the Joint Chiefs of Staff Martin Dempsey tried to use their contacts with the military to dissuade it (Hudson, 2013). The administration also used diplomatic channels, including through Gulf states with good relations with the organization, to try to get Morsi and the Brotherhood to compromise, form an inclusive government and thus keep the transition alive (Lynch, 2013a). Up to the July 2013 coup, the administration tried to broker a resolution, saying that it was engaging both sides so as not to be seen as trying to dictate events (*Democracy Digest*, 2013). Perhaps these efforts were doomed to fail, given the intensity of the political conflict, the unwillingness of the Brotherhood and military to compromise, and the mistrust by both sides of the United States (Dunne, 2013; Lynch, 2013a). Nevertheless, it is unclear just how hard an administration that had become disillusioned with the Brotherhood, for its incompetence in governing as much as for its illiberalism, was pushing it in private to accommodate its opponents or pushing the military not to mount a coup. In the last months of Morsi's presidency, the United States seemed more aloof and ambivalent about developments in Egypt, which may in part reflect the latter's declining importance in the most pressing issues confronting the US in the region as well as a degree of 'Egypt' fatigue (*New York Times*, 2013a). The administration did not welcome a coup but it seemed relatively untroubled by the prospect or by its apparent inability to prevent one. American leverage on Egypt's political actors was less than what some believed, but another set of policy-makers might have tried harder and more visibly to prevent the coup.

The political situation deteriorated further after the coup. The regime severely curtailed political and civil rights, used lethal force against protesters, arrested thousands and issued prison or death sentences for opponents, 'disappeared' others and tortured detainees (Amnesty International, 2015). Independent media and civil society have been systematically suppressed. Some have called the situation worse than anything under Mubarak or said that one needs to go back to the Nasser era for an equivalent (Dunne, 2015a; Mandour, 2015). In 2013 the military issued a road map for restoring democracy. While it did move ahead with a new constitution and a presidential election, the deeply flawed constitutional process and presidential poll cast doubt over its intentions (Brown, 2014). Parliamentary elections, delayed until late 2015, were marked by repression, low turnout and irregularities – and, in the absence of the Muslim Brotherhood and other opposition parties, were dominated by regime loyalists. In fact the military has removed checks on its influence and appears to be rebuilding the Mubarak-era system in which it held ultimate power in the background (Cook, 2015a; Mandour 2015). After leading the coup, Sisi left the army to run for president but in office has shown no commitment to democratic politics and governance (Dunne, 2015a).

The Obama administration did not react strongly to Morsi's removal or call for his restoration (Carothers, 2014). It was reported to want to give the military a window to stabilize the country, implying approval for the latter's line that it had intervened between the Brotherhood and its opponents rather than been central to the opposition to it (*Democracy Digest*, 2013). But Secretary of State John Kerry's statement a month after the coup that the military was restoring democracy sounded more like an endorsement than a reluctance to criticize (*New York Times*, 2013b). Not much later, at the United Nations General Assembly, Obama criticized Morsi for how he and the Brotherhood had governed and said the military had responded to popular dissatisfaction. He added that America had deliberately not chosen sides and would continue constructive relations with the interim government, but that US support would depend on democratic progress (Obama, 2013). Immediately after the coup and fearing more violence and radicalization, the administration worked with the EU, Qatar and the United Arab Emirates to encourage national reconciliation and to press the military not to crack down violently on large Islamist protests (*New York Times*, 2013c). But as human rights abuses mounted (especially the mass killing of protesters at Cairo's Rabaa Square), it became slightly more critical and began to suspend delivery of military equipment (Carothers, 2014; Dunne, 2014a). Following Rabaa, Obama said there could not be a 'return to business as usual' and lamented that the military had spurned diplomatic efforts to encourage reconciliation (*Hill*, 2013). Using aid as leverage for progress on democracy dominated the policy debate for months after the coup. So as not to trigger an automatic suspension of military assistance, the administration fudged the issue by arguing unconvincingly that it did not have to make a legally mandated determination of whether there had been a coup or not. Nevertheless, with backsliding in Egypt and pressure from Congress, a post-coup review of aid led to a decision to tweak economic support and withhold some military assistance (US Government Accountability Office, 2015: 18). The message was undermined, though, by senior officials, including Kerry and Hagel, expressing approval for the new regime and hope of restoring military assistance, which the Departments of State and Defense had wanted to preserve in the first place (*Daily Beast*, 2013; Dunne, 2014a).

At the same time, a White House review of MENA policy led to a tighter focus on Iran, Syria and Israel–Palestine to the detriment of other issues, including Egypt (*New York Times*, 2013d). Spelled out by Obama at the United Nations in October 2013, this appeared to abandon the democracy-oriented approach he had set out in 2011 and to characterize democracy as secondary to core security interests in Egypt, stressing the need sometimes to cooperate with governments regardless of human rights. Yet the president also described democracy as America's 'overriding interest' in Egypt and stated that the administration would keep asserting universal principles with its partners (Obama, 2013). In the following months Obama and other officials kept using a transition rhetoric while there was a gradual erosion of democratic conditionality and some military assistance was released. Human rights violations were condemned as setbacks in the military's road map rather than as part of a reversion to authoritarianism (Hawthorne, 2014). The administration, alongside the EU and international observers, described the political environment for the 2014 presidential election as restrictive and unfair, yet it welcomed Sisi's win with 96.91 per cent of the vote. In late 2014 Obama placed the fight against Islamic State and violent extremism more squarely at the core of MENA policy, and the administration began stressing more frequently the tradeoffs between security and human rights and democracy in region, especially with reference to Egypt (*New York Times*, 2015; Obama, 2014). There was also a growing normalization of relations in 2014–15, with a mix of human rights criticism and praise for progress under Sisi. The suspension of military assistance was ended in April 2015 on national security grounds, at the same time as the Department of State was unable to certify improvements in democracy and strongly criticized Egypt's human rights situation (US Department of State, 2015). In practice, the administration only half-heartedly tried to leverage military aid for democratic progress and this achieved nothing positive. It eventually and unconditionally supplied most of it, publicly downplayed the suspension and repeatedly indicated that it was temporary (McInerney and Bockenfeld, 2015). When it was lifted, though, the administration announced plans for changes in how assistance is structured, which might in the long run give America real conditionality leverage (Cofman Wittes, 2015; Dunne, 2015b; McInerney and Bockenfeld, 2015). Overall, in 2015 the approach towards Egypt effectively returned to accepting and supporting whoever is in power as long they are aligned with US interests in the region (Hawthorne, 2015).

Conclusion

In 2009–10, the Obama administration's policy towards Egypt was cautious and mostly replicated the traditional US approach, but it was not empty of democracy concerns. There was low-key and unpublicized engagement with the issue, which could have been stronger without affecting Obama's overarching effort to pull back from Bush's positions. The reaction to the 2011 revolution was as good as could be expected. It was ad hoc and reactive, but it is hard to see how it could have been much better. The change of policy towards Mubarak showed a quick adjustment to a changing situation in favour of democracy, which compares well with US reactions to similar cases in the past. In 2011–13, the administration made a genuine effort to support Egypt's attempted transition, although hampered by a curtailed ability to provide large-scale economic assistance. The engagement with elected Islamists was a major break with previous policy. But then there came the gradual failure of this policy and failure to keep up with a deteriorating situation shaped by the democratic shortcomings of the Muslim Brotherhood and the military. Underestimating the danger of the situation in the lead-up to the coup and reacting too late to try to dissuade the military from it was also a partial failure for the administration. The decision not to call Morsi's removal a coup was the greater failure. It may be understandable in the wider security context, but purely in terms of democracy promotion this refusal to apply a minimal standard regarding the fate of an elected leader undermined US credibility in this field globally. It left the United States once more open to the criticism of hypocrisy and double standards over democracy. Since the coup it is hard to find anything positive in US policy with regard to democracy and human rights. There has been little evidence that the US global stance against the closing space has led to a rethink as to how to support democratic civil society against the wishes of the vociferously nationalistic regime.

There has been a pattern in which the United States initially soft-pedalled the issue of democracy as it engaged with whichever Egyptian rulers it was faced with at any point before becoming disillusioned with them and more critical. As Obama entered his final year in office, however, the second part of this pattern had not been noticed in relation to Sisi. The occasional criticism of the regime has not been high-profile, especially when placed alongside the frequent praise by senior officials like Kerry, including for supposedly implementing the democracy road map. It will be interesting to see in the coming years whether the decline in the strategic importance of the US–Egyptian relationship and Egypt's growing reliance on patrons among the Gulf states will mean more freedom for Washington to be critical of the country's political situation. Starting with not making a coup determination, Obama's choice has been to live with an unsatisfactory Egyptian status quo in which democracy lost out. The administration may not like the post-coup political situation and Sisi's actions but, so far, they do not constitute an acute enough problem for the United States to warrant changing radically a bilateral relationship that is now heavily framed by the CVE agenda. The danger in this, however, for the United States and for Egypt is that the coup and the ensuing widespread repression have galvanized violent radical Islamists, notably in the Sinai peninsula, and led to a rise in jihadi attacks against state targets and the prospect of a wider armed rebellion (Awad and Hashem, 2015). Obama has backed away from the hard choice in Egypt and in the region, which would be to take the long-term democracy bet, and instead has taken the easier, reflexive short-term security option.

Following the end of the Cold War, the United States chose greater inclusion of democracy promotion in foreign policy, including eventually towards the MENA. Obama's second term may have witnessed the start of a turning away from that choice in the region, with Egypt exemplifying the initial opening to and subsequent abandonment of democracy promotion, and the United States mostly returning to its Mubarak-era policy. Given the security situation in the region and the increasingly dominant CVE agenda, it looks as though the MENA exception may be back for the foreseeable future. If this is confirmed in the coming years, this might even prove a harbinger for US democracy promotion globally since the questions of hard choices between democracy and other interests, and of declining US leverage, are likely to be replicated in other regions in light of the long-term power shifts in favour of other states at the global and regional levels. The presidents who come after Obama could find themselves confronted with a world in which democracy promotion exceptions may have to be applied elsewhere and even become the norm.

However, while the Obama administration has retreated in democracy promotion compared to its engagement in Egypt in the immediate aftermath of the 2011 revolution, it is premature to say that the pendulum has swung completely back. For one thing the experiences of the Arab Spring, good and bad, cannot be erased and the United States will eventually have no choice but to factor into its foreign policy the popular political aspirations in the region. However repressed these may be now, they will not go away. It is unlikely that Obama's successor will be able simply to go back to the status quo ante in the region. Furthermore, the greater realism or pessimism regarding democracy promotion witnessed in Obama's second term with regard to the MENA does not mean that this policy field will be discarded altogether, which would be the purely realist choice. It might instead indicate the early stage of a new phase in democracy promotion that sees the United States transition from the approach it took from the end of the Cold War to a more realistic one that looks at this policy field in new ways. This would acknowledge previous misreadings of important perennial issues pertaining to democratization and international relations, and be more attuned to changes in the global political environment in what has been described as the new 'global marketplace of political change' (Carothers and Samet-Marram, 2015).

References

Amnesty International (2015) *The State of the World's Human Rights*, London: Amnesty International.

Awad, M. and Hashem, M. (2015) *Egypt's Escalating Islamist Insurgency*, Washington, DC: Carnegie Endowment for International Peace.

Betts, R. (2015) 'Realism Is an Attitude, Not a Doctrine', *National Interest*, 24 August.

Bouchet, N. (2011) 'Barack Obama's Democracy Promotion at Midterm', *International Journal of Human Rights*, Vol. 15, No. 4.

Bouchet, N. (2013) 'The Democracy Tradition in US Foreign Policy and the Obama Presidency', *International Affairs*, Vol. 89, No. 1.

Bouchet, N. (2015) *Democracy Promotion as US Foreign Policy: Bill Clinton and Democratic Enlargement*, Abingdon: Routledge.

Brown, N. J. (2013) 'Egypt's Failed Transition', *Journal of Democracy*, Vol. 24, No. 4, October.

Brown, N. J. (2014) 'Grading Egypt's Roadmap Toward Democracy', *Foreign Policy*, 5 May.

Brownlee, J. (2012) *Democracy Prevention: The Politics of the U.S.–Egyptian Alliance*, Cambridge: Cambridge University Press.

Carothers, T. (2014) 'What the United States Wants in Egypt', *Al Masry Al Youm*, 1 May.

Carothers, T. and Brown, N. J. (2013) 'Recalibrating U.S. Policy in Egypt', *Washington Post*, 3 May.

Carothers, T. and Samet-Marram, O. (2015) *The New Global Marketplace of Political Change*, Washington, DC: Carnegie Endowment for International Peace.

Clinton, H. (2011) 'Remarks at Forum for the Future', Doha, 13 January.

Cofman Wittes, T. (2015) 'The Politics of Restoring Egypt's Military Aid', *Washington Post*, 2 April.

Cook, S. A. (2015a) 'Egypt's Coming Chaos', *Foreign Policy*, 3 July.

Cook, S. A. (2015b) 'The Middle Eastern Revolutions That Never Were', *American Interest*, 26 October.

Daily Beast (2013) 'John Kerry Defies the White House on Egypt Policy', 13 November.

Democracy Digest (2013) 'Egypt Crisis is "Tricky Diplomatic Geometry" for Obama Administration', 3 July.

Dueck, C. (2011) 'The Accommodator: Obama's Foreign Policy', *Policy Review*, No. 169.

Dunne, C. (2012) 'Confronting Egypt's Counterrevolution', Freedom House, 20 June, www.freedomhouse.org/blog/confronting-egypt's-counterrevolution.

Dunne, M. (2013) 'With Morsi's Ouster, Time for a New U.S. Policy Toward Egypt', *Washington Post*, 4 July.

Dunne, M. (2014a) 'US Policy Struggles with an Egypt in Turmoil', Arab Reform Initiative, 22 May.

Dunne, M. (2014b) 'A U.S. Strategy toward Egypt under Sisi', Carnegie Endowment for International Peace, Washington, DC, 5 June.

Dunne, M. (2015a) 'Egypt's Nationalists Dominate in a Politics-Free Zone', Carnegie Endowment for International Peace, Washington, DC, 15 April.

Dunne, M. (2015b) 'Washington's Egypt Dilemma (Interview)', Council on Foreign Relations, Washington, DC, 23 June.

Hamid, S. (2011) 'The Struggle for Middle East Democracy', *Cairo Review of Global Affairs*, 26 April.

Hassan, O. (2012) *Constructing America's Freedom Agenda for the Middle East: Democracy or Domination*, Abingdon: Routledge.

Hawthorne, A. (2013) 'Opportunities and Responsibilities for Transatlantic Powers in the MENA Region after the Arab Revolutions: The Case of the United States, EU, and Egypt Post-Morsi', Washington, DC: German Marshall Fund of the United States.

Hawthorne, A. (2014) 'Wishful Thinking: The Obama Administration's Rhetoric on Democracy and Human Rights in Egypt', Washington, DC: Atlantic Council, 4 April.

Hawthorne, A. (2015) 'The U.S.–Egypt Strategic Dialogue: Drift Along the Nile', Washington, DC: Council on Foreign Relations, 29 July.

Hill (2013) 'Obama: US "Can't Return to Business as Usual" with Egypt after Crackdown', 23 August.

Hudson, J. (2013) 'Kerry Now Loves the Cairo Coup America Tried to Stop', *Foreign Policy*, 18 July.

Kaplan, F. (2014) 'The Realist', *Politico*, 27 February.

Lizza, R. (2011) 'The Consequentialist: How the Arab Spring Remade Obama's Foreign Policy', *New Yorker*, 2 May.

Lynch, M. (2013a) 'Enough Is Enough', *Foreign Policy*, 14 August.

Lynch, M. (2013b) 'Promotion Demotion', *Foreign Policy*, 7 October.

Lynch, M. (2015) 'Obama and the Middle East: Rightsizing the U.S. Role', *Foreign Affairs*, September/October.

McInerney, S. and Bockenfeld, C. (2015) 'The Federal Budget and Appropriations for Fiscal Year 2016: Democracy, Governance, and Human Rights in the Middle East and North Africa', Washington, DC: Project on Middle East Democracy, May.

Mandour, M. (2015) 'Repression in Egypt from Mubarak to Sisi', *Sada*, 11 August.

Mann, J. (2012) *The Obamians: The Struggle Inside the White House to Redefine American Power*, New York: Viking.

New York Times (2013a) 'Egypt Crisis Finds Washington Largely Ambivalent and Aloof', 5 July.

New York Times (2013b) 'Kerry Says Egypt's Military Was "Restoring Democracy" in Ousting Morsi', 1 August.

New York Times (2013c) 'How American Hopes for a Deal in Egypt Were Undercut', 17 August.

New York Times (2013d) 'Rice Offers a More Modest Strategy for Mideast', 26 October.

New York Times (2015) 'Obama Calls for Expansion of Human Rights to Combat Extremism', 29 February.

Obama, B. (2011) 'A Moment of Opportunity', Remarks at the Department of State, Washington, DC, 19 May.

Obama, B. (2013) 'Remarks in Address to the United Nations General Assembly', New York, 23 September.

Obama, B. (2014) 'Remarks at Clinton Global Initiative', New York, 23 September.

Rose, G. (2015) 'What Obama Gets Right', *Foreign Affairs*, September/October.

Rothkopf, D. (2014) 'National Insecurity: Can Obama's Foreign Policy Be Saved?', *Foreign Policy*, 9 September.

Sanger, D. E. (2012) *Confront and Conceal: Obama's Secret Wars and Surprising Use of American Power*, New York: Crown.

Sestanovich, S. (2014) *Maximalist: America in the World from Truman to Obama*, New York: Knopf Doubleday.

Smith, T. (2013) 'Democracy Promotion from Wilson to Obama', in Cox, M., Lynch, T. J. and Bouchet, N. (eds), *US Foreign Policy and Democracy Promotion: From Theodore Roosevelt to Barack Obama*, Abingdon: Routledge.

Traub, J. (2013) 'Speak Softly and Carry No Stick', *Foreign Policy*, 15 August.

US Department of State (2015) 'Country Report on Human Rights Practices (Egypt) for 2014', Washington, DC.

US Government Accountability Office (2015) 'Egypt: U.S. Government Should Examine Options for Using Unobligated Funds and Evaluating Security Assistance Programs', Washington, DC, February.

Zakaria, F. (2009) 'Obama the Realist', *Newsweek*, 4 December.

11 US–Russia relations in Obama's second term

A damage limitation exercise

Maxine David

This chapter examines President Barack Obama's Russia policy in his second term in office, arguing that the policy approach has consistently reflected both doctrine and legacy. When Barack Obama began his first presidential term in 2008, he was to preside over an attempt to reset a relationship with Russia that was then experiencing its worst decline since the end of the Cold War. Near to the end of his second term, however, relations with Russia were at an even lower point than when Obama first became President. Indeed, even by the beginning of his second term, hopes for the reset had dwindled. It was in this context that the Obama administration settled on what is best described as a 'damage limitation policy', recognising the impossibility of positively influencing Putin's foreign policy, seeking instead to do the least amount of damage in the hope of keeping the doors open for a more productive relationship with Putin's successor.

Seen in the shorter term, it is all too easy to conclude that Obama's foreign policy towards Russia has both failed and acknowledged its failures. This chapter contemplates, however, the possibility that, properly contextualised and viewed over the longer term, Obama's Russia policy will be judged more favourably. This possibility is considered by treating the reasons for the current state of poor relations as various and complex, falling into one or more of the following categories: (1) intervening external events, even shocks; (2) Russian President Putin's perception of his own agency; (3) domestic political structural constraints; and (4) failings in Obama's own foreign policy focus and perceptions. The concluding summary argues, to rely on the distinction between politics and diplomacy made by *Yes Minister*'s Sir Humphrey Appleby, that Obama has rejected the pursuit of short-term political gains in favour of pursuing a more enduring diplomatic relationship. In this sense, there is continuity of doctrine across the first and second terms as Obama has striven over the length of his presidency to redress the wrongs caused by his predecessor's foreign policy and to leave, in the case of US–Russia relations at least, a foundation upon which his successor can build a more constructive relationship.

The chapter proceeds as follows. It begins by identifying the context in which US–Russia relations were conducted when Obama began his second and Putin his third term in office, demonstrating how Putin's rhetoric and actions set the scene for the relationship. Much has been made in recent times of the ways in which Putin has outplayed Obama in the foreign policy game. In this section, therefore, a little time is spent on consideration of the constraints and freedoms experienced by both leaders, in terms of their own perceptions and domestic political structures. In the next section, the first of the four categories, external events, is considered through an examination of the Ukrainian and Syrian conflicts. In this section too, the other categories, particularly those relating to the two leaders' perceptions of their foreign policy agency, are factors in their decisions and actions; Obama was held back to a large extent by his own doctrine and preferred approach, while Putin saw himself as relatively free to shape and conduct his foreign policy as he wished. In the third section, the US's attempts to counter Russia's foray into the use of soft power are analysed; this section is important for understanding wider perceptions about these two foreign policy actors. The chapter concludes that certain aspects of Obama's doctrine can only be judged in the interim: until time enough has passed for the legacy of his foreign policy to be assessed rather than simply asserted, we cannot know what the consequences for US–Russia relations will be. It argues, however, that other aspects can be evaluated – and in a positive light. Kennan's mid-twentieth-century diplomatic advice is as relevant today as then: 'what is important in the relations between governments is not just, or even predominantly, the "what" but rather the "how" – the approach, the posture, the manner, the style of action' (Kennan, 1961). In the longer term, it will be the 'how' in Obama's foreign policy that will be assessed most favourably. While his second term in office will see US–Russia relations end on no better note than did George W. Bush's, the manner in which Obama's Russia policy has been conducted stands in marked contrast to the openly hostile, demonising approach of Bush. The next incumbent of the White House will be working with a relationship that has suffered far less damage than it might have and in which messages have been clearly sent that there is a willingness in certain quarters in the US to work with rather than against Russia.

From reset to damage limitation

The reset in US–Russia relations was a demonstration both of the normativity and the pragmatism that Obama's campaigning for the White House had suggested would be pursued. It signalled an acknowledgement of the mistakes made by previous US administrations in relations with Russia but acknowledged too that Obama recognised the importance of Russia to the resolution of significant geopolitical problems. These acknowledgements were significant in that they spoke to Putin's persistent and widely expressed view that the US had failed to accord Russia the respect and place that it warranted in global affairs. The reset additionally reflected the perception that the US faced greater threats and was presented with better opportunities elsewhere, as demonstrated by the so-called pivot to Asia (Campbell and Andrews, 2013).

Both the normativity and pragmatism drew criticism, at home from the Republican camp (Kramer, 2010) and abroad from certain European allies.

However, that criticism did not always reflect the divisions that existed over certain matters. A case in point was Obama's decision not to move forward with a missile defence programme, which would have seen the US placing weapons in the Czech Republic and Poland; this had long divided opinion, not least because it might send out all the wrong signals to Russia (Hildreth and Ek, 2009), which viewed the programme as a direct threat. Without engaging in counter-factuals, determining the wisdom of Obama's concessionary approach on missile defence and the reset more generally is problematic, the evidence contradictory. Events in Syria and Ukraine since then and Putin's increasingly bellicose discourse on the US suggest the approach was naïve, based on a misperception of Russian foreign policy objectives and capacity to achieve them. However, as others have pointed out (Deyermond, 2013), some gains were made by this new approach to Russia, notably on Iran, the signing of the new START and in cooperation on Afghanistan.[1] In the event, this first administration admitted that some work had to be done before the values gap could be closed, saying: 'While seeking to engage the Russian government and Russian civil society in ways to promote universal values, the Obama Administration has not shied away from criticizing human rights abuses' (White House, 2010). Thus, the administration adopted what it called 'dual track engagement in support of universal values' (White House, 2010) and treated the Kremlin incumbent at the time, President Medvedev, as a moderniser serious about resolving some of the more intractable problems facing Russia, especially corruption and the rule of law. The White House simultaneously directed efforts towards civil society within Russia, including through the use of the US Agency for International Development (USAID). Matters were rather different once Putin returned to the Kremlin and set Russia on a course of challenging US dominance in international affairs.

Here, Obama's perception of Russia and the resources available to it took on great significance. The characterisation of Russia as a 'regional power' that was acting out of weakness rather than strength (Obama, 2014) is revealing of a failure to understand the creative capacities of President Putin, whose foreign policy successes have exceeded expectations derived from an analysis of tangible resources, as well as the extent to which he would go in pursuit of his objectives. Additionally, Obama's second term is a demonstration of the way in which a values gap between two significant global actors can constrain one and liberate another, as Putin's contradictory accounts of Russian troop involvement show.

There are good reasons to focus on the role of leadership in foreign policy, of course. However, it should not be forgotten either that a role is also played by domestic political structures, which dictate the extent to which any leader can dominate foreign policy-making processes. Given the verticalisation of power in Russia and the narrowed circle of political advisers now surrounding Putin, he must be seen as the dominant decision-maker in Russian foreign policy (Saltzman, 2012). It is for this reason that so much space is given in Russian foreign policy analysis to the person of Putin himself (Anon, 2015; Nixey, 2014; Sakwa, 2012). This contrasts sharply with Obama whose name may dominate in article titles but who has consistently had to fight off the Republican challenge to his decision-making (Deyermond, 2012). That became particularly evident in respect of the making of the 2015 Iran deal (Wong, 2015) but it is true too of the US's relations with Russia where Obama and his team have not been insulated from the clamour of voices advising that neither Putin nor Russia can be trusted (*Washington Post* Staff, 2013). This is not to deny that structural factors, for instance Russia's economic difficulties or its competing domestic groups, are irrelevant (Kuchins and Zevelev, 2012). However, Putin's crackdown on dissent at home, for instance, was *his* choice of response to an evident need for political reform, rather than the only choice or one arrived at through proper parliamentary processes. His third term in office has been marked by a consistent pattern of reference to conservative, traditional values that have rightly been criticised as regressive (Ryzhkov, 2013) and that expand even further the values gap between Russia and the West, as now discussed.

Poor omens at the start of the second term

Obama began his second term in office in January 2013, just eight months after Putin's return to the Kremlin in May 2012 and after the interim presidency of Dmitry Medvedev. Even before the March 2012 Russian presidential elections that returned Putin to the Kremlin two months later, Obama had reason aplenty to believe that the reset in relations had produced little that was enduring. The US was accused by Putin of causing the protests that had swept many streets in Russia following parliamentary and presidential elections in December 2011 (Cullison, 2011). By the beginning of October 2012, USAID had been banned from operating in Russia, one of the early casualties of Putin's work to limit the activities of external actors in the country. There had been plenty of other signs too that the values gap would widen rather than close with Putin back in the Kremlin. This was significant in the context of US–Russia relations given the explicit and implicit references to the US as a relevant factor in the evolution of Russian domestic as well as foreign policy.

Legislative blows to the pragmatic approach

A wave of legislation followed Putin's return to the Kremlin in May 2012. Three laws in particular tested Obama's pragmatism and meant an effective end to the dual track approach. Amendments to what has come to be known as the foreign agents law[2] were signed into law by Putin in July 2012. All organisations in receipt of foreign funding and engaging in political activities were at first required to register as foreign agents before a later amendment gave the Ministry of Justice power to register them itself. Human Rights Watch reported in July 2015 that eighty organisations had been registered, while an additional twelve chose to shut down rather than bear the ignominy of the label. The Russian response to criticism has been typical in pointing out that it merely follows the Western model: in 2013, the Russian Embassy to the UK argued that the 'blueprint for the Russian law' was 'America's Foreign Agents Registration Act, FARA, 1938' (Russian Embassy to the UK, 2013).

A second piece of legislation, the Dima Yakovlev Law[3] signed in December 2012, directly targeted the US. This was a tit for tat response to the US passing the Sergei Magnitsky Rule of Law Accountability Act in the previous month. Magnitsky was a Russian lawyer arrested following his investigations on behalf of the foreign-owned Hermitage Capital Management into massive fraud said to involve the police, judiciary, tax officials and bankers. Magnitsky died in prison in 2009 having allegedly been deprived of medical treatment while awaiting trial. Hermitage's CEO, the American Bill Browder, mounted a long campaign for justice on Magnitsky's behalf. The Act imposed various sanctions, including visa bans and the freezing of assets, on those Russian elites deemed complicit in Magnitsky's death. It was also inextricably linked to the repeal of the Jackson–Vanik amendment, a provision in the 1974 US Trade Act, which had been a source of much irritation to the Russians who understandably felt its continued place on US law books was an outdated hangover from the Cold War. Its repeal signalled the start of permanent normal trade relations (PNTR) with Russia. Any diplomatic benefits this change might have brought were lost by the fact that the repeal of the one was not possible without the passing of the other.[4] In retaliation, the Russians passed the Dima Yakovlev Law, named after a Russian child who died in the US after being adopted by Americans. It targeted citizens of the US, banning those alleged to have violated human rights from entering Russia, working in Russia or with non-profit organisations in Russia, and also from adopting children who are Russian nationals (Council on Foreign Relations, 2012). Even within Russia itself, the law met with disapprobation, sparking the 'March against Scoundrels' in January 2013.

The third legislative blow, ostensibly aimed at the protection of children,[5] was signed into law in June 2013. This legislation 'sets the legal basis and administrative liability for promoting non-traditional sexual relations among minors' (President of Russia, 2013) and was controversial for at least two reasons. First, it made clear that child protection laws could and would be used to impose a higher level of censorship on Russians and so to quiet dissent. Second, the focus on 'non-traditional sexual relationships' effected a ban on LGBT rallies and on distribution of information about non-traditional sexual relations to minors, over a range of media including the internet and advertisements. This move was consistent with Putin's ever closer relationship with the Russian Orthodox Church and emphasis on the need to uphold traditional Russian values. It also served to underline the widening of the values gap that Obama sought to close. With Russia due to host the Winter Olympics in Sochi in 2014, the anti-gay law, as it came to be known, received mass media attention and LGBT communities in various countries, including Russia, called for the games to be boycotted. Obama's reaction was swift and condemnatory but it also revealed one of the major problems the US encounters when tackling Putin's regressive values base, i.e. accusations of hypocrisy. Indeed, any Western critique of Russian foreign policy is inevitably met with a 'whataboutist' set of comments that point out the West's failings, not least because of the activities of the Kremlin trolls

(Subbotovska, 2015). It is true too, however, that the US is particularly vulnerable to accusations of hypocrisy. One analyst expressed surprise at Obama's impatient response to the anti-gay law, saying: 'In case anyone forgot, we're very close military and political allies with Saudi Arabia, Kuwait, the UAE, and numerous other countries in which homosexuality is not only illegal but it [*sic*] sometimes punished with the death penalty' (Adomanis, 2013). This is to ignore, however, the unpleasant exigencies underpinning much foreign policy, and to ignore too that Obama's reaction to Russia was indicative of a belief even then that Russia was/is/could be more like 'us' than could the UAE. In common with other US and European administrations, therefore, Obama's was no less immune to a sense that the West had lost Russia (Trenin, 2006).

Whatever attempts had been made to pretend all was well with the US's relations with Russia came to an end when Edward Snowden was granted asylum in Russia in July 2013. Snowden, who blew the whistle on the covert surveillance activities of the US National Security Agency, was wanted by the US authorities on charges of espionage and theft of government property. In the August, Obama cancelled the US–Russia Summit scheduled for that September. Citing insufficient progress in their agenda, the press statement was cast in regretful tones that acknowledged that: 'Russia's disappointing decision to grant Edward Snowden temporary asylum was also a factor' (White House, 2013). This sent a clear message about the US's view of Russia harbouring Snowden, even while dialogue continued at the ministerial level and in the context of international fora such as the G8. Russia became the subject of speculation in relation to what further might be extracted from Snowden but ultimately it was the US that was on the wrong side of wider diplomatic and public opinion, as European partners vigorously expressed their anger at the US's actions. This was precisely the picture of the US that Russia has sought to depict and Obama to redress.

A new foreign policy concept

Shortly after the start of Obama's second term, in February 2013, Russia issued a new Foreign Policy Concept (FPC), replacing the 2008 Concept from the Medvedev years. The 2013 version did not mark a radical break with earlier FPCs, although a noticeable change was an absence for the first time of any reference to the Cold War (Lukyanov, 2013; Ministry of Foreign Affairs, 2013). The Concept makes many references to globalisation, to change, and to the need to adopt new approaches in response to it. The West is presented as being on the defensive and as contributing to instability as it attempts to hold on to 'traditional positions'. Reference is also made to civilisational clashes and competitions and much is said about regional integration as a stabilising force in the face of increasing competition. While the US is rarely invoked directly, seen in the background of Putin's and Russian Foreign Minister Sergei Lavrov's wider discourse, the shadow of previous US actions lies heavy over the Concept. Reference is made, for instance, to 'unacceptable' military and other interventions under the 'pretext' of implementing the concept of 'responsibility to protect', while much is made of Russia's commitment to the United Nations and adherence to international law. In the section dedicated to regional priorities, Russia's immediate neighbourhood takes top priority, including the Commonwealth of Independent States (CIS), Collective Security Treaty Organisation (CSTO), and Eurasian Economic Union (EEU) amongst others. In contrast to the 2008 FPC, Ukraine warrants a line of its own, something which obviously takes on deeper meaning in the context of events from 2014 onwards. The US is spoken of specifically at the bottom of the list of Euro-Atlantic actors. Russia is portrayed as occupying an equal responsibility with the US for 'global strategic stability and international security as a whole'. Specific mention is made of the intention 'to prevent the USA from imposing unilateral extraterritorial sanctions against Russian citizens and legal entities', a clear nod to the Magnitsky Act and the Dima Yakovlev Law.

In late 2012, Lavrov had hinted about what the FPC would include. He too referred to the existence of different civilisational identities and to a 'multiplicity of centers of power and influence'. In an intriguing use of history, he compared the US to the Soviet Union as an exporter of revolution, attempting to 'impose' its model of development, instead inducing an opposite, potentially extremist reaction (Lavrov, 2012). In that context, Lavrov also said that 'Russia simply cannot exist as a subordinate country of a world leader' but rather viewed itself as 'one of the centers of the new polycentric world'. Evidence of just how much more the relationship had deteriorated came on 31 December 2015, when Putin signed a new Security Strategy in which the US is referenced multiple times as a threat to the Russian national interest and its ambitions, not least by reason of its actions in Ukraine.[6] This mirrored the US Security Strategy of February 2015, which made reference no fewer than seven times specifically to Russian 'aggression' (White House, 2015a).

The legacy and practice of international intervention

One of the external events that has derailed Obama's ambitions for improving US–Russia relations is the conflict that has afflicted the Ukrainian state since 2014 and which, in early 2016, is being held under a fragile ceasefire. Despite originally denying that Russian troops played an active role in Crimea and then Ukraine more widely, Putin admitted relatively early on that they had intervened in Crimea (Putin, 2014) and, much later, admitted this had been the case elsewhere too (Walker, 2015). These interventions are consistent with the Russian vision of 'Ukraine as a priority partner within the CIS' (Ministry of Foreign Affairs of the Russian Federation, 2013) and Putin's frequent references to the fact that '[s]upport for the Russian diaspora is one of the most important policies of our state' (President of Russia, 2012). They are consistent too with Russia's continued fears about the encroachment of US influence onto what it sees as its sphere of influence. This worry has been a constant since 1991, especially in relation to NATO's enlargement, fed further by the Colour Revolutions, particularly those in Georgia (2003) and Ukraine (2005), that are seen by the Kremlin as the outcome of Western, especially US, interference in the region.

This consistency in ambition is not matched by consistency of rhetoric in relation to what constitutes appropriate behaviour, however. In fact, Russia is left in the not unironic, even hypocritical, position of mirroring that which it so long criticised in US foreign policy (David, 2015). Criticism of the US's perceived interventionist tendencies has long permeated the Russian discourse, reflecting the shadow cast by the interventions in Kosovo (1999) and Iraq (2003). In March 2014, following Russia's annexation of Crimea but prior to Russian troops' involvement in Ukraine's conflict in the east of the country, Obama said it was 'important for everybody to be clear and strip away some of the possible excuses for a potential Russian action', rejecting the analogy to Kosovo as 'a comparison that makes absolutely no sense' (Obama, 2014). This was in response to the by now usual Russian reference to US actions in Kosovo as setting a standard for unauthorised intervention that others could follow on the grounds of human rights protection. As a result, the US has felt justified in levying sanctions against Russia, most particularly after the downing of the Malaysian Airlines flight MH17 over separatist-held territory in eastern Ukraine in July 2014. While the US has inevitably become embroiled in the Ukrainian conflict, Obama's administration has preferred to give room to the EU to take point in the search for a diplomatic solution. Further, Obama has resisted the provocation that has constituted much Russian activity in and around Ukraine. In March 2014, for instance, Obama acknowledged Russia was behaving in an intimidating fashion by lining its troops along Ukraine's border but pointed out also that it was within its sovereign rights to do so. Obama's strategy has been to send a clear message about the consequences of interference in a neighbouring state, without getting drawn too far in, the US's own legacy of 'illegal but legitimate' intervention[7] a major hindrance.

At the same time, the US has led the charge in ensuring there is a concerted effort to punish Russia for its alleged breaches of international law. Obama is justified in saying that the international response to Russian actions in Ukraine has been more robust than in relation to Georgia, that Russia was more isolated in 2014 than it had been as a result of its actions in Georgia in 2008. Still, Obama will remain vulnerable to criticisms that Putin acted as he did in Ukraine precisely because he saw the US was orientated elsewhere and therefore that Russia could win, ultimately, in Ukraine.

Thus, Obama has been rather caught between the proverbial rock and hard place: trying to avoid the foreign interventionist mistakes of previous US administrations but criticised too for a lack of effective action in relation to Ukraine (Anon, 2015), even while being accused by Russia of exacerbating the situation. The problem has been that the pragmatic (for US interests) rather than normative agenda has been privileged. For instance, the failure to defend Ukraine in more robust fashion has made a mockery of the diplomatic promise that was the Budapest Memorandum and called into question the point of such agreements and treaties. Thus, defence of the US reputation and interests has come at the expense of wider diplomatic relations, the legacy of which may yet prove severe. Nevertheless, the virtues of a policy that gives Putin enough rope to hang himself have been under-explored in comparisons of Obama's and Putin's foreign policy. As a consequence of its foreign adventures, Russia's reputation has suffered enormous damage, a widely held perception emerging that nothing Russia says can be trusted.[8]

In reality, though, Obama has had little interest in committing too many resources to Ukraine. It is in the Middle East that Russia has proved the biggest obstacle to Obama achieving his foreign policy objectives. As a result of the 2011 Libya intervention, for which Russia has criticised the West for overstepping the bounds of UN Security Council Resolution 1973 (2011), Russia (with China) has consistently thwarted the US's attempts to win UN Security Council authorisation for action in Syria. As a result of failure to mobilise support in the UN Security Council, Obama turned to Congress. In August and September 2013, he failed in his bid to build support at home or abroad for a military response to Assad's use of chemical weapons against his own people, one that would not involve troops on the ground but which would deter future use of chemical weapons while also degrading the regime's chemical weapons capacity. This cloud, however, did have its silver lining, which came in the form of the US and Russia agreeing a framework through which the Assad regime could destroy its chemical weapons stockpiles and Syria accede to the Chemical Weapons Convention. This was a rare success in relation to this conflict. The Obama administration, like others, has failed to find an effective way forward in Syria, not least because it has failed to bring Russia round to its way of thinking. US action has largely been restricted to air strikes on suspected so-called Islamic State (IS) targets and to arming and training 'moderate' rebels in Syria; neither action is bearing fruitful results. At the time of writing, Russia and the US are, effectively, supporting competing forces in Syria; the Russians, at Assad's invitation, conducting air strikes as often, it is commonly reported, against the moderate rebels the US supports as against IS.

But Obama, it is worth reiterating, has been stymied not only by Russia. In regard to the third category of domestic political constraints, the Senate Hearing on the Syrian Crisis of 3 September 2013 revealed the differences in US political opinion about how to deal with Russia and therefore the constraining structures within which Obama's team had to work. These have sometimes driven Obama's Secretary of State, John Kerry, to be overly uncritical in his assessment of the Russian position. At the same Hearing, in answer to a question about why Russia was not supportive of the proposed US action, Kerry was forced into something of a defence of Russia, reinforcing the need to remember that it was being cooperative on a number of issues, including Iran and North Korea, and spoke of a need too to 'deal with this thoughtfully' and to hope that Obama's upcoming meeting with Putin and the sharing of evidence about chemical weapons usage would bring a change of mind (*Washington Post* Staff, 2013). At the same time, Kerry counselled the need to do something regardless of the Russian reaction because of the more terrible consequences that doing nothing would bring. In response to questions about the likely Russian response, Kerry argued that Russia was not ideologically committed to supporting the Assad regime and that as long as it did not feel it would experience a loss of a market for arms export there would not be a 'major confrontation'. The exchange at least showed calculations about likely reactions were being made, even if events in the dying months of 2015 – Russia engaged in overt military action in Syria, conducting air strikes on behalf of the ailing Assad regime, bombing those the US continues to support, and Russia–Turkey relations at a dangerously low ebb – render Kerry's analysis optimistic at best, deluded at worst.

Nevertheless, in terms of ensuring doors remain open, Kerry's relatively delicate rhetoric towards Russia has to be credited. More commonly heard on the Hill are demands for explicit and barbed condemnation of Russia, as this assertion from a Democrat Senator, Tim Vaine, illustrates:

> We should make them wear being [*sic*] the pro-chemical weapons like a rotting carcass around their neck in every instance we can so that at some point they'll ask themselves the question: Do we really want to be the nation that is pro use of chemical weapons against a civilian population?
>
> (*Washington Post* Staff, 2013)

This kind of language in reference to Russia is an example of the uphill battle that Obama has had in trying to normalise relations with Moscow. The substance of the wider Hearing also functions as a good example of why it would be wrong to cast Russia as the only obstacle to attempts to intervene in Syria's terrible, costly conflict. Russia, and others, have legitimate concerns that Obama's administration, like Cameron's in the UK, has not been able to allay. That is in large part a symptom of the intervention fatigue that has been the outcome of the long years spent in Iraq and Afghanistan, as well as an understanding that military intervention, and regime change in particular, can have unforeseen and terrible consequences. In this way, the US's past foreign policy actions have become constraining factors which, in the case of Syria at least, Obama has not been able to overcome. This has given space for Russia to take the driving seat, leading to the erroneous impression that Putin is strong, Obama weak.

Two of the major tools Putin has had at his disposal to reinforce this impression are the Kremlin's dominance of mainstream media outlets in Russia and its use of legislation to shut down dissenting voices on social media sites.

A war of information

Since the mid-2000s, Russia has been speaking of and attempting to exercise soft power in its external relations. Ensuring provision of Russian sources of information that promote Russianness and Russian achievements has formed an extensive part of its foreign policy. According to the 2013 FPC: 'In its public diplomacy, Russia will … develop its own effective means of information influence on public opinion abroad … and take necessary measures to counteract information threats to its sovereignty and security'. Russia has certainly achieved this. RT is just the most visible of its efforts to present the official Russian vision of the world. Also well known is the work of the Kremlin's troll factory (Subbotovska, 2015).

The US has struggled to counter Russian efforts here and the Obama administration has come under fire from the House Foreign Affairs Committee for its failures. In February 2015, in his opening statement to the Committee, the Chairman spoke both of Russia 'gobbling up Ukraine' and of how it is spending more than half a billion US dollars annually 'to mislead audiences, to sow divisions, to push conspiracy theories out over RT television' (Royce, 2015). Royce went on to describe as dysfunctional the agency charged with responding to this, the Broadcasting Board of Governors. In an appearance before the Senate Foreign Relations Committee, John Kerry agreed the Russian information war was a major problem, arguing the US was simply not allocating the necessary funds to counter the Russians. In the same hearings, Kerry agreed with criticism that there was over-reliance on OCO (Overseas Contingency Operations) funds, stating a need to institutionalise OCO and more widely to ensure that there was 'multi-year authority to do multi-authority tasks' (Kerry, 2015). In this, Kerry exposed a wider failure in US foreign policy to ensure coherence across responsible bodies, to build longer-term strategies and to allocate sufficient budget considering the extent and range of threat. In relation to Russia's propaganda war, Kerry spoke of how Russia 'floods' 'frontline states' (Kerry, 2015) such as the Baltics, Bulgaria and Poland and stated frankly that the US$350 million currently allocated to countering Russian pressure is insufficient. As a consequence, many Russian speakers living outside Russia in eastern Europe believed Russia when it cast the US as the problem in Ukraine because there is nothing to counter its message. One response has been Voice of America's (VOA) production of a Russian-language programme, *Current Time*, available on various digital platforms and aired in Georgia, Latvia, Lithuania, Moldova and Ukraine since 2014 (*News on News*, 2015).

However, Russia's information war may already be showing signs of backfiring. A Pew Survey conducted in March–May 2015 reveals damage has been done to Russia's reputation. Public attitudes to Russia are largely unfavourable across large parts of the world and it trails well behind the US everywhere except the Middle East where the US was only marginally better received than Russia (29 versus 25 per cent expressing favourable opinions (Stokes, 2015)). Admittedly, the survey did not include those countries where Russia has focused many of its efforts, including the western Balkans, Bulgaria and Hungary. Nevertheless, it is other European states that are key to Russia's economy and its standing in the world. Reflecting the shift in Germany's foreign policy towards Russia, in Germany 70 per cent of those surveyed expressed an unfavourable view of Russia, compared to 50 per cent in 2010. In Italy too, another traditionally strong supporter of Russia, 69 per cent were unfavourable in 2015 (Stokes, 2015). In terms of leadership, Obama scored consistently higher than Putin everywhere. Notably too, Obama is viewed far more favourably than his predecessor, George W. Bush, implying he has gone some way to rehabilitate the US's image across the world.

Worrying for future US–Russia relations, however, is that within Russia itself the trend is very much in the other direction, reflecting Kremlin control of the media (and therefore information) within the country. By 2015, only 15 per cent held a favourable view of the US, compared to 51 per cent in 2013 (Bershidsky, 2015). And Obama fared little better, experiencing a fall in Russian public confidence in his foreign policy from 41 per cent in 2011 to just 11 per cent in 2015, comparable to Bush back in 2003 with 8 per cent (Stokes, 2015). At the same time, such large shifts one way mean they are relatively easily reversible and it is vital that the US leaves ground for a rapprochement with a future successor to Putin.

More immediately, the US *is* beginning to formulate a strategy for overcoming Russia's gains in this war of information. The 2016 budget includes an undisclosed amount of financing for 'Countering Russian Pressure and Aggressive Action Together with our European Allies' (White House, 2015b). While there has been relatively little comment on Russian activities in the western Balkans, Bulgaria, Hungary and others, the proposed allocation of finance in 2016 'to support efforts to bolster democracy and good governance, increase the capabilities of security forces, strengthen the rule of law and anti-corruption measures, and promote European Union integration, trade, and energy security' (White House, 2015b) suggests the Obama administration is alive to Russia's utilisation of soft power to win influence in certain EU member and candidate states. It suggests also that Obama has understood the need to send a range of confidence-building messages to eastern European states, in marked contrast to his first term when confidence measures were directed at Russia.

Conclusion

This chapter has argued that Obama's doctrine in respect of the US–Russia relationship has been one of 'damage limitation', marking a shift from the 'reset' that had been pursued in his first term in office. This second term doctrine, however, was driven less by Obama's preferences than by his perception of what was possible considering the constraints he faced. These included external events, especially the Syrian and Ukrainian conflicts; Putin's ruthless pursuit of his foreign policy objectives, no matter, seemingly, the cost; the structures within which Obama had to formulate and find support for his foreign policy; and, finally, with some circularity, Obama's own perception of Russia and what was achievable in this foreign policy relationship.

Also considered was the longer-term effect of Obama's Russia policy and the legacy of that for his successors. Here, the 'how' (Kennan, 1961) of Obama's Russia policy was the focus. In a sense, Obama's legacy will be the lesson given of how to maintain a foreign policy relationship in the face of extreme provocation. Obama has condemned Russian actions roundly where that is warranted, and resorted to legal and economic rather than purely military tools to sanction such actions. The 'dual track' currently being pursued is one of sanction accompanied by offers of dialogue and cooperation, the latter symptomatic of Obama's attempt to leave the ground prepared for a later, more constructive US–Russia relationship. Even while Obama has been subjected to much criticism, his foreign policy compared unfavourably with Putin's, the Pew Survey results indicate Obama has managed to restore some faith in US foreign policy, while Russia has suffered damage. In overcoming the negative historical legacy of previous administrations, Obama has created a space in which the US is more rather than less likely to achieve future foreign policy objectives. Some credit is due given this has been achieved in the context of the intractable challenges presented by the Syrian and Ukrainian conflicts, and a determinedly aggressive Russian foreign policy.

That said, this positive legacy cannot be perceived as secure. First, as events in Ukraine and Syria have amply demonstrated to Obama, any leader is subject to the vagaries of circumstance, which can derail a preferred policy course. These two conflicts have laid bare and extended the values gap between Obama's administration and Putin's. There is little reason to be optimistic that either conflict will be fully resolved before Obama leaves the White House and his successor may be either unwilling or unable (or both) to avoid a more overtly conflictual relationship with Russia. Second, Putin could outlast even Obama's successor and few in the West believe Russia–West relations will improve as long as Putin occupies the Kremlin (see, for instance, Nixey, 2014). Legacies, in short, are hostage to other fortunes, not least the actions of those who come after and the perceptions of the other actors with whom any foreign policy relationship is conducted.

On the credit sheet too should reside Obama's consistent drive to have Europeans take greater responsibility for their security. The EU's so far collective reaction to events in Ukraine demonstrates that this strategy has some merit. Further, we have witnessed Germany taking an unprecedented foreign policy lead on Ukraine, while the failure of other European actors, most notably the UK, to follow that lead cannot be regarded as the US's failure. Little analysis has focused on the idea that Obama's foreign policy incorporates an attempt to wean Europe off its dependency on the US and to free the US from the willingness of Western partners to try and keep their own hands clean and leave the USA to bear the blame. It is the case that Russia's actions in Ukraine have thwarted the Obama administration's attempt to reduce its allocation of resources to Europe. However, Obama has not been diverted from his determination to play the diplomatic versus the political game, giving Russia time and space to make mistakes and bear the consequences of them. Russia's lack of popularity as revealed by the Pew Survey, to say nothing of the deteriorating relationship with Turkey, are signs of the damage wreaked by Putin's foreign policy. Obama therefore has delivered a reminder of an important foreign policy message: time is often diplomacy's friend.

While there are some positives in Obama's second term Russia policy, it has also been a demonstration of how a leader's perception of another actor frames his or her view of what is possible. In the last year of his second term, seeking to secure his domestic legacy, and with Congress populated with many of his most vocal critics (Deyermond, 2012), it is understandable that Obama now looks set to ride out the storm with Putin. It is worth emphasising, however, that external events, Putin's intransigence and Congress's hurdles do not combine to shield

Obama from full culpability for his failed Russia policy. Obama's vision of Russia as a mere weak, regional power gave Putin the advantage of surprise. Ultimately, both the political and the diplomatic have to be balanced in foreign policy and Obama has ceded much of the political ground to Putin. The consequences of this are seen most clearly in Syria, where Putin's positioning of Russia ensures it will occupy a prominent position in peace negotiations.

Notes

1 See the White House (2010) for the administration's June 2010 account of the 'facts' behind the reset.
2 The official name is Federal Law on Introducing Amendments to Certain Legislative Acts of the Russian Federation Regarding the Regulation of Activities of Non-commercial Organizations Performing the Function of Foreign Agents.
3 The official name is On Sanctions for Individuals Violating Fundamental Human Rights and Freedoms of the Citizens of the Russian Federation.
4 The Magnistsky Act was essentially the price that Congress demanded for the repeal of the Jackson–Vanik Amendment.
5 The official name is Amendments to the Law Protecting Children from Information Harmful to their Health and Development.
6 The text is available in Russian at: http://static.kremlin.ru/media/events/files/ru/l8iXkR8XLAtxeilX7JK3XXy6Y0AsHD5v.pdf, last accessed 7 May 2016.
7 This was the eventual consensus accepted by the UN in relation to NATO air strikes against Belgrade in 1999.
8 This is a point that has been made in successive private conversations with foreign policy advisers since 2014 and in meetings attended by the author and held under the Chatham House Rule.

References

Adomanis, M. (2013) 'Barack Obama's Surprising Lack of Patience for Russia's Anti-Gay Laws'. *Forbes*, Aug 9 2013. Available online: www.forbes.com/sites/markadomanis/2013/08/09/barack-obamas-surpsrising-lack-of-patience-for-russias-anti-gay-laws/ (last accessed 20 August 2015).

Anon (2015) 'Putin's War on the West'. *The Economist*, 14 February. Available online: www.economist.com/news/leaders/21643189-ukraine-suffers-it-time-recognise-gravity-russian-threatand-counter (last accessed 20 November 2015).

Bershidsky, L. (2015) 'The World Hates Russia. Russia Hates It Back'. *Bloomberg View*, 5 August 2015. Available online: www.bloombergview.com/articles/2015–08–05/the-world-hates-russia-russia-hates-it-back (last accessed 20 August 2015).

Borger, J. (2014) 'Barack Obama: Russia is a Regional Power Showing Weakness over Ukraine'. *Guardian*, 25 March. Available online: www.theguardian.com/world/2014/mar/25/barack-obama-russia-regional-power-ukraine-weakness?CMP=twt_gu (last accessed 20 August 2015).

Campbell, K. and Andrews, B. (2013) *Explaining the US 'Pivot' to Asia.* London: Chatham House. Available online: www.chathamhouse.org/sites/files/chathamhouse/public/Research/Americas/0813pp_pivottoasia.pdf (last accessed 4 December 2015).

Council on Foreign Relations (2012) Dima Yakovlev Law, Moscow, December. Available online: www.cfr.org/russian-federation/dima-yakovlev-law-december-2012/p29756 (last accessed 20 August 2015).

Cullison, A. (2011) 'Putin Blames U.S. for Protests'. *Wall Street Journal*, 9 December 2011. Available online: www.wsj.com/articles/SB1000142405297020350130457708608112108 3576 (last accessed 20 August 2015).

David, M. (2015) 'Transitional Times: Russian Agency and International Intervention'. *Comillas Journal of International Relations*, 3: 100–115.

Deyermond, R. (2012) 'The Republican Challenge to Obama's Russia Policy'. *Survival: Global Politics and Strategy*, 54 (5): 67–92.

Deyermond, R. (2013) 'Assessing the Reset: Successes and Failures in the Obama Administration's Russia Policy, 2009–2012'. *European Security*, 22 (4): 500–523.

Hildreth, S. A. and Ek, C. (2009) *Long-Range Ballistic Missile Defense in Europe.* Washington DC: Congressional Research Service. Available online: www.fas.org/sgp/crs/weapons/RL34051.pdf (last accessed 4 December 2015).

Human Rights Watch (2015) *Russia: Government against Rights Groups.* Available online: www.hrw.org/news/2015/07/24/russia-government-against-rights-groups (last accessed 20 August 2015).

Kennan, G. (1961) 'George Kennan on Diplomacy as a Profession'. Washington DC: American Foreign Service Association. Available online: www.afsa.org/george-kennan-diplomacy-profession (last accessed 20 August 2015).

Kerry, J. (2015) 'John Kerry Testifies Before Senate Foreign Relations'. *YouTube.* 24 February. Available online: www.youtube.com/watch?v=L5I73MsYEOo (last accessed 20 August 2015).

Kramer, D. (2010) 'America's Silence Makes Us Complicit in Russia's Crimes'. *Washington Post*, 20 September. Available online: www.washingtonpost.com/wp-dyn/content/article/2010/09/19/AR2010091902893.html (last accessed 20 August 2015).

Kuchins, A. C. and Zevelev, I. A. (2012) 'Russian Foreign Policy: Continuity in Change'. *The Washington Quarterly*, 35 (1): 147–161.

Lavrov, S. (2012) 'Russia in the 21st-Century World of Power'. *Russia in Global Affairs*, 27 December. Available online: http://eng.globalaffairs.ru/number/Russia-in-the-21st-Century-World-of-Power-15809 (last accessed 20 August 2015).

Lukyanov, F. (2013) 'Russian Diplomats Move in to the Real World'. *Russia in Global Affairs*, 1 March. Available online http://eng.globalaffairs.ru/redcol/Russian-Diplomats-Move-in-to-the-Real-World-15860 (last accessed 20 August 2015).

Ministry of Foreign Affairs of the Russian Federation (2013) *Russian Foreign Policy Concept.* Moscow. Available online: http://archive.mid.ru//brp_4.nsf/0/76389FEC168189ED44257B2E0039B16D (last accessed 20 August 2015).

News on News (2015) 'VOA's Russian Language *Current Time* Launches Weekend Edition', 26 May. Available online: http://newsonnews.com/story/260515–508 (last accessed 20 August 2015).

Nixey, J. (2014) *Responding to Putin's Latest Ruse.* London: Chatham House, 11 May. Available online: www.chathamhouse.org/expert/comment/14291 (last accessed 04 December 2015).

Obama, B. (2014) 'Remarks by President Obama and Prime Minister Rutte of The Netherlands in a Joint Press Conference', 25 March. Available online: www.state.gov/documents/organization/235513.pdf (last accessed 20 August 2015).

President of Russia (2012) Vladimir Putin's Address to the Participants of the Fourth World Congress of Compatriots. Moscow, 26 October. Available online: http://en.kremlin.ru/events/president/news/16719 (last accessed 20 August 2015).

President of Russia (2013) Amendments to the Law Protecting Children from Information Harmful to their Health and Development. Moscow. Available online: http://en.kremlin.ru/acts/news/18423 (last accessed 20 August 2015).

Putin, V. (2014) Full Text of Putin's Speech on Crimea. *Prague Post*, 19 March. Available online: http://praguepost.com/eu-news/37854-full-text-of-putin-s-speech-on-crimea (last accessed 20 August 2015).

Royce, E. (2015) 'Chairman Royce Opens Hearing on 2016 State Department Budget w Secretary of State John Kerry'. *YouTube*. Available online: www.youtube.com/watch? v=RTu_4VW0mdM&feature=youtu.be (last accessed 20 August 2015).

Russian Embassy to the UK (2013) *Russian Embassy: On the Activity of Foreign-funded NGOs in Russia*. London. Press Release 10 April. Available online: www.rusemb.org. uk/press/1167 (last accessed 20 August 2015).

Ryzhkov, V. (2013) 'Anti-Gay Bill Takes Russia Back to Middle Ages'. *Moscow Times*, 12 February 2013. Available online: www.themoscowtimes.com/opinion/article/anti-gay-bill-takes-russia-back-to-middle-ages/475364.html (last accessed 20 August 2015).

Sakwa, R. (2012) 'Putin Redux: Continuity and Change'. *oDR Russia and Beyond*, 14 September. Available online: www.opendemocracy.net/od-russia/richard-sakwa/putin-redux-continuity-and-change (last accessed 20 November 2015).

Saltzman, I. Z. (2012) 'Russian Grand Strategy and the United States in the 21st Century'. *Orbis*, 56 (4): 547–564.

Stokes, B. (2015) 'Russia, Putin Held in Low Regard around the World'. Washington DC: Pew Research Center. Available online: www.pewglobal.org/files/2015/08/Pew-Research-Center-Russia-Image-Report-FINAL-August-5–2015.pdf (last accessed 20 August 2015).

Subbotovska, I. (2015) 'Russia Steps up Propaganda Push with Online "Kremlin Trolls"'. *San Diego Union Tribune*, 28 May. Available online: www.sandiegouniontribune.com/news/2015/may/28/russia-steps-up-propaganda-push-with-online/ (last accessed 20 August 2015).

Trenin, D. (2006) 'Russia Leaves the West'. *Foreign Affairs*, 85: 87–96.

Walker, S. (2015) 'Russia Admits Russian Military Presence in Ukraine for First Time.' *Guardian*, 17 December. Available online: www.theguardian.com/world/2015/dec/17/vladimir-putin-admits-russian-military-presence-ukraine (last accessed 28 December 2015).

Washington Post Staff (2013) 'FULL TRANSCRIPT: Kerry, Hagel and Dempsey Testify at Senate Foreign Relations Committee Hearing on Syria'. *Washington Post*, 3 September. Available online: www.washingtonpost.com/politics/2013/09/03/35ae1048–14ca-11e3-b182–1b3bb2eb474c_story.html (last accessed 20 August 2015).

White House (2010) *U.S.–Russia Relations: 'Reset' Fact Sheet*, 24 June. Available online: www.whitehouse.gov/the-press-office/us-russia-relations-reset-fact-sheet (last accessed 20 August 2015).

White House (2013) Statement by the Press Secretary on the President's Travel to Russia, 7 August. Available online: www.whitehouse.gov/the-press-office/2013/08/07/statement-press-secretary-president-s-travel-russia (last accessed 20 August 2015).

White House (2015a) *National Security Strategy*. Available online: www.whitehouse. gov/sites/default/files/docs/2015_national_security_strategy.pdf (last accessed 20 November 2015).

White House (2015b) 'The President's Budget for Fiscal Year 2016'. Office of Management and Budget. Available online: www.whitehouse.gov/omb/budget/ (last accessed 20 August 2015).

Wong, K. (2015) 'Obama, GOP Grapple over Iran'. *The Hill*, 3 September. Available online: http://thehill.com/homenews/senate/235149-obama-gop-vie-for-supremacy-on-iran (last accessed 20 November 2015).

12 The US and China

Obama's cautious engagement

Oliver Turner

In mid-1996 the US Congress voted to renew China's Most Favoured Nation status, ensuring that trade between the two countries could continue along 'normal' lines for at least another twelve months. In response, President Bill Clinton stated:

> [e]ngagement, not isolation, is the best way to advance America's interests with China as elsewhere. This positive vote helps us continue to engage China on a broad range of issues, including human rights, nonproliferation, trade, regional security, and relations with Taiwan. It enables us to continue to strengthen cooperation while firmly addressing our differences.
>
> (Clinton, 1996a)

At the time, the United States was in the midst of its 'unipolar moment' in which it was imagined to hold unrivalled economic and military power. Yet with high economic growth rates, increasing military expenditures, and concerted political and diplomatic efforts to enhance its presence in the workings of global affairs, China was already attracting attention as a 'rising power' of the first order.

Eighteen years later, in late 2014, President Barack Obama described the United States' twenty-first-century approach towards China:

> The United States will continue to pursue a constructive relationship with China.... [If] China is playing the role of a responsible actor ... that is good for this region, it's good for the world, it's good for the United States. So we'll pursue cooperation with China.... And in this engagement we will continue to be frank about where there are differences, because America will continue to stand up for our interests and principles.
>
> (White House, 2014)

In the nearly two decades between these presidential assessments, China's place in the world has evolved dramatically. Its GDP (by purchasing power parity) increased seven-fold, from around $2 trillion then to around $16 trillion now. The United States', by contrast, roughly doubled. As a share of world total, China's GDP increased from just less than 6 per cent in 1996 to around 16.5 per cent today, while the United States' declined from over 23 per cent to around 19 per cent (calculated from IMF, 2013). Concomitantly, China's military resources have grown exponentially. Its presence in existing organizations and institutions of global governance has deepened and widened and it has become the architect of new ones; it is a leader in scientific research and development; it has a mature space programme; a costly and expansive 'soft power' strategy to promote its culture abroad; and has advanced and developed in innumerable other ways besides. Yet despite this unprecedented rise, the words of Clinton and Obama reflect a certain long-term consistency towards China over at least the past twenty years. This approach can perhaps best be described as one of 'cautious engagement', based primarily around dialogue and cooperation rather than active hostility and containment, with careful manoeuvres around long-standing sites of tension and disagreement.

This chapter traces the key developments in US–China relations throughout the two-term presidency of Barack Obama, along with the approaches adopted in Washington designed to manage that relationship. It is argued that the lack of significant deviation in post-Cold War US China policy points to the overall lack of a discernible Obama Doctrine towards China. It is shown that China recaptured a more prominent place in American imaginations around the time of Obama's election in 2008, as attention was purposefully diverted away from the Bush administration's 'War on Terror'. Moreover, the sense of 'Hope' Obama inspired during his election campaign, which endured throughout the first months and years of his presidency, was reflected in his early dealings with Beijing. Over the course of Obama's time in office, however, tensions returned over such familiar issue areas as Tibet and Taiwan, along with those more specific to the contemporary global environment such as climate change and cybersecurity. The broad absence of an Obama Doctrine and continuation of cautious engagement is explained in part by the pragmatic need for Washington to retain cooperative relations with an increasingly wealthy and powerful state actor. In addition, however, it is explained by the changing patterns and structures of contemporary global power and its dispersal away from the nation state, which have limited the range of more radical options and which will almost certainly continue to impact Obama's immediate successor.

From Bush to Obama: China's return to the American imaginary

Obama's promising dawn...

In April 2001 a US EP-3 surveillance aircraft collided with a Chinese fighter jet over the island of Hainan. The incident strained US–China relations, with both sides attributing culpability to the other. It also came just two years after China's embassy in Belgrade was mistakenly destroyed by the US military during its operations against the Serbian forces occupying neighbouring Kosovo, resulting in the deaths of three Chinese citizens and widespread protests against the United

States. This period, characterized by sharp words and animosity, was abruptly resolved with the events of 11 September. China expressed sympathy for, and solidarity with, the United States in its new 'war' on Islamic extremism (some argue, to help justify its suppression of Muslim Uyghurs in western China; see for example Clarke, 2010), and China was identified as one of the 'important partners in the global coalition against terror' (Department of State, 2001). Islamic terrorism was elevated to the highest echelons of US security discourse, which manufactured the 'truth' that civilization itself was in peril. Understandings of the threats posed by a 'rising' China,[1] which had begun circulating more prominently throughout the 1990s, were subsumed by the newly imagined 'realities' of the post-9/11 world.

Throughout the long history of Sino-US relations 'truths' about China, as a friend, a threat, an opportunity and so on, have been socially constructed rather than self-evident (Turner, 2014a). In the post-Cold War 1990s, for example, China was 'the "best candidate" the United States could find' to fill the threat vacuum after the disappearance of the Soviet Union (Pan, 2004, p. 313). For nearly four decades China has been growing strongly and consistently so that its significance to the United States has fluctuated not simply from changes in its material physicalities, but from (re)constructions and (re)interpretations *of* those physicalities. This was evident in the aftermath of 9/11 when China was reimagined as a cooperative ally in the fight against terrorism, and then (to a lesser extent) during the period of Obama's election in 2008.

Around this time three especially notable developments had recently shaped, or were in the process of shaping, American perceptions of, and policy towards, China. First, the 2008 Summer Olympic Games in Beijing were highly symbolic in that they were widely interpreted to signal China's 'arrival' as a modern and influential global actor. They were designed for precisely that purpose; Beijing devoted $40 billion to the Olympics (Gratton *et al.*, 2015), with the aim of confirming China's great power status alongside the United States, Japan, Europe and others. Second, the US and wider West were in the midst of an economic depression and financial crisis. China escaped largely unharmed, maintaining high annual growth rates (which had peaked in 2007 at 14 per cent) to intensify debate about the 'rise' of China and the terminal 'decline' of the United States.

Third, and perhaps most importantly, the 2008 presidential election campaign between Obama and John McCain was dominated by concerns over the ailing domestic economy, but foreign policy debate broadly centred on withdrawing from Iraq and Afghanistan and winding down the 'War on Terror'. The financial crisis had also helped convince many that the US needed to scale back its Bush-era commitments and the 'War' was seen to have cost the United States (including its reputation) too dearly. Obama's promise of 'Hope' was in part intended to win over a war-weary public, and offer an escape from the politics of fear which had characterized the Bush presidency and its fanatical concern with terrorism. From 2009 newly elected Obama sought to steer attention towards Asia and the Asia Pacific as key sites of future US attention. Rising China – while never missing from US political discourse – resurfaced in American imaginations. Obama's administration also recognized the feeling across large parts of East and South-East Asia that Washington had paid scant diplomatic attention to the region over at least the past five to ten years, focusing instead on its anti-terror campaigns. This is neatly illustrated by the absence of Secretary of State Condoleezza Rice from two annual meetings of the Association of South-East Asian Nations (ASEAN) in her four-year term from 2005 to 2009 (see Bader, 2012, p. 2).

Historically, China has rarely been the uppermost priority of American politics or even foreign policy. Across the three televised presidential debates of 2008, for instance, China only appeared fleetingly behind Iraq, Afghanistan, Russia and Iran. Moreover, while Obama was keen to distance himself from the practices and worldview of the Bush administration and open a new chapter in US foreign policy, 30,000 extra troops were soon deployed to Afghanistan. In the Middle East of course the US still operates today, thirteen years after 'Mission accomplished' was infamously announced (Bush, 2003). Nonetheless, and in line with Obama's intention to repair America's damaged reputation abroad through a recommitment to global partnerships and multilateralism, the president and his cabinet were keen to quickly secure and redefine Washington's relationship with Beijing.

In April 2009 the US–China Strategic Economic Dialogue established under the Bush administration, the focus of which was on bilateral economic matters, was quickly rebranded and upgraded. By accommodating representatives of the State as well as the Treasury Department, along with their Chinese counterparts, Obama gave political and security issues in the forum more weight (Bader, 2012, pp. 21–22). The new Strategic and Economic Dialogue was announced at the G20 Summit in London, where Obama and China's president Hu Jintao cooperated to help bring about a coordinated international response to the economic downturn which had affected large parts of the world. Around this time the notion of a collaborative and more institutionalized US–China relationship in the form of a 'G2', which could increasingly shape the landscape of global affairs, gained wider credence.

As First Lady in 1995, Hillary Clinton had vocally emphasized the inextricability of women's rights from human rights in a thinly veiled attack on female infanticide and forced sterilization and abortion in China (*New York Times*, 1995). As Obama's first Secretary of State she visited China in early 2009 and adopted a far more measured tone, demoting China's record on human rights below other critical matters of the day. '[O]ur pressing on those issues [of human rights] can't interfere with the global economic crisis, the global climate change crisis, and the security crisis', she asserted 'It is essential that the United States and China have a positive, cooperative relationship' (CNN, 2009).

... *before familiar storm clouds return*

The first strains in the Obama administration's 'new' relations with China came in late 2009 and early 2010. At the UN Climate Change Conference in Copenhagen, Washington and Beijing found themselves on opposing sides of a familiar rift between the more developed global North and less developed global South, with each blaming the other for the failure of the event to produce any meaning- ful commitments to protect the global environment. A few months later China protested the sale of US military equipment to Taiwan, a deal struck in the final months of the Bush administration for billions of dollars worth of military heli- copters, mine-hunting ships and other advanced supplies. Since the middle of the last century Taiwan has represented the most consistently contentious issue in US–China relations. The US would not risk its own security in the protection of any small island a third of the way around the world, but it does so for one which constitutes an extension of democratic American identity on the doorstep of a large communist neighbour (see Turner, 2014a, ch. 4).

In February 2010 Obama also met with Tibet's Dalai Lama, again to the irri- tation of Beijing. A planned meeting had been postponed until after Obama's first visit to China in November 2009 to help secure the platform of Sino-US relations (*Washington Post*, 2009). Nevertheless, the issue of Tibetan independ- ence/autonomy has long been the second key site of enduring contention in US– China relations. Beijing insists that the region – like Taiwan – is an integral part of China, making the Chinese Communist Party, rather than the Dalai Lama, its rightful representative. The Dalai Lama has been a regular visitor to Washington in recent decades and Obama's journey along the path of cautious engagement with Tibet continued. It extended also to Taiwan; while the sale of arms went ahead it is important to note that Taiwan requested more from the deal, including F-16 fighter jets, but Washington refused in an attempt to avoid escalating ten- sions with Beijing.

Following China's communist revolution of 1949, Mao Zedong famously proclaimed that 'the Chinese have stood up'. After centuries of European and Japanese suppression the CCP claimed to have successfully reunified China, securing its territorial integrity. China's 'Century of Humiliation' remains embedded in the national psyche, with the fundamental desire for status and prestige inextricably linked to the prioritization of sovereignty and perceived encroachment by others, not least by China's main Cold War adversary, the United States. An understanding of this past helps explain Chinese intransigence over Taiwan and Tibet, along with such strategies as its recent construction of new islands in the South China Sea (discussed shortly), to regional protest; China is typically most inflexible and resolute on matters of territorial security. Accordingly, the Obama administration's 'pivot' – or 'rebalance' – to the Asia Pacific, announced in 2011, has generated less vocal objection from Beijing than many expected, though more has emanated from Chinese media and society (Swaine, 2012).

The stated aim of the 'rebalance' is to redirect US attention and resources away from Afghanistan and the Middle East and towards the Asia Pacific (see Turner, 2014b). Of course, the US has maintained a heavy presence across the region for decades, with current and former military bases in South Korea, Japan, the Philippines and elsewhere, and close trade, diplomatic and security relations with others. This precludes the need or even the capacity for a radical escalation of resources and, indeed, the 'rebalance' has developed more slowly than Washington's regular restatements of intent would have us believe. Thus in many respects the power of the policy lies mainly in the message it is designed to convey. To reintroduce former President Clinton in reflection of the long-term consistencies in US–China policy, articulations of the 'rebalance' are to inform everyone concerned that 'the United States has a continuing interest and a continuing presence in the Asia-Pacific region and … we're not going anywhere' (Clinton, 1996b). This message is reinforced by Obama's support for the vast and far-reaching Trans-Pacific Partnership, a proposed free trade deal between twelve Pacific Rim nations the terms of which were agreed in October 2015. China's control over state-owned enterprises precluded its involvement, and so the deal has been interpreted as a way for the US to prevent China from rewriting the regional economic system according to its own rules and values (*Wall Street Journal*, 2015).

Statements on the 'rebalance' have always had three key audiences. The first is the United States' allies in the Asia Pacific (and wider Asian region) and the second is China. The third, and arguably the most significant, is the American public and the announcement of the policy in late 2011 was auspiciously timed in advance of Obama's 2012 re-election campaign. Successive presidential candidates have talked tough on China before moderating their stance in office. For instance, Obama endorsed the proposed China Currency Manipulation Act and labelled George W. Bush's inactivity on the issue 'unacceptable' during his own campaign of 2008 (Reuters, 2008). As president in 2012 Obama resisted calls from his own challenger Mitt Romney to label China a currency manipulator. Romney accused Obama of weakness (Commission on Presidential Debates, 2012) at a time when 68 per cent of the American public, when asked if they considered China trustworthy, responded either 'not too much' or 'not at all'. Crucially, 45 per cent expressed the belief that Obama had not been tough enough on China (Pew Research Center, 2012). The 'rebalance' was thus emphasized in part to bolster the president's image as a defender of American interests in Asia.

Obama's second term

Extending the path of cautious engagement

In many respects, the contours of Obama's relationship with China in the first four years of his presidency mirrored those of his first term in office as a whole. The platform of 'Hope' on which he was elected offered great promise, as illustrated in his articulation of an alternative role for the United States in which military force would be complemented by multilateral cooperation, diplomacy and statecraft (White House, 2010). However as traditional sites of antagonism in US–China relations returned – like the Middle East, Afghanistan and other foreign policy priorities – Obama failed to steer the United States in a distinctively new direction. The path of cautious engagement Obama soon found with

China was already well trodden by Bush and Clinton, and it led directly into his second term.

To help cultivate an advanced understanding with China's new leader Xi Jinping, who became president in late 2012, Obama had transferred much of the responsibility for China policy from the State and Treasury Departments to Vice-President Joe Biden earlier that year. In June 2013 Obama met Xi for two days of talks in California, billed as 'the most important meeting between an American president and a Chinese leader in 40 years, since Nixon and Mao' (Nye, quoted in the *New York Times*, 2013). In the months preceding the visit the Chinese had been pushing for a joint declaration with the US of a 'new model of major country relations',[2] in a sign of the importance still attached to status and prestige in Beijing. Obama resisted, partly to avoid alienating others such as Japan and in Europe, and opted instead to describe this latest chapter as a 'new model of cooperation' (White House, 2013a). The two leaders agreed to work jointly towards the denuclearization of the Korean Peninsula and, more than three years after the failure of Copenhagen, towards slowing the rate of global climate change (White House, 2013b). The informal summit was widely regarded as a success, with a number of agreements made. Both leaders expressed a belief that cooperation over conflict serves the interests of both sides in the long run.

In the same year Xi proposed the creation of an 'Asian infrastructure bank'. The Asian Development Bank (ADB) has operated since the 1960s and the World Bank is active in Asia. However, with the ADB dominated by Japan and the World Bank by the United States, China was determined to lead its own influential multilateral organization, particularly given the acute need for improved infrastructure throughout the less developed parts of Asia. By early 2015 fifty-seven nations from around the world had become prospective founding members of the new Asian Infrastructure Investment Bank (AIIB), based in Shanghai. The most notable absentee was the United States which, along with Japan, did not apply for membership, citing concerns over transparency, governance standards and accounting methods (White House, 2015a).

Each tied into broader American fears about the weakening of the so-called 'Washington consensus' which promotes such neoliberal values as free markets, privatization and deregulation, and of organizations such as the World Bank which endorse them. Fears of an emerging 'Beijing consensus' defined by an alternative, Chinese-led value system, have grown in recent years and in an unsuccessful effort to undermine the legitimacy of the Bank the US lobbied the UK, Australia, South Korea and others to abstain (*Financial Times*, 2015). Former US Secretary of State Madeleine Albright argued that Washington had 'screwed up' in its AIIB strategy and had been left isolated (Center for Strategic and International Studies, 2012). Ultimately, the episode had little serious impact on wider US–China relations and Obama has left the door open to membership in the future.

A key site of tension around this time, however, and one which was primarily responsible for souring diplomatic relations in the months before the California summit, was – and remains – cybersecurity. In 2012 Obama wrote an editorial for the *Wall Street Journal* (2012) in which he emphasized the threats cyber-attacks posed to national security, stopping short of blaming a particular country or organization. China has been linked with large-scale cyberespionage since Obama's early years in office, but just a month before the talks in California his administration became markedly more explicit in its accusations; the Department of Defense asserted that the Chinese government and military had been respons-ible for numerous attacks since 2012 (Department of Defense, 2013). Beijing refuted the allegations and little progress was made on the matter during the presidential talks in June.

Along with cybersecurity, China's construction of new islands in disputed areas of the South China Sea has become far more prominent in regional US security discourse. The reclamations, which began in early 2014, expanded rapidly and while their intended purpose remains undeclared, it is likely that they will serve a military function and it is certain that they are designed to strengthen China's territorial claims to the area. Commitments by the United States to retain a strong presence in the region, notably via its planned 'rebalance', have been broadly welcomed by regional actors, not least those such as the Philippines and Taiwan with which the US has close ties, and which seek support in their mari-time disputes with Beijing in the South China Sea. In May 2015 Washington took the unusual step of inviting a news agency onto a surveillance flight over the islands to witness what were reported to be hostile communications with Chinese personnel, to promote the image of a China which is acting beyond the realms of acceptable behaviour (CNN, 2015).

Certainly, it is all but impossible to condone China's belligerent construction of the islands, not least because it is a signatory to the Declaration on the Conduct of Parties in the South China Sea (ASEAN, 2002). Equally, however, and as the Wikileaks organization and former CIA contractor Edward Snowden have recently helped demonstrate, the US under Obama remains guilty of many of the transgressions frequently attributed to China, including human rights abuses and widespread surveillance and 'cyberwarfare'. The discursive construc-tion of a self-evidently disruptive and threatening China in contradistinction to a benevolent United States as a defender of the status quo, in other words, con-tinues to frame American (and wider Western) interpretations of US–China rela-tions in ways not dissimilar to previous eras (see Turner, 2013).

Obama, China and shifting patterns of global power

US–China relations have been compared to 'great power' dynamics of the past, particularly those of the Cold War between the United States and the Soviet Union, with firm predictions made of the increasing likelihood (Kirshner, 2010) or even inevitability (Mearsheimer, 2006) of conflict. Indeed, the US Depart-ment of Defense (2014, pp. 15–16) observes that Obama's 'rebalance' to the Asia Pacific has been interpreted by China's government officials and wider population alike as 'further proof of "Cold War thinking" and a US effort to "contain" China's rise'. Yet such comparisons – unless heavily qualified – can be inaccurate and misleading. The US and China today, unlike the US and Soviet Union (and even China) during that period, communicate formally and regularly in multilateral and bilateral arenas; share intensive societal and cultural relations; and acknowledge (and in some cases jointly manage) shared strategic interests. Perhaps most importantly, they are locked into an economic and financial relationship – coined 'Chimerica' – on which both fundamentally rely. Unlike during the Cold War, American business is unashamedly pro-China, which has helped generate a Sino-US trade relationship of around US$600 billion (Morrison, 2015).

What this points to is the changing patterns and structures of global power. As noted at the outset, the broad absence of a discernible Obama Doctrine towards China and the continuation of cautious engagement may be explained in part by the need for Washington to retain positive and cooperative relations with a rapidly rising state actor; China is now wealthier and more influential, and its expanding capabilities are prominent considerations for US policy makers across the issue areas explored so far. Power in the international arena is commonly defined as the material (typically economic and military) capabilities of states. Yet particularly in the modern world power is fluid, dynamic and dispersed, and analyses of global affairs can be weak when understandings of power are restricted to assessments of state capability (Barnett and Duvall, 2005). In addition, then, Obama's cautious engagement of China is explained by the shifting nature of global power which partially limits the range of more radical political possibilities available to Washington.

In the presidential debates of 2012, for example, where China featured more prominently than in 2008, Mitt Romney pledged to toughen Washington's stance and 'crack down on China' to stem American job losses due to outsourcing. His stated intention was to label China a currency manipulator and impose tariffs on its goods (Commission on Presidential Debates, 2012). The problem – aside from Obama's observation that Romney had a record of investing in companies which outsource to China – is that such punitive measures risk triggering larger trade disputes, helping to explain the unwillingness of politicians, including Obama, to resort to such tactics in the past. A similar discourse played out during the 2010 mid-term elections in which China was represented as an economic threat to US employment (Turner, 2014a, pp. 155–158), with politicians making familiar promises to 'toughen up' on China. But of course, China does not take US corporations hostage or 'steal' American jobs. American business owners and managers choose to outsource their operations to China (and elsewhere) and so, in this sense at least, the economic 'threat' emanates not from China but from within the United States itself.

Obama resisted calls from Romney to label China a currency manipulator because of the wider ramifications it would have. A 'crackdown on China' from Washington would be inflammatory but also misdirected, given the ability of multinational corporations and small and medium-sized businesses to exploit the opportunities of an increasingly interconnected world. During the Cold War successive US presidents implemented an aggressive state-led containment strategy towards the Soviet Union to control its expansion and lessen its capabilities. In the 1990s the debate was often over whether Washington should repeat this containment, or engage with Beijing to work towards a mutually beneficial relationship. However, with China having long been embedded in, and a key beneficiary of, the intricate global structures of political and economic governance, the latter question was already redundant and cautious engagement became the only viable option.

The Obama administration has also been relatively cautious in its response to China's land reclamation in the South China Sea. Nations such as the Philippines and Vietnam are vocal in their criticism because of their overlapping territorial claims. Manila has taken the issue to the Permanent Court of Arbitration in The Hague and so, for some, US support and intervention are welcome. Many without comparable claims, however, including Thailand, Indonesia and Singapore, are less motivated to condemn China and a priority for them is to maintain an otherwise largely stable regional environment. Indeed, with China having established itself as the largest, or among the largest, trading partners of many Asian nations in and around the South China Sea, its neighbours are working to retain positive diplomatic relations with Beijing even when problems arise.

During the Cold War of course Asia was divided more cleanly. While no single 'communism' existed – as evidenced by the Sino-Soviet split of the 1960s – there was a neater division between those who welcomed communism and rejected American influence, and those whose allegiances lay implicitly or explicitly with Washington and the wider West. In the post-Cold War world the region's contours are more interwoven and complex. China has numerous interdependent, symbiotic relationships in Asia as well as with the United States, contributing to a more tentative strategy than those adopted by US presidents of the past, even while it aggressively stakes its claims to disputed territory. In June 2015 Obama labelled China's construction of new islands in the South China Sea 'aggressive' and 'counter-productive', but suggested that its territorial claims may in fact be legitimate (White House, 2015b).

Thus while China's tensions with the United States persist, the two nations are bound by a mutual reliance on one another for continued economic gain. By following the path of cautious engagement Obama has worked to sustain a relationship with China which – individual nuances aside – he essentially inherited in 2008 and which Bill Clinton left for George W. Bush in 2000. The absence of a distinctive Obama Doctrine towards Beijing has not been surprising, but it has helped challenge the opinions of those who have long predicted an inevitable deterioration of US–China relations and their descent into open hostility and conflict.

Conclusion

Obama is sometimes labelled a pragmatist (Milne, 2012) and even a realist (Walt, 2014), often to dislocate him from the idealism and moralism of George W. Bush. However, this chapter has described a broad continuation of the approach towards

China established by both Obama's immediate predecessors. The enduring strategy of cautious engagement, pursued for the most part by Clinton and Bush, highlights the overall lack of an identifiable Obama Doctrine towards China. A promising dawn emerged in 2009/10 when an early understanding seemed to have been cultivated with Beijing, reflecting the wider sense of newfound American 'Hope'. Yet expected sources of tension such as Taiwan and Tibet, along with those more characteristic of the early twenty-first century such as climate change and cyber-security, quickly (re)surfaced. Certainly then, Washington's relations with Beijing have wavered across Obama's eight years in office and throughout his second term in particular US rhetoric became more hard-edged. Generally speaking, however, the relationship has traversed familiar ground, veering only within relatively narrow extremes where broadly cooperative and occasionally positive dynamics have prevailed over almost routine episodes of tension and disagreement.

China's modern day physical rise – historically unprecedented in its pace and scope – has been a key motivation for the cautious engagement of post-Cold War presidents. So too have shifting patterns of global power which in certain important respects have limited the range of more radical possibilities in Washington. The US and China are two states separated by political-cultural differences and enduring sites of tension, and yet bound by an encompassing web of complex interdependence. Obama has had to tread carefully to avoid destabilizing the United States' relations with China, but equally those China shares with local actors whose priority is an absence of instability. Moreover, the mutual dependence of all these relations is unlikely to unravel in the near future, presenting Obama's successor with a familiar and yet rapidly evolving set of challenges. Indeed, while China overtook the United States by at least one economic measure in late 2014 (BBC, 2014), that successor will almost certainly be on duty when China passes many more significant milestones.

The past eight years have informed us that with Washington's policy makers largely impotent to slow or contain China's rise, a two-term strategy of cautious engagement has helped maintain the peace where many said it would fail. To this extent at least history will likely judge Obama favourably. That period also provides an important lesson for the next occupant of the White House. The election campaign and presidential debates will almost inevitably feature the usual China bashing for the sake of political point scoring. Yet the question for the next president, and even the presidential nominees – as in many ways it was for Obama – should be not so much 'how to manage China?', but how to manage and challenge the demands of those who argue that 'toughening up' or 'cracking down' on China is the starting position from which the interests of the United States and others are best served.

Notes

1 Inverted commas are used around the word 'rising' because it is not a neutral descriptor but heavily loaded, with connotations of a problem to be resolved. See Turner (2014a, pp. 152–153).
2 Sometimes translated as 'a new kind of great power relationship'.

References

ASEAN (2002), Declaration on the Conduct of Parties in the South China Sea. Available at: www.asean.org/asean/external-relations/china/item/declaration-on-the-conduct-of-parties-in-the-south-china-sea.

Bader, J. (2012), *Obama and China's Rise: An Insider's Account of America's Asia Strategy* (Washington DC: Brookings Institution Press).

Barnett, M. and Duvall, R. (2005), 'Power in International Politics', *International Organization* 59:1, 39–75.

BBC (2014), 'Is China's Economy Really the Largest in the World?', 16 December. Available at: www.bbc.co.uk/news/magazine-30483762.

Bush, G.W. (2003), 'Remarks by the President from Speech on the USS *Abraham Lincoln* on the Cessation of Combat Operations in Iraq', in National Review, *On War, Terrorism and Freedom: We Will Prevail* (New York: Continuum Books), 259–263.

Center for Strategic and International Studies (2012), 'Navigating Choppy Waters: China's Economic Decision-Making at a Time of Transition'. Available at http://csos/prg/files/publication/150327_navigating_choppy_waters.pdf.

Clarke, M. (2010), 'Widening the Net: China's Anti-Terror Laws and Human Rights in the Xinjiang Uyghur Autonomous Region', *The International Journal of Human Rights*, 14:4, 542–558.

Clinton, B. (1996a), 'Statement on House of Representatives Action on Most-Favored-Nation Trade Status for China', in Public Papers of the President of the United States: William J. Clinton (Washington DC: Government Printing Office), 988.

Clinton, B. (1996b), Press Briefing by David Johnson, Deputy White House Press Secretary and Senior Director of Public Affairs for the National Security Council, 3 July 1996. Available at: The American Presidency Project, www.presidency.ucsb.edu/ws/?pid=59401.

CNN (2009), 'Clinton: Chinese Human Rights Can't Interfere with Other Crises', 22 February. Available at: http://edition.cnn.com/2009/POLITICS/02/21/clinton.china.asia/.

CNN (2015), 'Exclusive: China Warns US Surveillance Plane', 27 May. Available at: http://edition.cnn.com/2015/05/20/politics/south-china-sea-navy-flight/.

Commission on Presidential Debates (2012), 'Debate Transcript', 16 October. Available at: www.debates.org/index.php?page=october-1–2012-the-second-obama-romney-presidential-debate.

Department of Defense (2013), *Annual Report to Congress: Military and Security Developments Involving the People's Republic of China 2013* (Washington DC: Government Printing Office).

Department of State (2001), 'US, China Stand Against Terrorism', 19 October. Available at: http://2001–2009.state.gov/s/ct/rls/rm/2001/5461.htm.

Department of Defense (2014), *Annual Report to Congress: Military and Security Developments Involving the People's Republic of China*. Available at: www.defense.gov/pubs/2014_DoD_China_Report.pdf.

Financial Times (2015), 'US Attacks UK's "Constant Accommodation" with China', 12 March. Available at: www.ft.com/cms/s/0/31c4880a-c8d2-11e4-bc64-00144feab7de.html#axzz3k21tnBQh.

Gratton, C., Preuss, H. and Liu, D. (2015), 'Economic Legacy to Cities From Hosting Mega Sports Events: A Case Study of Beijing 2008', in Richard Holt and Dino Ruta (eds), *Routledge Handbook of Sport and Legacy: Meeting the Challenge of Major Sports Events* (London: Routledge), 46–58.

IMF (2013) World Economic Outlook Database, October. Available at: www.imf.org/external/pubs/ft/weo/2013/02/weodata/index.aspx.

Kirshner, J. (2010) 'The Tragedy of Offensive Realism: Classical Realism and the Rise of China', *European Journal of International Relations*, 18:1, 53–75.

Mearsheimer, J. (2006), 'China's Unpeaceful Rise', *Current History*, 105, 160–162.

Milne, D. (2012), 'Pragmatist or What? The Future of US Foreign Policy', *International Affairs* 88:5, 935–951.

Morrison, W. (2015), 'China–US Trade Issues', Congressional Research Service Report, 17 March. Available at: www.fas.org/sgp/crs/row/RL33536.pdf.

New York Times (1995), 'Hillary Clinton, in China, Details Abuse of Women', 6 September. Available at: www.nytimes.com/1995/09/06/world/hillary-clinton-in-china-details-abuse-of-women.html.

New York Times (2013), 'Obama and Xi Try to Avoid a Cold War Mentality', 9 June. Available at: www.nytimes.com/2013/06/10/world/asia/obama-and-xi-try-to-avoid-a-cold-war-mentality.html?pagewanted=all.

Pan, C. (2004), 'The "China Threat" in American Self-Imagination: The Discursive Construction of Other as Power Politics', *Alternatives: Global, Local, Political*, 29, 305–331.

Pew Research Center (2012), 'How Americans and Chinese View Each Other'. Available at: www.pewglobal.org/2012/11/01/how-americans-and-chinese-view-each-other/.

Reuters (2008), 'Obama, Clinton, Back Senate Trade Bill on China Currency', 1 May. Available at: www.reuters.com/article/2008/05/01/usa-china-currency-idUSN0144032720080501.

Swaine, M. (2012), 'Chinese Leadership and Elite Responses to the US Pacific Pivot', *China Leadership Monitor*, 38. Available at: http://carnegieendowment.org/files/CLM38MS.pdf.

Turner, O. (2013), '"Threatening" China and US Security: The International Politics of Identity', *Review of International Studies*, 39:4, 903–924.

Turner, O. (2014a) *American Images of China: Identity, Power, Policy* (London: Routledge).

Turner, O. (2014b), 'The US "Pivot" to the Asia Pacific', in Inderjeet Parmar, Linda B. Miller and Mark Ledwidge (eds), *Obama and the World: New Directions in US Foreign Policy*, second edition (London: Routledge), 219–230.

Wall Street Journal (2012), 'Taking the Cyber Attack Threat Seriously', 19 July. Available at: www.wsj.com/articles/SB10000872396390444330904577535492693044650.

Wall Street Journal (2015), 'Trans-Pacific Trade Deal a Setback for China', 5 October. Available at: www.wsj.com/articles/trade-deal-a-setback-for-china-1444046962.

Walt, S. (2014), 'Is Barack Obama More of a Realist than I Am?', *Foreign Policy*, 19 August. Available at: http://foreignpolicy.com/2014/08/19/is-barack-obama-more-of-a-realist-than-i-am/.

Washington Post (2009), 'Obama's Meeting with the Dalai Lama is Delayed', 5 October. Available at: www.washingtonpost.com/wp-dyn/content/article/2009/10/04/AR2009100403262.html.

White House (2010), Remarks by the President at United States Military Academy at West Point Commencement, 22 May. Available at: www.whitehouse.gov/the-press-office/remarks-president-united-states-military-academy-west-point-commencement (accessed 27 February 2015).

White House (2013a), Remarks by President Obama and President Xi Jinping of the People's Republic of China Before Bilateral Meeting, 7 June. Available at: www.whitehouse.gov/the-press-office/2013/06/07/remarks-president-obama-and-president-xi-jinping-peoples-republic-china-.

White House (2013b), White House Briefing on Meetings Between Obama, China's Xi, 8 June. Available at: http://london.usembassy.gov/china049.html.

White House (2014), Remarks by President Obama at the University of Queensland, 15 November. Available at: www.whitehouse.gov/the-press-office/2014/11/15/remarks-president-obama-university-queensland.

White House (2015a), Remarks by President Obama and Prime Minister Abe of Japan in Joint Press Conference, 28 April. Available at: www.whitehouse.gov/the-press-office/2015/04/28/remarks-president-obama-and-prime-minister-abe-japan-joint-press-confere.

White House (2015b), Remarks by the President in Town Hall with YSEALI Initiative Fellows, 2 June. Available at: www.whitehouse.gov/the-press-office/2015/06/02/remarks-president-town-hall-yseali-initiative-fellows.

13 Energy security under Obama

Some hope, but not much change

Jonna Nyman

As the United States geared up for election in the spring and summer of 2012, I spent three months in Washington DC interviewing experts and policy makers working on energy security and energy policy. I attended talks and roundtable discussions focused on energy from every ideological angle. Energy played an important role in debates leading up to the election, and talk of the shale revolution was high on the agenda. With growth in American energy production, energy independence and reducing oil imports were at the forefront of commitments by both Barack Obama and Mitt Romney. However, they disagreed on what role the government should play in the energy system, on environmental regulation of the energy industry, and on the proposed Keystone XL pipeline. Despite this, one of the results of bringing up energy security and energy policy in Washington is immediate cries of: 'but the US doesn't have an energy policy!'. In some cases, this claim is based on the idea that the US energy system is independent of government; in other cases, it's a complaint that federal energy policy isn't clear enough. It may be true that US energy security strategy and policy are uncoordinated and unclear, but the government does routinely pursue policy in the name of energy security. Meanwhile, the supposed independence of the energy industry is a fiction. First, fossil fuel lobbies exert a huge amount of influence on government, through donations, lobbying and other pressure tactics. Second, the federal government intervenes in the energy market in myriad ways: sometimes directly, as during the Unocal affair in 2005 (Nyman 2014) and through bilateral energy agreements with foreign nations, and other times less directly, through subsidies, regulation and legislation on energy which all affect energy production and consumption. As noted by Bamberger, 'not only does the nation have an energy policy, it has adopted several distinct policy approaches over the years' (2003: 1).

Energy security is usually considered to be made up of two parts: security of supply (access to secure and reliable energy supplies) and price security (reliable or stable energy prices). While the meaning of energy security is increasingly debated, most discussions in the United States relate back to these two concerns and centre heavily on fossil fuels. It is particularly ingrained in US thinking because the country has a history of energy *in*security in these terms: the 1970s oil crises caused shortages and price hikes at a time when the country was used to energy abundance, and the effects still resonate. Indeed, every president since Nixon has endorsed energy independence to control supply and prices. As a result, energy is generally considered an issue of high politics in the United States. The term energy security is commonly used, and energy is generally considered an issue of national security (Nyman 2014). However, this notion of energy security leaves a dilemma: the energy resources focused on are finite, so any 'security' achieved is inherently time limited. Moreover, fossil fuel production and consumption represent the largest single contributor to climate change, which itself poses new and unpredictable security concerns. Barack Obama has campaigned both for changing energy policy and for taking action on climate change. However, initial promises of change have given way to reticence: climate change was hardly mentioned during the 2012 election campaign, and increasing fossil fuel production has become key in Obama's energy strategy. While speaking about the evils of dependence on foreign oil, Obama has enthusiastically praised the benefits of fracking and drilling, and expanding domestic pipelines.

This chapter argues that there is a fundamental conflict between Obama's energy policy and his position on climate change, that the two are incompatible. The chapter will analyse administration policy in the second term to show that Obama's energy security strategy has since 2012 seen not only continued but *expanded* exploration and exploitation of conventional and unconventional fossil fuels. Thus, while Obama came to power in 2008 on a wave of promises of hope and change, when it comes to energy security, the Obama administration has represented more continuity than change. Although his stance on climate change represents a welcome departure from his predecessor, his continued emphasis on fossil and nuclear energy industries devalues his environmental commitments. The chapter begins with a brief assessment of Obama's early years, outlining his pre-election and first term approach to energy security, before moving on to discuss his second term, comparing the discourse and practice of the administration and outlining some of the limits to change.

In the beginning, there was hope

In 2008, Obama was elected on a platform of hope and change. Energy was an important issue during the election and in Obama's campaign it was often explicitly linked to climate change. New energy and reducing consumption were key in the Democratic platform, alongside calls for global cooperation on energy and climate change. While the Republican platform supported fossil fuels strongly, advocating 'accelerated exploration, drilling and development', the Democratic platform argued that 'We can't drill our way to energy independence' (*New York Times* 2008). Obama promised that his presidency would mark 'a new chapter in America's leadership on climate change that will strengthen our security'. He spoke out loudly in favour of action on climate change, and even campaigned on cap and trade legislation to limit carbon emissions. He recognised the impact of energy choices on climate change. He went further to label climate change a shared security issue, stating that 'our dependence on oil and gas … puts the future of our planet in peril' – it is not only 'a security threat', but also 'a moral challenge of our time'. In response, he proposed investments to 'transform our energy economy', focusing on alternative energy as 'we need to do more than drill' (Obama 2008a). Obama's *Blueprint for change*, outlining his policy vision for the election campaign, contained a similar message. Energy was picked out as a key issue, with promises of relief from high gas prices, reduced dependence on foreign oil, green jobs and action on climate change, alongside 'promoting the responsible domestic production of oil and gas' (Obama and Biden 2008: 37–9). On the whole, the focus was on new, alternative and cleaner energies, fitting with his vision on climate change, and though he did also support increasing oil and gas production in the third election debate (Obama 2008b) this was not a focus of discussion. Overall, Obama's campaign and election promised change, both in energy policy and on climate change.

As Obama came into power, the focus was on the economy and one of the first measures taken was the Recovery Act, an economic stimulus package passed by Congress in February 2009 formally known as the American Recovery and Reinvestment Act of 2009. This included specific provisions to fund renewable energy and energy efficiency developments, as well as a (much smaller) provision for fossil fuel research and development (Recovery Act 2009). Obama also established a White House Office of Energy and Climate Change to coordinate policy, suggesting a new approach to both. However, he soon ran into resistance. His attempt to push through cap and trade legislation failed to pass through Congress. Despite his aims to establish the US as a global leader on climate change, the United Nations Climate Change negotiations in Copenhagen in 2009 were widely seen as a failure. The world had hoped to develop a binding framework to replace the Kyoto Protocol, but the negotiations resulted in a weak, non-binding agreement. Congressional resistance to commit on climate change left the US in a weak negotiating position, and Obama's last-ditch attempt to strengthen negotiations by arriving in person was not sufficient to strike a more ambitious agreement. He has made multiple failed attempts to cut federal subsidies for fossil fuels. Overall, Obama did focus more on climate change in the first couple of years of his administration, but the recession shifted the political climate. As a result, the focus was on clean energy as a jobs creator and a way to restart the economy, rather than the threat of climate change, discussion of which largely disappeared from Obama's political discourse. The resistance he faced did not help: according to Open Secrets, an independent organisation tracking money in US politics, the oil and gas industries alone spent $175 million lobbying against climate legislation in 2009 alone (Mackinder 2010). Moreover, the global context changed with the Libyan revolution and the spike in oil prices that followed in 2011, and the administration shifted focus to the oil market and to fossil fuels more broadly.

The shift is well illustrated in Obama's 2012 State of the Union speech, where he announced that 'this country needs an all-out, all-of-the-above strategy that develops every available source of American energy' (Obama 2012a). With this,

Obama and his first Secretary of Energy Steven Chu put everything on the table, allowing a refocus on fossil fuels. This was a clear change from previous Democratic administrations which tended to focus more on efficiency and renewables. Compared to previous Democratic administrations, they also made a stronger, unequivocal commitment to nuclear energy. In practice, the 'all-out, all-of-the-above' approach involved a refocus on traditional sources of energy, increased drilling for oil and gas, and more 'clean' coal and nuclear, while continuing the focus on efficiency/clean energy. The mood had shifted, and energy became key. This is not to say that the administration gave up all ambitions on climate change, but the prevailing atmosphere suggested that focusing on clean energy, green jobs and economic growth was the solution: climate change would get dealt with along the way. As one interviewee noted during my own research, 'dealing with energy, you're not allowed to say climate change anymore'. However, despite the focus on clean energy, the administration also continued support for non-renewable and fossil energy industries.

Before turning to Obama's second term, it's worth noting the level of continuity between his energy policy and that of the preceding Bush administration. The two are often seen as representing opposing sides of the energy/climate spectrum. Of course, Bush was more sceptical of climate change, especially during his first administration, and more committed to the fossil fuel industries. However, there is more continuity between the two in terms of energy policy than is usually recognised. They both focused strongly on reducing dependence on foreign oil, and emphasised increasing domestic production as a response. While Obama has taken more of a regulatory approach and has placed more emphasis on renewable energy, the support for domestic fossil fuel industries has remained. In 2011, Obama boasted that 'last year, American oil production reached its highest level since 2003' (Obama 2011). Despite his emphasis on climate change, Obama has not only permitted but actively promoted and pursued expanded domestic fossil fuel production. This is also recognised in an Oxford Institute for Energy Studies report, which notes that throughout Obama's first administration 'the public message has been more about energy security and creating jobs than about climate change. To the extent that these objectives were in conflict, the priority was not climate change' (Robinson 2013: 3).

Re-election: 'we've added enough new oil and gas pipeline to encircle the Earth and then some'

In 2012, Obama's election campaign exemplified the changing focus of the administration. With the world (and oil prices) in turmoil as the Arab Spring gained force and the country still suffering from the recession, climate change was not a vote winner. Energy was key in the campaign, following the new energy strategy announced in the 2012 State of the Union address. During a campaign speech in a TransCanada pipeline yard in the oil town of Cushing, Oklahoma, Obama noted that 'producing more oil and gas here at home has been, and will continue to be, a critical part of an all-of-the-above energy strategy'. He went on to add,

Now, under my administration, America is producing more oil today than at any time in the last eight years. [Applause.] That's important to know. Over the last three years, I've directed my administration to open up millions of acres for gas and oil exploration across 23 different states. We're opening up more than 75 percent of our potential oil resources offshore. We've quadrupled the number of operating rigs to a record high. We've added enough new oil and gas pipeline to encircle the Earth and then some.... And as long as I'm President, we're going to keep on encouraging oil development and infrastructure.

(Obama 2012b)

In May 2012, after poor results in a Democratic primary in West Virginia, a state 'heavily reliant on the coal industry', the Obama campaign quietly added 'clean coal' to its energy policy website (Markay 2012). Having already shifted away from a stronger public stance on climate change, Obama's 2012 campaign focused heavily on energy while climate change was largely absent both from the campaign and from the election debates. At the same time, the shale revolution was also gaining force, with 2012 seeing frequent discussions and debates over the possibilities for American energy independence with growing shale oil and gas production. Obama seized on this opportunity to showcase his energy and economic growth agenda. Shale gas in particular was continually represented as environmentally friendly, compared with coal. However, in practice shale gas often replaced renewable energy production rather than coal production, so the climate benefit is debatable, especially given the potential environmental impacts of shale production (particularly methane leaks and groundwater contamination). Indeed, a 2011 study suggested that if we look at long-term impacts, shale gas has a larger greenhouse gas footprint than either conventional gas or oil, or coal (Howarth *et al.* 2011). Again, during the election debates there was discussion on offshore drilling and coal, but no focus on climate change.

Obama's second administration saw a growing conflict between his energy policy and supposed climate commitments. As will be discussed later, climate change does resurface in 2013, but Obama's enduring commitment to fossil fuel exploitation undermines his climate agenda. He has achieved some changes in energy policy, notably some increases in domestic renewable energy production and energy efficiency. However, without a more substantial change in energy policy his climate strategy will have little substantive impact. The rest of this section will discuss Obama's second term positions on energy and climate change, beginning by detailing his discourse on the issues before outlining and comparing the discourse to his policies.

Part one: discourse

Energy security has been key in Obama's second term agenda: he has continued his all-of-the-above energy strategy in the name of sustainable economic growth and energy independence. The importance of both energy and climate change in the discourse of the Obama administration can be seen in Obama's State of the Union speech in January 2013. Here, both issues were central: Obama directed his Cabinet to come up with measures to 'reduce pollution, prepare our communities for the consequences of climate change, and speed the transition to more sustainable forms of energy' (Fox-Penner 2013). He also proposed an Energy Security Trust, to support research into shifting trucks and cars off oil (Obama 2013c).

A key 40-page document released on the strategy in 2014 spends the first 30 pages detailing the ways in which the strategy has driven the energy revolution and the economic recovery, and it's only on page 31 that the document turns to the need for a low carbon future (White House 2014a). Even here, there is continued emphasis on nuclear energy and clean coal. In the summary, the benefits of the strategy are listed in the order of economic growth, energy security, and then, lastly, reducing emissions (White House 2014a: 2). The document also notes that 'The United States has emerged as the world's leading producer of petroleum and natural gas. In 2013, combined production of petroleum, natural gas, and other liquid fuels in the United States exceeded that of Saudi Arabia and Russia', and the strategy aims to continue this (White House 2014a: 3). It takes an unusual approach in that it defines energy security explicitly, which is rarely the case in official policy documents (Littlefield 2013). Here, it states that 'the term energy security is used to mean different things in different contexts, and broadly covers energy supply availability, reliability, affordability, and geopolitical considerations' (White House 2014a: 20). Interestingly, this is followed by a footnote referencing a joint statement by the G7 energy ministers on energy security. However, there is an important difference between the two definitions: the joint statement includes reducing greenhouse gas emissions as part of creating enduring energy security, something which disappears in the definition in the White House document.

Indeed, expanding oil and gas production is explicitly raised as key to national security in both of Obama's National Security Strategies (White House 2015a, 2010). Overall, Obama's discourse on energy security shows a significant amount of continuity with previous administrations, particularly in the continued focus on energy independence through the all-of-the-above strategy. This strategy has led to some progress on clean energy and renewables, but the overall commitment to increasing domestic production of fossil fuel energy sources as well as nuclear power suggests that climate change remains a secondary priority. Herbstreuth (2014) has studied the focus on energy independence in the United States, and suggests that the discourse on energy dependence and independence is constructed on particular geographical/spatial delineations, where energy independence doesn't actually necessarily mean only domestic production, but includes imports from 'safe' countries, namely Canada and Mexico. Thus, dependence is constructed as negative, but is strongly linked with cultural representations of the Middle East as foreign and other. Thus, 'foreign' oil is only a problem when it comes from particular countries or regions: in other cases it represents mutually beneficial economic interdependence (Herbstreuth 2014).

Genuine American energy independence is often dismissed by experts as either impossible, unnecessary, or both: yet consecutive presidents continue to consider it a goal.

While climate change was downplayed during the 2012 election campaign, Obama moved quite swiftly to reposition the issue in his 2013 State of the Union speech, and unveiled a major new Climate Action Plan in June 2013. The Climate Action Plan is an impressive document outlining the climate strategy of Obama's second administration. The language in the plan is strong: 'we have a moral obligation to future generations to leave them a planet that is not polluted and damaged … climate change is no longer a distant threat – we are already feeling its impacts across the country and the world' (White House 2013: 4). It sets clear targets, and one of the key pillars on which it is based is to cut carbon pollution in the United States. It recognises that 'Climate change represents one of the greatest challenges of our time' (White House 2013: 5) – a far cry from the early George W. Bush years. Even the energy strategy discussed above recognises that 'Approximately 87 percent of U.S. anthropogenic emissions of all greenhouse gases are energy-related' (White House 2014a: 31). The plan also talks specifically about climate security, and there is a broader shift in Obama's discourse on climate change in 2013 to emphasise the security implications.

In the State of the Union speech, he noted the need to 'act before it's too late' on climate change, suggesting that this means he may need to act without Congressional approval (Obama 2013c). However, the commitment to domestic fossil fuel production was retained with a promise to 'keep cutting red tape and speeding up new oil and gas permits' (Obama 2013c). In a speech in Berlin, Obama called for joint action on climate change, explicitly labelling it 'the global threat of our time' (Obama 2013a). He presented a new plan 'to lead the world in a coordinated assault on a changing climate' (Obama 2013b). Here, he created a sense of urgency and emergency associated with security discourse. On the other hand, the 2014 State of the Union address noted the continuing 'commitment to American energy', the all-of-the-above energy strategy and energy independence, as well as continued increases in natural gas (Obama 2014). While Obama's framing of climate change as a security issue is important, it is continually undermined by his energy policy. However, in his second administration he has taken a stronger position on climate change, together with efficiency and environmental regulations, some of which will be discussed under policy, below.

Overall, Obama's second term discourse shows some hope, and some change. The Climate Action Plan, together with the repositioning of climate change as a key issue, suggests that climate change has come back into focus. However, the discourse on energy security makes it difficult to take this seriously: the continued emphasis on increasing domestic fossil energy production in the name of national security and energy independence calls Obama's climate commitment into question. Some of the language around energy security is particularly problematic, framing it as a national security issue in ways that make it seem as if boosting domestic production is the cure for all ills.

Part two: policy

In many ways Obama's 'all-out, all of the above' approach to energy security has represented a return to a fossil- and nuclear-focused policy rather than the shift towards sustainability promised. His strategy has tried to depoliticise the issue, appointing two scientists as his consecutive Secretaries of Energy. The second National Security Strategy also highlights a growing focus on energy as a national security issue. Energy is frequently framed either in security terms or as an issue of economic growth: and both are seen to necessitate a strategy centred on domestic production of fossil fuels (Nyman 2016). The 2014 Energy Security Strategy emphasises the energy revolution, highlighting the impact increasing oil and gas production has had on economic growth and jobs creation (White House 2014a: 3). Obama has embraced the shale gas industry, viewing gas as a key bridging fuel for moving towards cleaner energies. However, while he has attempted to phase out fossil fuel subsidies, Congressional resistance has made this impossible and in practice the growth of the industries has meant that subsidies for oil and gas exploration actually doubled between 2009 and 2013 (Leber 2014). Obama has opened more areas, offshore and onshore, for oil and gas exploration, and presided over an unprecedented expansion in production. A White House blogpost from 2014 heralds growing US oil and gas production. It notes:

> Onshore, nearly 36.1 million acres of federal land were under lease to oil and gas companies last year. Of that land, over 12.6 million acres were actively producing oil and gas – the highest acreage under production since 2008. Last year, the Interior Department's Bureau of Land Management (BLM) held 30 separate oil and gas lease sales, offering 5.7 million acres for lease by industry, the most in a decade. Even as sales have gone up, processing time for onshore drilling permits has gone down – last year, it took an average of 194 days to process an APD [application for permit to drill], down from 228 in 2012 and faster than any time since 2005. Offshore, the Interior Department's Bureau of Ocean Energy Management (BOEM) offered 59 million acres for lease by industry in the Gulf of Mexico last year, and industry submitted bids on 3 percent of these acres, resulting in $1.3 billion in high bids. The current Five Year Offshore Oil and Gas Leasing Program includes 15 potential lease sales in six planning areas that comprise some of the richest and most promising areas for oil and gas exploration and development.
>
> (White House 2014c)

Overall, there's been a lack of new legislation on energy because of Congressional resistance, and as a result oil and gas industries in particular continue to be treated very favourably. Under Obama, the focus remains on reducing dependence on *foreign* oil, rather than on dirty sources of energy altogether (White House 2015b). The administration has opened up huge new areas for oil and gas exploration and continued to invest federal money in dirty sources of energy: all in the name of energy independence.

Alongside this, Obama has included a focus on renewable sources of energy in his second term strategy. He has pursued a number of initiatives supported by the Recovery Act. Overall, 'total energy obtained from wind, solar, and geothermal sources has more than doubled since 2009' (White House 2014a: 2; see also White House 2014b, 2012). The administration has also introduced important efficiency standards for vehicles, homes and appliances (White House 2014a: 8). To an extent, these policies have been successful, and Obama has managed an increase in renewable energy production and consumption, as well as energy efficiency (Nyman 2016: 22). After a long waiting period, he also vetoed the controversial Keystone XL pipeline, citing its potential environmental impacts as a core reason. However, as the United States increases renewable energy production, there is also a growing debate over oil, gas and coal exports. For example, the US continues to export a large amount of coal (EIA 2015), which negates the net climate benefit of US consumers shifting from coal to renewables.

Some of Obama's initiatives on climate change have been significant, however. The Climate Action Plan from 2013 has three pillars: cutting carbon pollution, preparing for the impacts of climate change, and leading international efforts on climate change (White House 2013: 5). It includes seventy-five climate targets, many of which it has already achieved and on all of which it has made some progress (Tubman 2015). It also announces a Presidential Memorandum directing the Environmental Protection Agency (EPA) to develop carbon pollution standards: an important sign of what was to come. Climate policy in Obama's first term was halted by Congressional resistance which has made it difficult to implement change. Even at that stage, however, Obama chose to use executive action to direct the EPA to regulate emissions. The initiatives taken under the new Climate Plan give the EPA further directives to regulate carbon pollution, and the vast majority of the Plan relies on executive action. Moreover, in 2014, Obama took further executive action on climate change, unilaterally pushing cap and trade regulation through the EPA in the face of continued Congressional resistance (Dumaine 2014). In some ways, action has been limited by Congressional resistance, and while the use of executive action has allowed Obama to push some of his policies anyway, the next president can reverse the changes just as easily.

The Energy Security Strategy notes that 'The United States has reduced its total carbon pollution since 2005 more than any other nation on Earth', a significant achievement, but it also recognises that projections suggest emissions may rise again (White House 2014a: 3). Energy-related CO_2 emissions have fallen by 10 per cent since 2007, partly due to cleaner energy and energy efficiency, but more than half of the reduction can be attributed to slowed economic activity with the recession (White House 2014a: 31). Problematically, the Climate Action Plan continues to endorses natural gas as a bridging fuel, which is dubious – even researchers from the National Oceanic and Atmospheric Administration (NOAA), a US federal agency, have called into question the climate benefits of natural gas (Romm 2013). It also calls for phasing out fossil fuel subsidies, which has still not been achieved.

In many ways, Obama's climate policy and climate commitments are impressive, and increasingly match his rhetoric on climate change – particularly since the release of the 2013 Climate Action Plan which has been followed by an impressive number of initiatives. His energy policy also matches his rhetoric, showing continued focus on increasing domestic fossil fuel production alongside cleaner sources of energy. However, what does not match up is Obama's approaches to energy security and climate change. Energy security policy focuses on energy independence, emphasising increasing domestic production in the name of national security and economic growth. However, continued focus on fossil fuels is clearly not sustainable, in any sense of the word. Despite some increases in renewable energy production, Obama's energy policy more generally continues to undermine his climate agenda. His approach to energy security is finite, and does not produce security in the longer term.

Change is difficult: there are many barriers and political resistance. There is clear evidence that climate change and energy security are best dealt with together (Jacobson 2009; McCollum *et al.* 2013). But Obama cannot be wholly blamed for his record. He has attempted to push climate change and renewable energy, but has faced a difficult context and institutional resistance. The recession placed the focus on economic growth, and Obama has tried to use this to push clean energy as a jobs and growth creator. To some degree, this has been successful: the Recovery Act provided funding for clean energy and energy efficiency measures. However, Vezirgiannidou's study of different ways of framing climate change in the United States found that the Obama administration consistently framed climate change in terms focused on energy security and economic growth (2013). In practice, she finds that rather than increasing support for climate change, such strategies allow other concerns to take over, effectively overriding climate considerations and 'the climate message loses its potency' (Vezirgiannidou 2013). So Obama's attempts to 'hide' climate change initiatives in energy security and growth strategies may not have been the most effective strategy.

Obama has also faced political resistance: both from Republicans in Congress and from the fossil fuel lobby which has used pressure tactics to resist climate legislation and attempts to cut subsidies. The effects also can be seen in the failed cap and trade bill and the failure of the Copenhagen negotiations. Obama's second term has faced a House and Senate dominated by Republicans. Even the Chair of the Senate Committee on the Environment, Senator Jim Inhofe, favours increased domestic energy production and has called climate change a hoax: he recently threw a snowball in the Senate to 'disprove' global warming. Energy security itself does not help: it's rarely clearly defined, and vague and imprecise terminology over energy prohibits genuine discussion and meaningful public debate, allowing different groups to hijack terms for their own ends (Littlefield 2013). Bang's study of the US political system found that while dealing with energy and climate issues together resulted in more climate-friendly policy, 'the established energy policy majority preferred to focus exclusively on energy security issues and disregard the effects for climate change, trying to keep it off the agenda' (2010: 1649). Ultimately, 'the design and structure of the political institutions and their voting rules prevented radical change away from the status quo' (Bang 2010: 1652). A persistent divide between staff working on energy and climate in key institutions also makes it hard to coordinate the issues (Nyman 2016).

House Republicans in particular have continued to push domestic fossil fuel production through the American Energy Initiative (House Committee on Natural Resources 2015). Initiatives have favoured lowering petrol prices, expanding fossil energy production, protecting coal mines, and removing barriers to offshore oil exploration (put in place after the Deepwater Horizon oil spill in the Gulf of Mexico in 2010). Funding was also cut for Obama's White House Office on Energy and Climate Change in 2011. Climate change remains deeply divisive and politicised. Despite this, Obama hasn't completely given up his climate agenda, pushing action through the EPA where possible.

Conclusion

Obama's record on energy security is significant. However, despite triumphant messages proclaiming 'America's new energy security', suggesting that the United States is more secure than ever (Yergin 2011), these policies may actually be making America less secure in the long term. For a president who sees action on climate change as key to his legacy, an energy policy which continues to support expanding domestic fossil fuel and nuclear energy production is shameful. Energy is frequently framed either in security terms or as an issue of economic growth: and both are seen to necessitate a strategy centred on domestic production of fossil fuels. However, boosting domestic production is not the panacea Obama presents it as. Experts argue that we cannot even extract all the oil and gas we have already discovered if we want to avoid the worst impacts of climate change. Climate change, in turn, is listed as a 'threat multiplier' by the United States' own Quadrennial Defense Review (US Department of Defense 2014: 8; see also US Department of Defense 2015). Thus, overall, Obama's approach to energy security has represented some hope, but not enough change.

References

Bamberger, R. (2003) 'Energy policy: historical overview, conceptual framework, and continuing issues', Congressional Research Service, published online at www.nation alaglawcenter.org/assets/crs/RL31720.pdf, accessed on 26 September 2012.

Bang, G. (2010) 'Energy security and climate change concerns: triggers for energy policy change in the United States?', *Energy Policy*, 38(4), 1645–53.

Dumaine, B. (2014) 'Why business will hate Obama's new cap-and-trade rules', *Fortune*, published online at http://fortune.com/2014/06/03/business-will-hate-obama-new-cap-and-trade-rule/, accessed on 3 August 2015.

EIA (2015) 'US coal exports Jan–March 2015', Energy Information Administration, published online at www.eia.gov/coal/production/quarterly/pdf/t7p01p1.pdf, accessed on 3 August 2015.

Fox-Penner, P. (2013) 'A high-energy State of the Union', *Huffington Post*, published online at www.huffingtonpost.com/peter-foxpenner-phd/a-highenergy-state-of-the-union_b_2689 389.html, accessed on 2 August 2015.

Herbstreuth, S. (2014) 'Constructing dependency: the United States and the problem of foreign oil', *Millennium – Journal of International Studies*, 43(1), 24–42.

House Committee on Natural Resources (2015) 'American energy', House Committee on Natural Resources, published online at http://naturalresources.house.gov/american energy/, accessed on 31 July 2015.

Howarth, R. W., Santoro, R. and Ingraffea, A. (2011) 'Methane and the greenhouse-gas footprint of natural gas from shale formations', *Climatic Change*, 106, 679–90.

Jacobson, M. Z. (2009) 'Review of solutions to global warming, air pollution, and energy security', *Energy & Environmental Science*, 2(2), 148–73.

Leber, R. (2014) 'Obama oil and gas subsidies', *New Republic*, published online at www.newrepublic.com/article/120239/us-subsidies-fossil-fuel-exploration-double-under-obamas-watch, accessed on 2 August 2015.

Littlefield, S. R. (2013) 'Security, independence, and sustainability: imprecise language and the manipulation of energy policy in the United States', *Energy Policy*, 52, 779–88.

McCollum, D. L., Krey, V., Riahi, K., Kolp, P., Grubler, A., Makowski, M. and Nakicenovic, N. (2013) 'Climate policies can help resolve energy security and air pollution challenges', *Climatic Change*, 119(2), 479–94.

Mackinder, E. (2010) 'Pro-environment groups outmatched, outspent in battle over climate change legislation', *Open Secrets*, published online at www.opensecrets.org/news/2010/08/pro-environment-groups-were-outmatc/, accessed on 23 July 2015.

Markay, L. (2012) 'Obama campaign quietly adds "clean coal" to energy policy website', *Daily Signal*, published online at http://dailysignal.com/2012/05/11/obama-campaign-quietly-adds-clean-coal-to-energy-policy-website/, accessed on 31 July 2015.

New York Times (2008) 'Party platforms 2008', *New York Times*, published online at http://elections.nytimes.com/2008/president/issues/party-platforms/index.html, accessed on 22 July 2015.

Nyman, J. (2014) 'Red storm ahead: securitisation of energy in US–China relations', *Millennium*, 43(1), 43–65.

Nyman, J. (2016) 'Rethinking energy, climate and security', *Journal of International Relations and Development*, published online at www.palgrave-journals.com/jird/journal/vaop/ncurrent/abs/jird201526a.html, accessed 4 May 2016.

Obama, B. (2008a) 'Obama addresses the Clinton global initiative', *Washington Post*, published online at www.washingtonpost.com/wp-dyn/content/article/2008/09/25/AR2008092501675_4.html, accessed on 21 July 2015.

Obama, B. (2008b) 'The third presidential debate [transcript]', *New York Times*, published online at http://elections.nytimes.com/2008/president/debates/transcripts/third-presidential-debate.html, accessed on 22 July 2015.

Obama, B. (2011) '2011.03.11 Obama news conference', *Washington Post*, published online at http://projects.washingtonpost.com/obama-speeches/speech/586/, accessed on 20 September 2012.

Obama, B. (2012a) '2012.01.24 Obama State of the Union', Office of the Press Secretary, published online at www.whitehouse.gov/the-press-office/2012/01/24/remarks-president-state-union-address, accessed on 21 September 2012.

Obama, B. (2012b) '2012.03.22 Obama in Cushing', White House, published online at www.whitehouse.gov/the-press-office/2012/03/22/remarks-president-american-made-energy, accessed on 31 July 2015.

Obama, B. (2013a) 'Remarks by Obama at the Brandenburg Gate', White House, published online at www.whitehouse.gov/the-press-office/2013/06/19/remarks-president-obama-brandenburg-gate-berlin-germany, accessed on 24 March 2014.

Obama, B. (2013b) 'Remarks by the President on climate change at Georgetown University', White House, published online at www.whitehouse.gov/the-press-office/2013/06/25/remarks-president-climate-change, accessed on 24 March 2014.

Obama, B. (2013c) 'State of the Union', White House, published online at www.white house.gov/the-press-office/2013/02/12/remarks-president-state-union-address, accessed on 24 March 2014.

Obama, B. (2014) 'State of the Union', White House, published online at www.white house.gov/the-press-office/2014/01/28/president-barack-obamas-state-union-address, accessed on 24 March 2014.

Obama, B. and Biden, J. (2008) *Blueprint for change: Obama and Biden's Plan for America*, published by the Obama campaign online at https://ia601003.us.archive. org/19/items/34612-obamablueprintchange.pdf, accessed on 4 May 2016.

Recovery Act (2009) 'American Recovery and Reinvestment Act of 2009', US Government Printing Office, published online at www.gpo.gov/fdsys/pkg/PLAW-111publ5/html/PLAW-111publ5.htm, accessed on 23 July 2015.

Robinson, D. (2013) 'US energy and climate change policies – Obama's second term', Oxford Institute for Energy Studies, published online at www.oxfordenergy.org/wpcms/wp-content/uploads/2013/03/US-energy-and-climate-change-policies-Obamas-Second-Term.pdf, accessed on 2 August 2015.

Romm, J. (2013) 'Bridge to nowhere? NOAA confirms high methane leakage rate up to 9% from gas fields, gutting climate benefit', *Think Progress*, published online at http://thinkprogress.org/climate/2013/01/02/1388021/bridge-to-nowhere-noaa-confirms-high-methane-leakage-rate-up-to-9-from-gas-fields-gutting-climate-benefit/, accessed on 2 August 2015.

Tubman, M. (2015) 'President Obama's Climate Action Plan: two years later', Center for Energy and Climate Solutions, published online at www.c2es.org/docUploads/climate-action-plan-2-year-update-06-15.pdf, accessed on 3 August 2015.

US Department of Defense (2014) 'Quadrennial Defense Review', Department of Defense, published online at www.defense.gov/pubs/2014_Quadrennial_Defense_Review.pdf, accessed on 29 September 2014.

US Department of Defense (2015) 'DoD releases report on security implications of climate change', Department of Defense, published online at www.defense.gov/news/newsarticle.aspx?id=129366, accessed on 3 August 2015.

Vezirgiannidou, S.-E. (2013) 'Climate and energy policy in the United States: the battle of ideas', *Environmental Politics*, 22(4), 593–609.

White House (2010) 'National Security Strategy 2010', White House, published online at www.whitehouse.gov/sites/default/files/rss_viewer/national_security_strategy.pdf, accessed on 9 February 2015.

White House (2012) '2012.03.12 A secure energy future: progress report', White House, published online at www.whitehouse.gov/sites/default/files/email-files/the_blueprint_for_a_secure_energy_future_oneyear_progress_report.pdf, accessed on 12 October 2012.

White House (2013) 'Climate Action Plan', White House, published online at www.whitehouse.gov/sites/default/files/image/president27sclimateactionplan.pdf, accessed on 2 August 2015.

White House (2014a) 'The all-of-the-above energy strategy as a path to sustainable economic growth', White House, published online at www.whitehouse.gov/sites/default/

files/docs/aota_energy_strategy_as_a_path_to_sustainable_economic_growth.pdf, accessed on 2 August 2015.

White House (2014b) 'The Recovery Act and renewable energy investments', White House, published online at www.whitehouse.gov/recovery/innovations/clean-renewable-energy, accessed on 1 October 2014.

White House (2014c) 'Safe and responsible oil and gas production as part of President Obama's all-of-the-above energy strategy', White House Blog, published online at www.whitehouse.gov/blog/2014/06/25/safe-and-responsible-oil-and-gas-production-part-president-obama-s-all-above-energy-, accessed on 2 August 2015.

White House (2015a) 'National Security Strategy 2015', White House, published online at www.whitehouse.gov/sites/default/files/docs/2015_national_security_strategy.pdf, accessed on 9 February 2015.

White House (2015b) 'Securing American energy', White House, published online at www.whitehouse.gov/energy/securing-american-energy, accessed on 3 August 2015.

Yergin, D. (2011) 'America's new energy security', *Wall Street Journal*, published online at http://online.wsj.com/article/SB10001424052970204449804577068932026951376.html, accessed on 11 October 2012.

Part IV
The Obama doctrine
Its place in history

14 For the record

(Re)constructing Obama's foreign policy legacy

Lee Jarvis and Michael Lister

It is, of course, too early to pronounce definitively on the foreign policy legacy that will be attached to the Obama presidency, for at least two reasons.[1] The first is that, at the time of writing,[2] Obama has one year left of his second term in office, and recent events in Paris are a timely reminder of the capacity of unforeseen developments to alter the shape and direction of (foreign) policy. It remains to be seen what longer-term effects the Paris attacks have (if any), and whether or not they result in a fundamental shift in US foreign policy with regard to Syria, Iraq and the 'Islamic State' (IS). It is, however, at least possible that such a shift (or others) are possible in the final months of Obama's time in office. A second reason for being cautious about definitive conclusions on Obama's legacy, perhaps even upon his leaving office, is that history often alters its judgements on presidential performance. Comparing the differences in the ways Woodrow Wilson and Teddy Roosevelt were perceived upon their departures (the former seen as a failure; the latter a success) with their influence and standing years later, Nye (2013: 6) notes that 'Even careful judgements change over time.... History does not produce final verdicts because each age reinterprets the past in the light of its own interests and preoccupations'.

As this suggests, any attempt to pronounce on the legacy of the Obama administration is necessarily provisional. And yet there are reasons to suppose that it would not be wildly speculative to forward some assessment on the likely shape it will begin to take on. The caveats noted above, for instance, can be weighed against identifiable characteristics of the Obama administration thus far. Thus, critics and supporters alike frequently characterise Obama's foreign policy as being marked by a conservative or pragmatic approach (Drezner, 2011; Indyk *et al.*, 2012, 2013; Rose, 2015). This, along with factors such as a hostile Congress and attention shifting to the next occupier of the Oval Office, suggests that a radical change of direction, whilst at least possible, is unlikely. Indeed, if Obama is to abide by his own maxim, 'don't do stupid shit', it would seem that future historians will form their judgements of the Obama presidency's legacy on a set of policies, speeches and interventions that remain broadly similar to those before us now.

In order to make some headway in interpreting this legacy, the chapter proceeds in two parts. Following a review of recent literature assessing and characterising how others see Obama's foreign policy and its likely legacy – considering on the way any 'Obama doctrine' and its potential significance – this chapter then turns to the words used by the administration itself in framing its own actions. Clearly, the assessments of academics, commentators and the media will have their own weight in contributing to Obama's legacy. Yet, as noted by Stuckey (cited in Murphy and Stuckey, 2002: 49), the president plays an important role as the 'interpreter-in-chief ... the nation's chief storyteller'. Woodrow Wilson similarly pointed out, 'there is but one national voice in the country and that is the voice of the president' (cited in Campbell and Jamieson, 1990: 13). Thus, we argue, it is important to consider the ways in which the administration itself seeks to characterise its own foreign policy and its own foreign policy legacy. To this end, we explore constructions of the major successes and failures of his presidency, as well as the grounds upon which these evaluations are made. Particular attention will be given to efforts to situate his administration's record historically. This will include explicit and implicit comparisons with previous administrations; uses of temporal metaphors and other discursive figures; reconstructions of the administration's ambitions prior to taking up office; and accounts of Obama's place within relevant constructed histories including those of the American nation and American presidents. The chapter will conclude by reflecting on the wider importance of claims relating to time and history within the administration's efforts to shape its historical legacy.

Assessing Obama's foreign policy

Discussions, evaluations and opinions about US foreign policy under Obama have not been in short supply. Whilst there is much that divides them, particularly in evaluative terms (compare, for example, Rose, 2015, and Stevens, 2015), there is also some high degree of agreement, especially concerning policy content. There are two broad themes around which a degree of agreement exists. The first is the balance between ambitious goals and caution/incrementalism, and the second concerns retrenchment.

Former National Security Advisor Zbigniew Brzezinski points to what many have seen as a key feature of Obama's foreign policy, namely the gap or disjuncture between the lofty rhetorical goals and the delivered outcomes (see also Guerlain, 2014). Brzezinski identifies a number of 'ambitious' (2010: 16) goals, such as redefining America's 'war on terror' and its relations with Islam, pursuing peace between Israel and Palestine, negotiating a deal with Iran over its nuclear ambitions, bringing China in as a geopolitical partner, and improving relations with Russia. Yet for all this sense of 'strategic direction' (2010: 17), he considers policy outcomes to have generated 'more expectations than strategic breakthroughs' (2010: 28). Similarly, Nye (2013: 10) considers Obama's foreign policy to be marked by 'transformational policy goals' followed by 'incremental policies'. Indyk *et al.* (2012: 30) likewise identify a disjuncture between Obama the candidate and Obama the president – between 'soaring rhetoric and desire for fundamental change, on the one hand, and his instinct for governing pragmatically, on the other' suggesting that 'pragmatism has dominated'. This pragmatic instinct, with its preference for a smaller footprint and incremental policies, has two potential sources: one, the result of innate caution from Obama himself; or two, the (perceived) constraints he has faced, such as a public weary of US overseas involvement, and economic and budgetary difficulties.

A second recurring theme within the literature on Obama's foreign policy concerns retrenchment. Drezner (2011: 58) argues that Obama, afflicted by the weariness and economic woes noted above, has pursued a foreign policy strategy of 'multilateral retrenchment'. Leading a country tired of dealing with the problems of other states and drained by the financial crisis of 2008, Obama, it is argued, sought to wind down a number of America's overseas commitments and draw in other partners to share some of the heavy lifting. The term 'leading from behind' came to encapsulate this approach to foreign affairs (even if the term was not used by Obama himself). In his first term, the Libyan intervention epitomised this approach. The continued hesitation over Syrian intervention, through his second term, also could be said to be marked by similar instincts. Indeed, as we shall see below, in certain ways Obama has been at pains to emphasise the difference and discontinuity of this approach with that of his predecessor.

For some authors, this emphasis on retrenchment is occasion for a sharply negative, and sometimes scathing, assessment of the effect of such policies. For Singh (2012: 4), Obama's foreign policy is understood as 'adhering strongly to a "post-American" conception of world order – one in which American primacy is steadily but inexorably ebbing, with the US President's task being not to stem and reverse, but rather to gracefully manage, that obvious and inevitable decline'. Similarly, Dueck (2015) argues that if the retrenchment in Obama's foreign policy was designed to shore up America's global position and improve relations with hitherto hostile countries, it has not been successful and, in his view, has allowed problems to fester which will have longer-term consequences. Stevens (2015: 16) argues that Obama's 'cramped' foreign policy has created power vacuums, filled by the likes of Islamic State, and emboldened enemies.

Others, however, agree that Obama has sought to pull back American foreign policy, yet interpret this differently. Drezner, for instance, argues that as well as retrenchment, there has been 'counterpunching', where the administration has been willing to assert 'influence and ideals across the globe when challenged by other countries, reassuring allies and signaling resolve to rivals' (Drezner, 2011: 58). The continued use of drone warfare and the killing of bin Laden could be seen as first term examples of this. The recent sailing of a US warship through disputed waters in the South China Sea and the decision to maintain US troops in Afghanistan could be seen as further examples in his second term in office. Other authors, such as Rose, have argued that Obama's retrenchment has been strategic and allowed the maintenance of the fundamentals of the liberal international system, from which the US has benefited for many years. As he puts it:

> The critics are right about the downsizing of the U.S. global role and the withdrawal from exposed forward positions. But what they miss is that Obama's retrenchment is not universal, his diffidence not complete. The

administration has not abandoned traditional U.S. grand strategy; it has tried to rescue it from its predecessor's mismanagement. Obama is prepared to save the core of the liberal order – but to do so, he is willing to sacrifice the periphery, both functional and regional.

(Rose, 2015: 7)

The Obama legacy? An assessment

In making the above arguments, authors frequently think beyond the temporal confines of the Obama administration, reflecting on the likely legacy of his presidency for the future of America and its foreign policy. For example, Rose (2015: 2) considers that Obama will leave a positive legacy for his successors, arguing: 'Obama will likely pass on to his successor an overall foreign policy agenda and national power position in better shape than when he entered office'. Others take a more critical position. Dueck (2015: 38), for example, suggests that Obama has 'kicked a few cans down the road', yet views his policies as lacking 'serious coherence' and leaving his successor with much to address. In making such arguments, authors (re)visit the longstanding question of continuity and change within US foreign policy. For some, American foreign policy exhibits broad continuity, irrespective of who holds the office (Lynch and Singh, 2008). Others see a cyclical pattern, whereby transformationalists are followed by incrementalists (Nye, 2013) or maximalists give way to retrenchers (Sestanovich, 2014). Others still, particularly those who identify presidential doctrines as important (Drezner, 2011; Murray, 2013), would point to the distinctive approach of a given president.

For those who adopt a position of broad continuity across American foreign policy, there can be little in the way of significant presidential legacies, at least in terms of shaping the policy agenda that is to follow. The material interests of the United States remain relatively constant, leading to continuity. 'American administrations actually differ very little when it comes to foreign policy and especially to national security; they tend to observe the behavioural patterns of their predecessors' (Lynch and Singh, 2008: 43). For Lynch and Singh, certain features, such as a desire to maximise influence and minimise interference alongside pragmatism and what they refer to as 'a la carte multilateralism' (2008: 43), combine in recurring administrations to produce an essential continuity. Others – focusing on the shift from Obama to Bush, for instance – have identified essential continuities in specific areas, such as counterterrorism (Jackson, 2011), democracy promotion (Boyle, 2011; Bouchet, 2013) or Middle East policy (Gerges, 2013). Such a view is also to be found in Rose's conception of a presidential administration not as a heroic and discrete endeavour, with singular achievements distinguishing a leader from both predecessors and successors. Rather, a president should be seen as 'a member of a relay team or a middle relief pitcher: somebody who takes over from a predecessor, does a hard job for a while and then passes things on to the next guy' (Rose, 2015: 2). For these 'pitchers', there is not (and perhaps cannot be) any distinctive Obama legacy, merely another 'shift' completed which maintains the essential continuity of US foreign policy. As we shall see below, we can perhaps see a similar sense of ongoing and enduring challenges in Obama's own sense of his foreign policy legacy, albeit one tempered by a highlighting of his own achievements and contributions to those challenges.

Against such conceptions with their emphasis on historical continuities sit alternative understandings which identify a repetitive process of oscillation at work. Nye (2013), for example, sees two (or four) types of presidential leadership: those with transformational and incremental ideals (he also distinguishes between transactional and inspirational styles). Sestanovich (2014: 9), similarly, argues that US foreign policy exhibits recurring shifts between maximalists and retrenchers:

> Strategies of 'maximalism' and 'retrenchment' bear an obvious cyclical relation to each other. Again and again, one has provided a corrective to the other's mistakes. When the maximalist overreaches, the retrencher comes in to pick up the pieces. Then when retrenchment fails to rebuild American power, meet new challenges, or compete effectively, the maximalist reappears, ready with ambitious formulas for doing so.

Here George W. Bush is cast as the maximalist, succumbing to over-reach, with Obama as the retrencher, scaling back and rebuilding. The implication for such arguments is that the legacy of the Obama administration may, counterintuitively, perhaps be a return to the policies pursued by his predecessor. As Sestanovich notes, 'Our look back over many decades tells us where Americans turn when they are dissatisfied with retrenchment: back to maximalism' (2014: 330). Further, he identifies two factors which are likely to yield to an enlarged US foreign policy, namely scepticism as to whether other states can 'step up' to the big global issues and problems, and – second – a lack of belief in the abilities of international institutions to do the same. This sits alongside the views of those such as Dueck (2015), who suggest that a drop in Obama's approval ratings over his handling of Syria/Iraq and Ukraine renders a more transformational/maximal foreign policy more politically appealing. On the other hand, Sestanovich questions whether a swift return to a more expansive policy agenda is likely to be immediately forthcoming. Looking at defence spending historically, he notes that periods of retrenchment often last much longer than the 'maximalist' periods of spending. For example, Kennedy and Johnson, he argues, provided an eight-year boost to defence spending, whilst the retrenchment from this lasted for more than a decade. Thus he concludes we 'should probably expect the unwinding of the Bush administration's buildup to take a solid decade or more. A strong aversion to large military operations may last considerably longer' (Sestanovich, 2014: 328). Thus, under this picture, Obama's legacy may be a return to a more interventionist, maximalist foreign policy, but not perhaps immediately.

Each of the above positions places considerable emphasis on the role of context or structure in determining the trajectory of foreign policy. Against this lie accounts which place greater emphasis on the actions and ideas of individual presidents. Those who argue for a discrete 'Obama doctrine', however identified (compare Drezner, 2011, with Murray, 2013), maintain that Obama has developed a distinctive style and approach in his term in office. For Drezner, as argued above, this coalesces around a multilateral retrenchment spiked with counterpunching. For Murray, the Obama doctrine is one which focuses on a belief in cooperation to deal with international crises, and the assertion of a pragmatic, multifaceted, limited strategy to deal with such crises; one which is sensitive to the longer-term implications of action. Although Obama is explicit in not rejecting the right or value of the US to 'go it alone' when necessary, this approach, clearly, sits in distinction to the Bush years and any Bush doctrine. As will be discussed further below, a strong, idealist, sense of the importance of values and idealism underpins this articulation.

Curiously, such positions may not lead us to a distinctive Obama legacy. For, despite Murray's (2013: 148) claim that the nature of presidential doctrines is such that their gestation exceeds the term of office ('it may be some time after the president leaves office before there is a consensus about what constitutes an Obama Doctrine'), it is also the case that doctrines rarely outlive their presidential namesakes. Brands (2006) points out that the Monroe doctrine is an outlier in that it has been unusually long-lived (with a lifespan of some 160 years), but that many others were rapidly superseded, either by circumstance or by subsequent administrations. This suggests that any 'Obama doctrine' is unlikely to be influential in American politics much beyond his term in office.

Although the three positions outlined above concerning continuity/change in US foreign policy offer different accounts, they point (perhaps depressingly for the Obama administration) in a similar direction. Whether due to an overriding and long-term continuity in interests and policy, or to an oscillation between maximalists and retrenchers, or, indeed, to the tendency of presidential doctrines to have a limited shelf-life, there is little in the above accounts to suggest that Obama's approach to foreign policy is likely to have much of an influence once he leaves the Oval Office. These accounts suggest either that his influence has been limited by long-term enduring processes (as will be that of past and future holders of the office); or that his influence will result in a swing back to an alternative by his successor; or that his influence will be rapidly overtaken by the next office holder and their own distinctive foreign policy doctrine.

(Re)writing Obama's legacy

In the remainder of this chapter, we turn to the ways in which President Obama has himself narrated his time in office and the likely legacies thereof. As demonstrated below, these efforts to tell the story of his successes (and, occasionally, failures) rely upon claims to both historical continuity and radical discontinuity with his immediate predecessor – George W. Bush – and, indeed, beyond. Claims to continuity, typically, highlight incremental progresses across foreign policy foci throughout his time in office, this period in power depicted as a story of gradual yet discernible improvement towards some posited end. On the US contribution to global environmental security, for example, Obama highlights that: 'over the last four years, our emissions of the dangerous carbon pollution that threatens our planet have actually fallen' (Obama, 2013a). Energy security – especially in the context of US reliance upon imported oil – offers a still more frequently repeated tale of progress, one which is framed around a gradual strengthening of traditional and renewable energy industries domestically. In Obama's 2013 State of the Union address, for instance, listeners were told 'we're finally poised to control our own energy future. We produce more oil at home than we have in 15 years' (Obama, 2013a). In the same centrepiece of presidential storytelling the following year, we heard that there is now: 'More oil produced at home than we buy from the rest of the world – the first time that's happened in nearly twenty years', such that 'America is closer to energy independence than we've been in decades … we're becoming a global leader in solar, too' (Obama, 2014a).

Looking at American external relationships, we see similar constructed temporalities at work in areas as diverse as border security, regional interests, and space exploration. On the former, political fortitude is invoked to explain successes in reducing illicit entrances to the US: 'we can build on the progress my administration has already made – putting more boots on the Southern border than at any time in our history and reducing illegal crossings to their lowest levels in 40 years' (Obama, 2013a). On the latter, a similar commitment to public investment explains the reinvigoration of a space programme: 'Last month we launched a new spacecraft as part of a reenergized space programme that will send American astronauts to Mars' (Obama, 2015a). In terms of regional interests, we see the frequent tethering of a continuity of commitments to circumstantial necessities, such that: 'Our alliance with Europe remains the strongest the world has ever known…. And we will continue to focus on the Asia Pacific, where we support our allies, shape a future of greater security and prosperity, and extend a hand to those devastated by disaster' (Obama, 2014a); and 'In the Asia Pacific, we are modernizing alliances while making sure that other nations play by the rules' (Obama, 2015a).

These constructions of continuity imply a conception of time as a 'process of gradual, incremental, transformation … [wherein] temporality possesses a traceable, knowable, and potentially even predictable directionality, with time unfolding as a structured, irreversible, dynamic of connected beginnings, middles, and ends' (Jarvis, 2009: 37). Decisions undertaken by Obama's administration are connected here to tangible outcomes – increased border or energy security, or modernised alliances, for instance – that constitute a quantitative transformation of some sort within America's role in the world. This effectively linear 'temporal shape' (Graham, 1997), however, is far from the only one evident in Obama's work as 'interpreter-in-chief', with constructions of temporal discontinuity equally prominent in his state-making practices. Most common here are references to the withdrawal of American troops from Afghanistan and the termination of this protracted conflict. As Obama described it in his statement marking the end of this combat mission: 'Today's ceremony in Kabul marks a milestone for our country ... our combat mission in Afghanistan is ending, and the longest war in American history is coming to a responsible conclusion' (Obama, 2014c). This is not – written thus – merely a gradual reduction in military commitments, or a winding down of activities in one theatre of conflict. Rather, the (planned) withdrawal from Afghanistan constitutes here a transition from an old time of war and insecurity to a new, post-conflict era. As Obama had earlier put it: 'After a decade of grinding war, our brave men and women in uniform are coming home' (Obama, 2013a), after which: 'in tight-knit communities across America, fathers and mothers will tuck in their kids, put an arm around their spouse, remember fallen comrades, and give thanks for being home from a war that, after twelve long years, is finally coming to an end' (Obama, 2014a).

Implicit in this particular construction of discontinuity between conflict and post-conflict are two additional claims. First is a distinction between Obama's successes and the failings of his immediate predecessor, such that:

> the United States is more secure. When I took office, nearly 180,000 Americans were serving in Iraq and Afghanistan. Today, all our troops are out of Iraq. More than 60,000 of our troops have already come home from Afghanistan [and] ... our troops have moved to a support role.
>
> (Obama, 2014a)

This construction had been a prominent feature in earlier stories of Obama's successes, especially in relation to the May 2011 killing of Osama bin Laden which was explained – in part – by a refocusing of the war on terror away from the distraction of Iraq (Jarvis and Holland, 2014). Second is a claim to a more pervasive, almost normative, transformation in the American embrace of militarism. In his 2014 State of the Union address, for instance, Obama argued: 'even as we aggressively pursue terrorist networks ... America must move off a permanent war footing' (Obama, 2014a). In his address to the UN General Assembly the previous year, this caution had been written larger still:

> Beyond bringing our troops home, we have limited the use of drones so they target only those who pose a continuing, imminent threat to the United States where capture is not feasible, and there is a near certainty of no civilian casualties.
>
> (Obama, 2013b)

These claims to temporal discontinuity depict the movement of history as a 'punctuated, disjunctive, dynamic' (Jarvis, 2009: 35). Here, a significant or novel event – the end of a war, the killing of an enemy – is positioned as a break or interval separating two qualitatively distinct eras. Such a construction is, of course, of likely appeal to statespeople, given the emphasis it places upon – and agency it attributes to – specific decisions or actions. We might, therefore, not be surprised to find this temporal shape invoked widely across Obama's second term in office, whether in relation to its destruction of al Qaeda as a security threat – 'the organization that attacked us on 9/11 is a shadow of its former self' (Obama, 2013a); its relationship with Cuba – 'we have to be strong enough to acknowledge when what you're doing is not working. For 50 years, the United States pursued a Cuba policy that failed to improve the lives of the Cuban people. We changed that' (Obama, 2015b); a refashioning of the liberty/security 'balance' in the use of intelligence –

> Just as we've reviewed how we deploy our extraordinary military capabilities in a way that lives up to our ideals, we've begun to review the way we gather intelligence, so that we properly balance the legitimate security concerns of our citizens and allies with the privacy concerns that all people share.
>
> (Obama, 2013b)

or intervention in the 'Arab Spring' –

> we chose to support those who called for change. And we did so based on the belief that while these transitions will be hard and take time societies based on democracy and openness and the dignity of the individual will ultimately be more stable, more prosperous and more peaceful.
>
> (Obama, 2013b)

These claims to the Obama presidency as a bringer of genuine, qualitative change in world politics at times draw upon an important construction of the US as a reflexive agent capable of learning from earlier errors. For instance: 'we've learned some costly lessons over the last 13 years.... Instead of sending large ground forces overseas, we're partnering with nations from South Asia to North Africa to deny safe haven to terrorists who threaten America' (Obama, 2015a). He continued, 'Instead of getting dragged into another ground war in the Middle East, we are leading a broad coalition, including Arab nations, to degrade and ultimately destroy this terrorist group' (Obama, 2015a). Particularly interesting in this context is discussion of the Iranian nuclear programme, and the successes of executive diplomacy (especially vis-à-vis legislative resistance) in addressing this challenge. As Obama put it in his 2014 State of the Union address: 'it is American diplomacy, backed by pressure, that has halted the progress of Iran's nuclear programme – and rolled parts of that programme back.... Unprecedented inspections help the world verify, every day, that Iran is not building a bomb' (Obama, 2014a). This claim was returned to more forcefully in a July 2015 statement, with two years of his administration's efforts presented here as an interval between an old time of antagonism-induced insecurity and a new, more mature, time of hope and security:

> Today, after two years of negotiations, the United States, together with our international partners, has achieved something that decades of animosity has not – a comprehensive, long-term deal with Iran that will prevent it from

obtaining a nuclear weapon. The deal demonstrates that American diplomacy can bring about real and meaningful change – change that makes our country, and the world, safer and more secure.

(Obama, 2015c)

These efforts to frame Obama's legacy in terms of continuity and discontinuity alike find their equivalent in reflection upon the future challenges likely to confront his remaining time in office and that of his successor(s). In some instances these challenges are discussed as part of an enduring threat – 'we will continue to take direct action against those terrorists who pose the gravest threat to Americans' (Obama, 2013a) – even if the specific incarnations of that threat might evolve over time:

> The fact is, that danger remains. While we have put al Qaeda's core leadership on a path to defeat, the threat has evolved, as al Qaeda affiliates and other extremists take root in different parts of the world. In Yemen, Somalia, Iraq and Mali, we have to keep working with partners.... In Syria, we'll support the opposition.
>
> (Obama, 2014a)

In others, it is the ramifications of current decisions and actions that occupy attention, and a continuity of American commitment to stay the course. As Obama put it in relation to the return of US troops to Afghanistan: 'our commitment to Afghanistan and its people endures. As Commander-in-Chief, I will not allow Afghanistan to be used as a safe haven for terrorists to attack our nation again' (Obama, 2015d). Environmental harm – 'we must do more to combat climate change' (Obama, 2013a); weapons of mass destruction – 'America will continue to lead the effort to prevent the spread of the world's most dangerous weapons' (Obama, 2013a); infectious diseases – 'we will continue to mobilize other countries to join us in making concrete commitments, significant commitments to fight this outbreak' (Obama, 2014b); and cybersecurity – 'We'll keep strengthening our defences and combat new threats like cyberattacks' (Obama, 2014a) – all emerge as future, broadly known, threats, requiring continued US attention. Indeed, in the case of the latter, there is scope for lesson learning and optimism based on recent successes in related areas, such that: 'we're making sure our government integrates intelligence to combat cyber threats, just as we have done to combat terrorism' (Obama, 2015a).

In the context of regional conflagrations, similarly, a combination of presidential and national determination brings genuine hope for successful future resolution. In relation to Syria, for instance: 'we will continue to work with the international community to usher in the future the Syrian people deserve – a future free of dictatorship, terror and fear' (Obama, 2014a), whereby: 'the United States will work with a broad coalition to dismantle this network of death ... we will demonstrate that the future belongs to those who build – not those who destroy' (Obama, 2014b). On Iran, similarly: 'My message to Iran's leaders and people has been simple and consistent. Do not let this opportunity pass. We can reach a solution' (Obama, 2014b). And, in relation to Israel, finally, Obama signalled a determination to help 'resolve a conflict that goes back even further than our differences with Iran, and that is the conflict between Palestinians and Israelis' (Obama, 2013b). Here, a continuity of problem might be addressed by a discontinuity of effort, such that: 'We will continue our unprecedented efforts to strengthen Israel's security – efforts that go beyond what any American administration has done before' (Obama, 2015c).

Although at times implicit, all of the above claims to past foreign policy successes, future challenges and so forth rely upon some positioning of the American self. A construction of national identity, in other words, is a vital element of these efforts to tell the story of his administration's record. In this rendition (compare with Campbell, 1992; Weldes, 1996), familiar political myths around the American dream – 'prosperity – broad, shared, built on a thriving middle class – that has always been the source of our progress at home. It's also the foundation of our power and influence throughout the world' (Obama, 2013a) – and American exceptionalism – 'I lead the strongest military that the world has ever known' (Obama, 2015b) – combine to draw an inside-out story of a country whose internal make-up influences its external behaviour. Written thus, the foreign policy legacy of Obama is – at foundation – a principled one, as the president outlined in his discussion of counterterrorism: 'we must enlist our values in the fight. That's why my administration has worked tirelessly to forge a durable legal and policy framework to guide our counterterrorism efforts ... we have kept Congress fully informed of our efforts (Obama, 2013a). A city upon a hill, 'America must remain a beacon to all who seek freedom during this period of historic change' (Obama, 2013a) in which enduring and universal moral commitments cannot but shape foreign policy behaviour:

> we do these things because they help promote our long-term security. And we do them because we believe in the inherent dignity and equality of every human being, regardless of race or religion, creed or sexual orientation.... on every issue the world turns to us ... because of the ideals we stand for, and the burdens we bear to advance them.
>
> (Obama, 2014a)

> As Americans, we respect human dignity even when we're threatened, which is why I have prohibited torture and worked to make sure our use of new technology like drones is properly constrained.... We do these things not only because they are the right thing to do, but because ultimately they will make us safer.
>
> (Obama, 2015a)

> As Americans we have a profound commitment to justice. So it makes no sense to spend $3 million per prisoner to keep open a prison that the world condemns and terrorists use to recruit.
>
> (Obama, 2015a)

In contrast to less principled actors – 'we're upholding the principle that bigger nations can't bully the small – by opposing Russian aggression, and supporting Ukraine's democracy, and reassuring our NATO allies' (Obama, 2015a) – the United States is here resolute in 'defend[ing] the democratic principles that allow societies to succeed ... some universal truths are self-evident' (Obama, 2015b). Thus, 'America is not the same as it was 100 years ago, or 50 years ago, or even a decade ago. Because we fight for our ideals, and we are willing to criticize ourselves when we fall short' (Obama, 2014b).

The importance of American/universal values (for these are frequently depicted as co-terminous) in Obama's foreign policy approach is complemented by America's status as a global power – 'our ability to influence others depends on our willingness to lead and meet our obligations' (Obama, 2013a) – yet is moderated by a pragmatic approach to dealing with emergent challenges where necessary: 'The United States will at times work with governments that do not meet, at least in our view, the highest international expectations.... Nevertheless, we will not stop asserting principles that are consistent with our ideals' (Obama, 2013b). A cosmopolitan ethics evidenced by American behaviour – 'America is exceptional – in part because we have shown a willingness through the sacrifice of blood and treasure to stand up not only for our own narrow self-interests, but for the interests of all' (Obama, 2013b) – is here matched by the personal conviction and courage of its current president. Thus, in relation to the use of military power, for instance:

> As Commander-in-Chief, I have used force when needed to protect the American people, and I will never hesitate to do so as long as I hold this office. But I will not send our troops into harm's way unless it's truly necessary; nor will I allow our sons and daughters to be mired in open-ended conflicts.
>
> (Obama, 2014a)

For, as Obama put it in the following year's State of the Union address:

> My first duty as Commander-in-Chief is to defend the United States of America. In doing so, the question is not whether America leads in the world, but how. When we make rash decisions, reacting to the headlines instead of using our heads; when the first response to a challenge is to send in our military – then we risk getting drawn into unnecessary conflicts.
>
> (Obama, 2015a)

Echoing the above discussion of ambitious pragmatism, Obama consistently portrays himself as willing to wield violence, but only where necessary:

> I've been President and Commander in Chief for over six years now. Time and again, I have faced decisions about whether or not to use military force. It's the gravest decision that any President has to make. Many times, in

multiple countries, I have decided to use force. And I will never hesitate to do so when it is in our national security interest.

(Obama, 2015c)

And:

I do not send you [troops returning to Afghanistan] into harm's way lightly. It's the most solemn decision I make. I know the wages of war in the wounded warriors I visit.... But as your Commander-in-Chief, I believe this mission is vital to our national security interests in preventing terrorist attacks against our citizens and our nation.... I have repeatedly argued against marching into open-ended military conflicts that do not serve our core security interests.

(Obama, 2015d)

If constructions of this legacy rely upon implicit articulations of history's passage, temporality also, at times, takes on a more explicit focus in Obama's foreign policy discourse. In the first instance, we see the use of historical analogies or references to variously explain or justify a chosen course of events. The possibility of diplomacy around the Iranian nuclear weapons programme, for instance, is evidenced by Cold War successes: 'If John F. Kennedy and Ronald Reagan could negotiate with the Soviet Union, then surely a strong and confident America can negotiate with less powerful adversaries today' (Obama, 2014a). Responding to Assad's use of chemical weapons, similarly, is imperative, given the shared experience of horrific past conflicts:

The ban against the use of chemical weapons, even in war, has been agreed to by 98 percent of humanity. It is strengthened by the searing memories of soldiers suffocating in the trenches; Jews slaughtered in gas chambers; Iranians poisoned in the many tens of thousands.

(Obama, 2013b)

Second, there are references to the passing of time itself as a carrier or conveyor of responsibilities. On the former, we see repeated reference to obligations that are owed to 'future generations' and the need to act in the present in order to meet these. On cybersecurity, for example, Obama notes: 'We cannot look back years from now and wonder why we did nothing in the face of real threats to our security and our economy' (Obama, 2013a). On global warming, similarly: 'Climate change is a fact. And when our children's children look us in the eye and ask if we did all we could to leave them a safer, more stable world, with new sources of energy, I want us to be able to say yes, we did' (Obama, 2014a). History also, however, emerges as a teacher or a repository of knowledge at times, whether in relation to democracy's triumph: 'The history of the last two decades proves that in today's world, dictatorships are unstable' (Obama, 2015b); or on the lessons of contemporary interconnectedness in a globalised world:

in the old ways of thinking, the plight of the powerless, the plight of refugees, the plight of the marginalized did not matter. They were on the periphery of the world's concerns. Today, our concern for them is driven not just by conscience, but should also be driven by self-interest.

(Obama, 2015b)

There are, to be sure, limitations to American agency (limitations learned by a reflexive actor): 'The United States has a hard-earned humility when it comes to our ability to determine events inside other countries.... The danger for the world is that the United States, after a decade of war ... may disengage' (Obama, 2013b). At the same time: 'History is littered with the failure of false prophets and fallen empires who believed that might always makes right, and that will continue to be the case' (Obama, 2015b).

A combination, perhaps, of historical providence, national character and presidential determination is that which – finally – explains Obama's certainties about the successful future awaiting the US. Returning, here, to a broadly linear conception of time in which the future's general direction might be known or predicted, we see repeated reference to good things ahead. As Obama put it in his 2013 address to the United Nations General Assembly, for instance:

I know what side of history I want the United States of America to be on. We're ready to meet tomorrow's challenges with you – firm in the belief that all men and women are in fact created equal, each individual possessed with a dignity and inalienable rights that cannot be denied. That is why we look to the future not with fear, but with hope. And that's why we remain convinced that this community of nations can deliver a more peaceful, prosperous and just world to the next generation.

(Obama, 2013b)

This was a theme he returned to in more detail at the same venue two years later: 'We can rollback preventable disease ... we can eradicate extreme poverty and erase barriers to opportunity.... We can promote growth through trade ... we can roll back the pollution that we put in our skies' (Obama, 2015b). If not quite teleological – given the importance of effort and possibility of setbacks – a clear sense emerges of his current foreign policy decisions being made with an eye on their far-reaching consequences. As he put it in a 2014 address – again at the United Nations:

on issue after issue, we cannot rely on a rule book written for a different century. If we lift our eyes beyond our borders – if we think globally and if we act cooperatively – we can shape the course of this century as our predecessors shaped the post-World War II age.

(Obama, 2014b)

Conclusion

The above exploration of Obama's framing of the legacies and future challenges of his time in office demonstrates, we suggest, three points on which we would like to finish. The first is the importance of specific claims to – or imaginations of – time and history within his efforts to write his own foreign policy record. The above analysis relies, of course, upon a small sample of speeches identified either for their symbolic significance – in the case of the State of the Union addresses and Obama's annual address to the United Nations General Assembly. Or – in the case of statements on Iran, Afghanistan and the Paris attacks – their conjunctural importance in the context of developments in his second term in office. In spite of this, however, we can see, amongst other things: quite powerful implicit and explicit constructions of temporality; widespread use of historical metaphors, comparisons and analogies; and the invocation of time or history as subjects (owing a responsibility to the future) or agents (history as a teacher). While there is much space for future work exploring such themes in greater detail, such research would undoubtedly benefit from a small but growing body of academic literature on time and international politics more widely (e.g. Noon, 2004; Hutchings, 2007; Hom, 2010; Solomon, 2014).

Second, Obama has relied upon quite different conceptions of time in his effort to make sense of – or perhaps to 'sell' (Holland, 2012) – his foreign policy record. Although this is interesting, it may not in itself be overly surprising. His predecessor, George W. Bush, for instance, was similarly catholic in this aspect of his rhetorical output, variously (re)producing time as a process of radical discontinuity, linearity or cyclicity (Jarvis, 2009). This variability might be explained in a number of ways, but there is, again, much scope for greater comparative work on the work that 'history' or 'time' does on the legacy-making practices of executives and others in the US and, indeed, beyond.

A third point to note is that there is some considerable overlap between contemporary academic debate on Obama's foreign policy record and his own framing thereof. Discussions of pragmatism, idealism and the like emerge across both of these discursive arenas. This points – perhaps – to the likely descriptive nature of foreign policy research focused on the present. It is beyond our own interests – as well as our focus in this chapter – to seek to resolve either this realm of academic debate or Obama's rhetorical inconsistencies, if, indeed, a resolution to either was even possible or desirable. Our hope – more modestly – is that we have simply pointed to the value of taking seriously Obama's framing of his own foreign policy, and the conceptions of temporality therein.

Notes

1 We are grateful to the editors – Michelle Bentley and Jack Holland – for their invitation to contribute to this book, and their support and suggestions along the way. Any outstanding errors are ours alone.
2 This chapter was completed in December 2015.

References

Bouchet, N. (2013) 'The democracy tradition in US foreign policy and the Obama presidency', *International Affairs*, 89 (1), pp. 31–51.

Boyle, M. J. (2011) 'Between freedom and fear: explaining the consensus on terrorism and democracy in US foreign policy', *International Politics*, 48 (2–3), pp. 412–33.

Brands, H. W. (2006) 'Presidential doctrines: an introduction', *Presidential Studies Quarterly*, 36 (1), pp. 1–4.

Brzezinski, Z. (2010) 'Hope to audacity: appraising Obama's foreign policy', *Foreign Affairs*, 89 (1), pp. 16–30.

Campbell, D. (1992) *Writing Security: United States Foreign Policy and the Politics of Identity*. Minneapolis: University of Minnesota Press.

Campbell, K. K. and Jamieson, K. H. (1990) *Deeds Done in Words: Presidential Rhetoric and the Genres of Governance*, Chicago: University of Chicago Press.

Drezner, D. W. (2011) 'Does Obama have a grand strategy? Why we need doctrines in uncertain times', *Foreign Affairs*, 90 (4), pp. 57–68.

Dueck, C. (2015) *The Obama Doctrine. American Grand Strategy Today*. Oxford: Oxford University Press.

Gerges, F. A. (2013) 'The Obama approach to the Middle East: the end of America's moment?', *International Affairs*, 89 (2), pp. 299–323.

Graham, G. (1997) *The Shape of the Past: A Philosophical Approach to History*. Oxford: Oxford University Press.

Guerlain, P. (2014) 'Obama's foreign policy: "smart power," realism and cynicism', *Society*, 51 (5), pp. 482–91.

Holland, J. (2012) *Selling the War on Terror: Foreign Policy Discourses after 9/11*. Abingdon: Routledge.

Hom, A. R. (2010) 'Hegemonic metronome: the ascendancy of Western standard time', *Review of International Studies*, 36 (4), pp. 1145–70.

Hutchings, K. (2007) 'Happy anniversary! Time and critique in international relations theory', *Review of International Studies*, 33 (S1), pp. 71–89.

Indyk, M. S., Lieberthal, K. G. and O'Hanlon, M. E. (2012) 'Scoring Obama's foreign policy: a progressive pragmatist tries to bend history', *Foreign Affairs*, 91 (3), pp. 29–43.

Indyk, M. S., Lieberthal, K. G. and O'Hanlon, M. E. (2013) *Bending History: Barack Obama's Foreign Policy*. Washington DC: Brookings Institution Press.

Jackson, R. (2011) 'Culture, identity and hegemony: continuity and (the lack of) change in US counterterrorism policy from Bush to Obama', *International Politics*, 48 (2–3), pp. 390–411.

Jarvis, L. (2009) *Times of Terror: Discourse, Temporality and the War on Terror*. Basingstoke: Palgrave.

Jarvis, L. and Holland, J. (2014) 'We [for]got him': remembering and forgetting in the narration of bin Laden's death', *Millennium: Journal of International Studies*, 42 (2), pp. 425–47.

Lynch, T. J. and Singh, R. S. (2008) *After Bush: The Case for Continuity in American Foreign Policy*. Cambridge: Cambridge University Press.

Murphy, J. M. and Stuckey, M. E. (2002) 'Never cared to say goodbye: presidential legacies and vice-presidential campaigns', *Presidential Studies Quarterly*, 32 (1), pp. 46–66.

Murray, D. (2013) 'Military action but not as we know it: Libya, Syria and the making of an Obama doctrine', *Contemporary Politics*, 19 (2), pp. 146–66.

Noon, D. H. (2004) 'Operation enduring analogy: World War II, the war on terror, and the uses of historical memory', *Rhetoric & Public Affairs* 7 (3), pp. 339–64.

Nye, J. S. (2013) *Presidential Leadership and the Creation of the American Era* Princeton, NJ: Princeton University Press.

Obama, B. (2013a) 'Remarks by the President in the State of the Union address', 12 February.

Obama, B. (2013b) 'Remarks by President Obama in address to the United Nations General Assembly', 24 September.

Obama, B. (2014a) 'President Barack Obama's State of the Union address', 28 January.

Obama, B. (2014b) 'Remarks by President Obama in address to the United Nations General Assembly', 24 September.

Obama, B. (2014c) 'Statement by the President on the end of the combat mission in Afghanistan', 28 December.

Obama, B. (2015a) 'Remarks by the President in State of the Union address', 20 January.

Obama, B. (2015b) 'Remarks by President Obama in address to the United Nations General Assembly', 28 September.

Obama, B. (2015c) 'Statement by the President on Iran', 14 July.

Obama, B. (2015d) 'Statement by the President on Afghanistan', 15 October.

Obama, B. (2015e) 'Statement by the President on the situation in Paris', 13 November.

Rose, G. (2015) 'What Obama gets right: keep calm and carry the liberal order on', *Foreign Affairs*, 94 (5), pp. 2–12.

Sestanovich, S. (2014) *Maximalist: America in the World from Truman to Obama.* New York: Alfred A. Knopf.

Singh, R. (2012) *Barack Obama's Post-American Foreign Policy: The Limits of Engagement.* London: Bloomsbury.

Solomon, T. (2014) 'Time and subjectivity in world politics', *International Studies Quarterly* 58 (4), pp. 671–81.

Stevens, B. (2015) 'What Obama gets wrong: no retreats no surrenders', *Foreign Affairs*, 94 (5), pp. 13–16.

Weldes, J. (1996) 'Constructing national security', *European Journal of International Relations*, 2(3), pp. 275–318.

Index

Taylor & Francis eBooks

Helping you to choose the right eBooks for your Library

Add Routledge titles to your library's digital collection today. Taylor and Francis ebooks contains over 50,000 titles in the Humanities, Social Sciences, Behavioural Sciences, Built Environment and Law.

Choose from a range of subject packages or create your own!

Benefits for you

» Free MARC records
» COUNTER-compliant usage statistics
» Flexible purchase and pricing options
» All titles DRM-free.

Benefits for your user

» Off-site, anytime access via Athens or referring URL
» Print or copy pages or chapters
» Full content search
» Bookmark, highlight and annotate text
» Access to thousands of pages of quality research at the click of a button.

REQUEST YOUR FREE INSTITUTIONAL TRIAL TODAY

Free Trials Available
We offer free trials to qualifying academic, corporate and government customers.

eCollections – Choose from over 30 subject eCollections, including:

Archaeology	Language Learning
Architecture	Law
Asian Studies	Literature
Business & Management	Media & Communication
Classical Studies	Middle East Studies
Construction	Music
Creative & Media Arts	Philosophy
Criminology & Criminal Justice	Planning
Economics	Politics
Education	Psychology & Mental Health
Energy	Religion
Engineering	Security
English Language & Linguistics	Social Work
Environment & Sustainability	Sociology
Geography	Sport
Health Studies	Theatre & Performance
History	Tourism, Hospitality & Events

For more information, pricing enquiries or to order a free trial, please contact your local sales team:
www.tandfebooks.com/page/sales

 Routledge
Taylor & Francis Group

The home of
Routledge books

www.tandfebooks.com